SUCCEED

How We Can Reach Our Goals

Heidi Grant Halvorson, Ph.D.

Foreword by Carol S. Dweck, Ph.D.

HUDSON
STREET
PRESS

HUDSON STREET PRESS
Published by the Penguin Group
Penguin Group (USA) Inc., 375 Hudson Street, New York, New York 10014, U.S.A.
Penguin Group (Canada), 90 Eglinton Avenue East, Suite 700, Toronto, Ontario, Canada M4P
2Y3 (a division of Pearson Penguin Canada Inc.) • Penguin Books Ltd., 80 Strand, London
WC2R 0RL, England • Penguin Ireland, 25 St. Stephen's Green, Dublin 2, Ireland (a division of
Penguin Books Ltd.) • Penguin Group (Australia), 250 Camberwell Road, Camberwell, Victoria
3124, Australia (a division of Pearson Australia Group Pty. Ltd.) • Penguin Books India Pvt. Ltd.,
11 Community Centre, Panchsheel Park, New Delhi – 110 017, India • Penguin Group (NZ),
67 Apollo Drive, Rosedale, North Shore 0632, New Zealand (a division of Pearson New Zealand
Ltd.) • Penguin Books (South Africa) (Pty.) Ltd., 24 Sturdee Avenue, Rosebank, Johannesburg
2196, South Africa

Penguin Books Ltd., Registered Offices: 80 Strand, London WC2R 0RL, England

First published by Hudson Street Press, a member of Penguin Group (USA) Inc.

First Printing, January 2011
10   9   8   7   6   5   4   3   2   1

REGISTERED TRADEMARK—MARCA REGISTRADA
HUDSON
STREET
PRESS

LIBRARY OF CONGRESS CATALOGING-IN-PUBLICATION DATA
Grant, Heidi, 1973-
    Succeed : how we can reach our goals / Heidi Grant Halvorson ; Foreword by Carol S. Dweck.
    p.   cm.
    Includes bibliographical references and index.
    ISBN 978-1-59463-073-6 (hardcover : alk. paper)   1. Goal (Psychology)   2. Success.   3.
Conduct of life.   I. Title.
    BF505.G6.G65   2011
153. 8—dc22   2010028136

Printed in the United States of America
Set in Fairfield LH • Designed by Eve Kirch

PUBLISHER'S NOTE

For my husband, Jonathan Halvorson
and our children, Annika and Maximilian
and for my mother, Sigrid Grant

Contents

Foreword by Carol S. Dweck, Ph.D.   ix

Introduction   xi

Part One. Get Ready

Chapter 1.   Do You Know Where You Are Going?   3

Chapter 2.   Do You Know Where Your Goals Come From?   31

Part Two. Get Set

Chapter 3.   The Goals That Keep You Moving Forward   55

Chapter 4.   Goals for Optimists and Goals for Pessimists   77

Chapter 5.   Goals Can Make You Happy   105

Chapter 6.   The Right Goal for You   125

Chapter 7.   The Right Goals for Them   141

Part Three. Go

Chapter 8.   Conquer the Goal Saboteurs   159

Chapter 9.   Make a Simple Plan   171

Chapter 10.   Build the Self-Control Muscle   183

Chapter 11.   Keep It Real   197

Chapter 12.   Know When to Hang On   209

Chapter 13.   Give the Right Feedback   223

Epilogue   237

Acknowledgments   239

Notes   241

Index   251

Foreword

by Carol S. Dweck, Ph.D.

HEIDI GRANT HALVORSON KNOWS JUST ABOUT EVERYTHING THERE IS to know about setting goals and reaching them. In this book, she shares this knowledge with you.

She takes all the latest research in psychology, distills it to its essence, and makes it practical. Why don't you stick to your New Year's resolutions? What's the best way to make sure you get started on the report that's due? Why can focusing on grades harm students' grades? How do you match your goals to your outlook on life? Why are some depressed people highly effective? She answers all of these questions (and many more) in ways you can use.

Dr. Grant Halvorson is not only a wonderful writer, she's also a researcher who did much of the research that appears in this book! She understood from the very start of her career that people's goals were at the center of their well-being and success, and in the course of her research, she has had extraordinary insights into why people set the goals they do and why they do or don't reach them. In fact, her research has answered every question I posed in the previous paragraph.

Dr. Grant Halvorson also has great taste in other people's research. She knows which research is important and meaningful, and she knows how to capture its essence and its practical applications. Psychological research can sometimes be rigorous without being meaningful, and it can sometimes address meaningful issues without being rigorous or trustworthy. All of the work you will read about here sheds light on the most basic processes of human motivation and has been held to the highest standards of research. That's what makes this book so exceptional.

The most important message of this book is that people can change. It's not necessarily easy, but it is possible with the right motivation and the right information about how to go about it. The problem has always been, Where do we go to get the right information? The solution is at hand; you need only turn the page.

I am proud to have been one of Dr. Grant Halvorson's mentors, but I have been even more excited to learn from her accomplishments, her knowledge, and her wisdom. As you read this book, you will see exactly what I mean.

Introduction

Why do we fail to reach our goals? Whether it's wanting to impress our bosses, find a loving relationship, straighten out our finances, or take better care of ourselves—we all feel that there is at least one part of our lives that is in real need of improvement. (And, in reality, it's usually more than just *one* part.) We want to do better, we even try to do better, but somehow we fall short or miss the mark—sometimes over and over again. So we go looking for something to blame for our failures, and most of the time we blame ourselves. We feel like we just don't have what it takes—whatever that is—to reach our goals. And we could not be more *wrong*.

As a social psychologist, I've spent years studying achievement. I've carefully observed thousands of research participants pursue goals at work, in the classroom, on the playing field, and in my own laboratory. I've asked people to fill out weeks of daily diary reports, telling me all about the goals they pursue in their everyday lives. I've reviewed hundreds and hundreds of studies on goals and motivation. And I've come to a few conclusions, two of which I'll share with you now.

Most of us blame our failures on the wrong things. Even very smart, accomplished people don't understand why they succeed or fail. Before I started studying this for a living, my intuitions about achievement were no better than anyone else's. I thought that I was good at school and disastrous at sports because I was born that way. I wasn't—actually, no one is simply "born that way." I had a lot to learn.

Another conclusion I've reached after all these years of studying achievement is that *anyone* can be more successful at reaching his or her goals. *Anyone* can. I really can't emphasize that enough. But the first step is to put aside your beliefs about why you've succeeded or failed in the past, because they are probably wrong. And the second step is to read this book.

You may not be aware that the government keeps track of this, but on its website www.USA.gov, you can find a list of the most popular perennial New Year's resolutions Americans make. On that list, you probably won't be surprised to find both "lose weight" and "quit smoking." Every January, millions of people—and like me, you may be one of them—have set one of these two goals for themselves, vowing that this is the year that they will finally get healthy, fit into their skinny jeans, or stop spending a small fortune on cigarettes.

According to the latest reports issued by the Centers for Disease Control and Prevention (CDC), two out of three Americans are overweight, and one in three is obese. The majority of these individuals would very much prefer to weigh less. Overweight individuals not only grapple with an increased susceptibility to heart disease and diabetes, but they contend with the self-esteem-crushing consequences of being heavy in a society in which thin is in. And yet, despite an abundance of diet books and plans, and a very real and powerful desire to be slim, relatively few people who set out to lose weight actually manage to lose it and keep it off long-term. We're not getting any thinner, and our skinny jeans are still waiting for us in our closets.

The CDC also keeps track of smokers—today, roughly one in five adult Americans smoke. In its surveys, seven out of ten smokers reported that they wanted to quit smoking completely, and nearly half of those who wanted to quit (over 19 million) had stopped smoking for at least one day in the previous twelve months in an attempt to kick the habit. Only about 3 million manage to make it last—that means that about 85 percent of the people who want to quit, and have actually set themselves the *goal* of quitting, fail. In spite of all the public awareness of the serious risks to one's health, nearly half a million Americans die every year from smoking-related illnesses. So if you're a smoker and you fail to quit smoking, you may well die as a result of it. And the 85 percent of people who try to quit and fail each year know it.

So, why the high failure rates? It's obviously not that the many who try to lose weight or quit smoking aren't motivated. There aren't many incentives more powerful than knowing "this could kill you." Why then do people fail, over and over again, to achieve goals that are vital to their well-being? The most common answer you'll hear, and probably the one you were thinking when I asked that question, is that it's about *willpower*. And by "willpower," I mean some innate quality of inner strength that allows those who have it to successfully avoid temptation. Most people believe that it's fundamentally a character issue. Some people have willpower (the thin, nonsmokers—and we admire them for it). Others don't, and we judge them accordingly. Those who don't are simply weaker, less successful people, with less admirable character traits.

Interestingly, that's not only how we describe the failures of others—it's also how we describe our own shortcomings. Countless times I've heard colleagues, students, and friends talk about how they "just can't stop" smoking, "just can't resist" the dessert cart, "just can't get going" on a difficult project. And once you've decided you just don't have the willpower to lose weight or quit smoking or stop procrastinating, why bother trying? What hope is there for you?

Well, the answer is that there is actually plenty of hope for you, because it turns out that willpower is *not what you think it is.* And it might be helpful to use a less lofty term for it, because what we are really talking about here is plain old self-control. Self-control is the ability to guide your actions in pursuit of a goal—to persevere and stay on course, despite temptations, distractions, and the demands of competing goals. It's really, really important—one of the critical elements necessary for achieving your goals that I'll be talking a lot about in this book. But it doesn't work the way you think it does.

Successful People and the Paradox of Self-Control

First of all, it's simply not the case that some people have it and others don't. If that were true, then you'd expect all the people in the world to break down very clearly into "winners" and "losers." Because they are in possession of the mighty power of self-control, successful people would be successful *all the time*, winning at everything they do. And unsuccessful people, the ones utterly lacking in this critical ability, would pretty much stink at everything they tried. Why, without any self-control, these people would find it nearly impossible just to get out of bed in the morning!

It's obvious that none of that is actually true. Winners don't win at everything, and no one is so lacking in self-control that they can't accomplish anything. It's true that some people may have more self-control than others, but everyone has some. And as it turns out, even

people with *a lot* of self-control sometimes run out. To vividly illustrate this point, all you need to do is think about all the very successful people—people who have risen to the very top of their game—who
have struggled publicly with one of these two difficult New Year's
resolutions.

Celebrities who have talked openly about their many attempts to
lose weight and keep it off include Grammy-winning musicians
(Janet Jackson, Wynonna Judd) and Oscar or Emmy-winning actors
(Oprah Winfrey, Roseanne Barr, Kirstie Alley, Rosie O'Donnell, Eliz-
abeth Taylor). As you've probably noticed in the checkout aisle, popular magazines are constantly splashing photos of these and other
well-known faces on their covers. Sometimes, the celebrity proudly
displays a slimmed-down body that is the hard-earned result of a
healthy diet and exercise. At other times, the photo reveals the consequences of a return to bad habits, along with some very unkind
comments. (If you're wondering why I listed only women celebrities,
it's not because successful men don't struggle with their weight, too.
Women are simply more likely to talk publicly about it.)

This is probably a good time to point out that while we do sometimes
fail to reach our goals because we don't know what we need to do to
reach them, it's more often the case that we know *exactly* what needs to
happen, and still we fail. Everyone knows that eating less and exercising
more will help you lose weight. But knowing is one thing, and actually
doing it is another thing entirely. Many of us can look at our own struggles with whatever it may be and see that very clearly—whether it's
weight loss, quitting smoking, realizing our potential at school or work,
repairing (or staying out of) dysfunctional relationships. We seem to
make the same mistakes over and over again, even though we feel we
know better—even when failing to reach our goal subjects us to unpleasant, often cruel public scrutiny.

Speaking of public scrutiny, there is perhaps no better example of how a very successful person can have a tough time conquering his New Year's resolutions than our current president and his on-again, off-again battle to quit smoking. In February 2007, then senator Obama told the *Chicago Tribune* that he had resolved to quit smoking once and for all.

> I've quit periodically over the last several years. I've got an ironclad demand from my wife that in the stresses of the campaign I don't succumb.

It didn't last. President-elect Obama told Tom Brokaw in late 2008 that he had stopped, but that "there are times when I've fallen off the wagon." As the *New York Times* reported in December 2008, "his good-humored waffling in various interviews about smoking made it plain that Mr. Obama, like many who have vowed to quit at this time of year, had not truly done so." There's really no way of knowing if or when the president kicks his habit—his staff doesn't discuss it, and he's not likely to be caught smoking on the White House lawn. I certainly hope he has quit; but it would hardly be surprising if he hasn't, given that it can take smokers as many as ten or more attempts before they finally quit for good.

Does President Obama lack self-control? Hardly. Barack Obama worked his way up from relatively modest beginnings to become arguably the most powerful man in the world. His meteoric rise from community organizer to *Harvard Law Review* president, state senator, U.S. senator, and finally president of the United States would be worthy of admiration were he the son of well-connected, New England bluebloods. But he isn't—he's the mixed-race child of a broken home and a family of average means, with no particular advantages other than his clearly extraordinary intelligence and determination. Even if you're not a fan, you've got to admit that this is a guy who knows something about reaching goals.

All the individuals I've mentioned have known extraordinary success. Many have overcome nearly insurmountable obstacles and adversity in order to achieve what they've achieved. Countless children dream of one day becoming an award-winning artist or a powerful world leader. Very few actually do it. No one achieves that kind of success without possessing *a lot* of self-control. Achieving even ordinary, garden-variety successes requires plenty of self-control. Think back to the achievements in your own life—the ones you are most proud of. I'll bet you needed to work hard, persist despite difficulty, and stay focused, when it would have been much easier for you to just relax and not bother. You needed to avoid temptation, when it would have been more fun to give in. And you probably needed to be critical and honest with yourself, when it would have been far more pleasant to just let yourself believe that you were awesome and needed no improvements. Each of those aspects of reaching a goal requires self-control. Undoubtedly, someone like President Obama is in possession of an *extraordinary* capacity for self-control. But the president has repeatedly quit smoking only to start up again. How can that make sense?

What Self-Control Is *Really* Like

Actually, it makes perfect sense if you understand the true nature of self-control. And recently, in light of some very interesting research findings, psychologists have come to understand that the capacity for self-control is very much like a muscle. That's right—like a bicep or tricep. I know that sounds odd, but let me explain.

Like a muscle, self-control can vary in its strength—not only from person to person, but *from moment to moment*. Even well-developed biceps sometimes get tired, and so too does your self-control muscle. In one of the earliest tests of this theory of self-control strength (or *self-regulatory* strength, as it is sometimes called), Roy Baumeister and his colleagues presented very hungry college students with a bowl of chocolates and a bowl of radishes.[1]

Both bowls were placed on a table in front of each student, who was then left alone to stare at the bowls. Some of the students were asked to eat two or three of the radishes during their alone time, and to not eat any of the chocolates. Others (the lucky ones) were asked to eat two or three chocolates, while avoiding the radishes. Compared to the chocolate eaters, the radish eaters should have had to use up a fair amount of self-control. It's hard enough for most people to eat a raw radish, or to not eat readily available chocolates—just imagine doing both.

Next, to see how much self-control the students in each group had used up, Baumeister gave them each a puzzle to work on. The puzzle was difficult—actually, it was unsolvable—but what interested Baumeister was how long the students would work on it before giving up. As the "muscle" theory would predict, he found that the radish eaters gave up much faster than the chocolate eaters. They even reported feeling more tired afterward.

So how does this relate to you and me, and to situations that don't necessarily involve radishes? Think of it this way—if you've just finished working out, chances are your muscles will be tired, and you'll have sapped some of the strength you started with when you arrived at the gym. If you've just finished doing something that requires a lot of self-control (like producing a television show or leading the free world), you've probably spent a lot of your self-control strength as well. Recent research shows that even everyday actions like making a decision or trying to make a good impression can sap this valuable resource. People who are very successful in one or more areas of their life are successful precisely because that's where they devote the bulk of their capacity for self-control. When you deal with a lot of stress all day, no matter who you are, you may find yourself depleted and vulnerable to goal failure.

In an article in *O* magazine, Oprah concludes a discussion of her most recent weight gain by observing:[2]

> What I've learned this year is that my weight issue isn't about eating less or working out harder . . . It's about my life being out of balance, with too much work and not enough play, not enough time to calm down. I let the well run dry.

I think that last remark is particularly insightful and right on the money. When you tax it too much, the well of self-control will certainly run dry.

What You Can Do about It

So perhaps now you're thinking, "Okay, my failure to lose weight isn't because I lack willpower in general, but because I've spent it all on other important goals, like succeeding at work. Great. How does that help me, exactly?" Fair enough. It helps you because, if you understand the kind of thing self-control is, you can plan accordingly. This brings us to another way in which self-control is like a muscle— namely, that if you rest it for a while, you get your strength back. Depletion is only temporary, and you are most vulnerable immediately after you've used up your self-control reserves. Did you ever notice how dealing with a temptation seems to get easier over time? It may feel like torture to forgo that dessert or cigarette, or to think about starting work on that project you've been dreading, but it doesn't keep torturing you quite so much as time passes. If you can get past that moment when your self-control is nearly spent and give it time to bounce back, you're probably going to be just fine.

There are other ways around this problem, too. A lack of self-control strength can sometimes be overcome with well-chosen incentives or rewards. Psychologists Mark Muraven and Elisaveta Slessareva told students participating in a study at Case Western Reserve University to watch a five-minute video clip of Robin Williams performing a particularly funny piece of stand-up.[3] Half of the students were told that they would be under observation and were instructed not to laugh or smile while watching the video. This took a lot of self-control (it was a *very* funny clip), and it sapped their willpower resources. To demonstrate this depletion, all of the students were then given a cup of orange Kool-Aid to drink—except instead of using sugar, the experimenters made it with vinegar. It was unpleasant, though drinkable if you forced yourself. If you've ever psyched yourself up to swallow cold medicine, you know that it's an act that requires significant self-control, but it's doable.

Muraven and Slessareva didn't stop there—they also varied how much the students would be paid for every ounce of vinegar Kool-Aid they managed to get down. When the students were receiving relatively low pay for drinking the vinegar Kool-Aid (one cent per ounce), those who had been allowed to laugh at Robin Williams drank twice as much as those who had to suppress their laughter, demonstrating that that latter group had indeed depleted their self-control strength. But among students who were paid well (twenty-five cents per ounce) the effect completely disappeared. Even the suppressors managed to drink down quite a lot of the gross concoction.

Does this mean that money can create self-control? Or, to put it differently, that rewards can replenish your willpower? Not exactly—it's probably more accurate to say that increasing your motivation through better rewards can help you compensate for a temporary loss of self-control. This is no doubt why so many successful dieters report that they used nonfood rewards as a key part of their diet strategies. Increasing your motivation, in whatever way works for you, is an excellent way to tip the scales back in your favor when you're just too tired to resist temptation.

Another way in which willpower, or self-control, is different than you may have imagined is that it's neither innate nor unchangeable. Self-control is learned, and developed and made stronger (or weaker) over time. If you want more self-control, you can get more. And you get more self-control the same way you get bigger muscles—you've got to give it regular workouts. Recent research has shown that engaging in daily activities such as exercising, keeping track of your finances or what you are eating—or even just remembering to sit up straight every time you think of it—can help you develop your overall self-control capacity. For example, in one study, students who were assigned to (and stuck to) a daily exercise program not only got physically healthier, but they also became more likely to wash dishes instead of leaving them in the sink, and less likely to impulsively spend money.

In another demonstration of how self-control strength can be increased through regular use, Matthew Gailliot and his colleagues asked participants in an experiment to spend two weeks using their nondominant hand to do things like brush their teeth, stir drinks, eat, open doors, and use the computer mouse.[4] (In another version of this study, they asked participants to refrain from cursing, only speak in complete sentences, say *yes* and *no* instead of *yeah* and *nope*, and avoid starting sentences with *I*.) After two weeks of training their self-control muscle, compared to a no-training group, they performed significantly better on a task that required self-control. Specifically, they were better able to avoid using any stereotypes when forming an impression of a person. Sadly, that turns out to be *very* hard to do, though that is a topic for another book.

The Topic of *This* Book

I've spent a lot of time in this introduction talking about self-control, not only because it's important, but because it's a great example of how our intuitions about things that seem obvious can sometimes fail us. And consequently, it's also a great example of how the science of psychology can be really useful—helping us to see not only what kind of thing willpower really is, but also how we can, if we want to, get our hands on some more of it.

This book isn't actually just about willpower, however. It's about achieving goals, and self-control is just one piece of that puzzle. Specifically, *Succeed* is about understanding how goals work, what tends to go wrong, and what you can do to reach your goals or to help others reach theirs.

Too much of the advice you'll typically hear about reaching your goals is both obvious and useless—we all know we're supposed to do things like "Stay Positive!" "Make a Plan!" and "Take Action!" But *why* do I need to stay positive? Is that even always true? (No.) And what kind of plan should I make? Does it matter? (Yes.) And *how* do I take action? I know that to lose weight I need to eat less and exercise more, but I never seem to actually do it. Can I fix that? (You bet.)

Some of the advice in this book may surprise you—in fact, I'm certain it will. But that advice is drawn from excellent sources—not only my own research on goals and motivation, but several decades and many hundreds of rigorous experimental and field studies, conducted by some of the world's leading scientific psychologists.

I wish that I could have called this book *Succeed: The Three Things You Need to Do to Reach All Your Goals.* At the very least, I'd probably sell more books that way. But it's not that simple—there are more than three things you need to know. For example, it turns out that there are many ways to frame the same goal in your mind. Do you think of getting that promotion as something you *ideally* would achieve, or as something you *ought* to achieve? Is mastering your classwork about developing skills or proving that you're smart? Those differences matter—differently framed goals need to be pursued with different strategies and are more or less vulnerable to different kinds of errors. Frame a goal one way, and the person pursuing it will work hard but never love what he is doing. Frame a goal another way, and you'll create interest and enjoyment—but to be honest, probably not spectacular performance (at least not in the short run). For some goals, confidence is essential, while for others it doesn't seem to matter if you're sure or shaky.

The important thing is that while achieving your goals is a bit more complicated than just doing "Three Things," it's not overly complicated, either. In Part 1 of the book, "Get Ready," I'll talk about the key principles of goal-setting that seem to be universally true, whether you're pursuing goals at work, in relationships, or for self-development. In Part 2, "Get Set," you'll learn about the different kinds of goals we set for ourselves, focusing on the few distinctions that seem to matter the most. I'll show you how to choose the goal that will work best for *you* personally in *your* situation. And you'll learn how to instill the most beneficial goals in your children, students, and employees. In Part 3, "Go," I'll take you step by step through the most common reasons why we fail to reach our goals once we've started pursuing them. And you'll learn effective, often simple and easy-to-implement strategies for avoiding these pitfalls in the future.

In the last decade or two, social psychologists have come to know a lot about how goals work. *Succeed* is my attempt to take that knowledge out of the academic journals and handbooks and spread it around a bit more so that it can do some good.

PART ONE

Get Ready

CHAPTER 1

Do You Know Where
You Are Going?

THE FIRST STEP TO GETTING ANYWHERE IS TO DECIDE WHERE YOU want to go. That seems so obvious that you may be wondering why I bothered to say it. Well, for one thing, despite its obviousness, you'd be surprised to learn just how often we completely forget to do it. Oh sure, you feel like you've set a lot of goals for yourself, *but have you really*? Or have you just thought about how you'd like to be happier, healthier, or more successful, without actually deciding what specifically you were going to do about it? You have desires, lots and lots of things that you *want* to happen, but how many of those wishes have you turned into real *goals*? Without being translated into goals, our desires remain just that—things we wish would happen. Imagine you want to take a nice vacation. If your planning never gets any further than "I'd like to go someplace warm," you're probably not going anywhere, are you?

So setting goals is important, and in this chapter I'll describe some research that shows us why. But that's not the whole story. Because *how* you set your goals—the way you think about whatever it is you want to do, and how you will get there—is every bit as important.

Success is more likely when you focus on the right details, in the right way.

Don't Do Your Best

Telling someone to "do your best" is a great way to motivate them, right? Most of us have said or heard this expression countless times. It's always meant well—*do your best* is supposed to inspire you without putting on too much pressure. It's supposed to bring out the best in you. Only it doesn't. It's a really lousy motivator.

And that's primarily because *do your best* is very, very vague. What *is* my best, exactly? Imagine you are a manager, and you've given your employee an assignment to investigate a possibly lucrative sales opportunity for your company. It's something that requires a lot of work. And it's really important. So you tell your employee, "Bob, do your best on this one." But what is Bob's best? How would you know it if you saw it? And for that matter, how would Bob? Does Bob even really know what his best looks like? Does *anyone*?

The reality is that no one hears *do your best* and thinks, "I will work on this until I can't possibly make it even the *tiniest* bit better." That would be silly and probably far too time-consuming to be of benefit to you or to Bob. Instead, we hear *do your best* and think, "I will do a good enough job so that my boss will believe this is my best and be happy with it." Not exactly inspiring stuff. In the absence of a specific goal, *do your best* somewhat ironically tends to produce work that is far from the best—it's a recipe for mediocrity.

So what's the alternative? The alternative is to set *specific, difficult goals*. Edwin Locke and Gary Latham, two eminent organizational psychologists, have spent several decades studying the extraordinary effectiveness of setting specific and difficult goals.[1] In more than one thousand studies conducted by researchers across the globe, they've found that goals that spell out *exactly* what needs to be accomplished, and that set the bar for achievement *high*, result in far superior performance than goals that are vague or that set the bar too low. And this is true regardless of whether the goal is something you adopt on your own, something you are assigned to complete, or something that you develop jointly with your parent, teacher, boss, or coworkers.

Why are specific, difficult goals more motivating than *do your best?* The *specific* part is relatively straightforward. Letting people know exactly what is expected of them (or deciding for yourself exactly what you want to achieve) removes the possibility of settling for less—of telling yourself that what you've done is "good enough." When what you're striving for is vague, it's too tempting to take the easy way out when you've gotten tired, discouraged, or bored. But there's just no fooling yourself if you've set a specific goal. You've either reached it or you haven't. And if you haven't, you've got little choice but to keep on trying if you want to succeed.

What about the *difficult* part? Isn't it dangerous to set difficult goals—aren't I asking for trouble if I set the bar high? Aren't I inviting disappointment and failure? Absolutely not! (And haven't you ever seen *Stand and Deliver*? If Mr. Escalante could teach calculus to remedial math students, imagine what you could achieve if you dared to try!) Of course, you shouldn't set goals that are not realistic or are impossible to reach. *Difficult but possible is the key.* That's because more difficult goals cause you to, often unconsciously, increase your effort, focus, and commitment to the goal; persist longer; and make better use of the most effective strategies.

Locke and Latham have shown this to be true in groups of people as diverse in their day-to-day goals as scientists, businessmen, truck drivers, unionized workers, and loggers. In one study conducted in the early 1970s, Latham found that log haulers were carrying loads to the mill that were 60 percent of the legal weight limit, on average—a situation that was wasting both time and company resources. But the log haulers did not have any specific goals about what they *should* be carrying for each load. So he assigned them the goal of carrying loads that were 94 percent of the legal limit instead. He returned after nine months and found that they were now averaging above 90 percent, saving the company what would be many millions in today's dollars.

So if you give log haulers the goal of carrying a lot more trees, it turns out they *carry a lot more trees.* People pretty much do what is asked of them, and rarely more. Ask for a great performance from someone, and as long as you're specific about what *great* is, you are much more likely to actually get it. Set yourself difficult goals, and your performance will rise to the challenge. In one study of nearly three thousand federal employees, those who agreed with statements like "my job is challenging" and "people in my work group are expected to work hard" were the ones that had the *highest* ratings on their annual performance reviews.

But they were miserable, right? Wrong. Setting and achieving challenging goals has other added benefits besides great performance. Think about a time in your life when you accomplished something really difficult, and compare that to how you felt when you pulled off something relatively easy. Which feels better? Succeeding at something hard is more pleasurable, gives greater satisfaction and happiness, and increases your overall sense of well-being. Succeeding at something easy is barely worth mentioning. A recent study in Germany showed that *only* those employees who felt their work was difficult reported increases in job satisfaction, happiness, and feelings of achievement over time.

You might be wondering if being satisfied at work leads to better performance, or if it's that better work performance creates satisfaction. The answer is that actually both are true—job satisfaction increases people's commitment to their organization and confidence in themselves, which leads them to challenge themselves more, which leads to better performance and more satisfaction, and so on and so on . . . setting specific, challenging goals creates a cycle of success and happiness that can repeat itself over and over again, creating what Locke and Latham call the "high performance cycle."[2]

You too can start this cycle in your own life—the first step is to set yourself some very specific and reasonably difficult goals. And you can further enhance your chances for success by thinking about those goals in the most motivating ways.

The Big Picture versus the Nitty-Gritty

Any action you take or goal you adopt can be described or thought about in a number of different ways. Using a vacuum can be called "keeping things clean" or "sucking up crumbs from the floor." Wanting to get an A on a math test can be thought of as wanting to "get almost all of the answers correct" or "master algebra." Working out regularly can be about "trying to lose 10 pounds" or "trying to become more fit."

How Do You Think about the Things You Do?

Before you read on, answer the questions below to see how *you* typically think about the things you do. Jot down your answers in a notebook or on a piece of paper. There are no *right, wrong,* or even *better* answers. Choose the description that best describes the behavior for *you*—the one that sounds right to your ears.

1. Making a list is
   a. getting organized
   b. writing things down

2. Cleaning the house is
   a. showing one's cleanliness
   b. vacuuming the floor
3. Paying the rent is
   a. maintaining a place to live
   b. writing a check
4. Locking a door is
   a. putting a key in the lock
   b. securing the house
5. Greeting someone is
   a. saying hello
   b. showing friendliness

To score, add up your choices to create a total score using the following numerical values:
1a = 2, 1b = 1, 2a = 2, 2b = 1, 3a = 2, 3b = 1, 4a = 1, 4b = 2, 5a = 1, 5b = 2[3]

If you scored 6 or higher, you are probably someone who tends to think about their own behavior in more *abstract* terms—when you think about the things you do each day, you describe them by focusing on *why* you are doing them. So pushing a vacuum around the house is about "keeping things clean"—wanting the house to be clean is the reason you are vacuuming, so that's how you think of it. If you scored a 5 or lower, you are probably someone who tends to think in more *concrete* terms. You think about your behavior in terms of *what* you are doing. So pushing the vacuum is about "sucking up crumbs"—it's what is actually happening, so that's how you think of it.

Both descriptions of vacuuming are accurate, so it's not as if one kind of description is right and the other is wrong. But they are different, and importantly so. Because it turns out that the abstract *why* and concrete *what* ways of thinking about your behavior have motivational pros and cons. Each mode of thinking, under different circumstances, can lead to greater achievement. The trick is to adjust your thinking according to your circumstances, and the good news is that it's not at all hard to do. You just need to learn when to think *why* and when to think *what*.

Let's start with the abstract, *why* kind of thinking. Thinking more abstractly about behavior can be very energizing because you are linking one particular, often small action to a greater meaning or purpose. Something that may not seem important or valuable on its own can be cast in a whole new light. For example, when staying that extra hour at work is thought of as "helping my career" rather than "typing for sixty more minutes," I'm much more likely to want to stay put and work hard. The *why* of what you do is incredibly motivating, so it's not surprising that many of us often prefer to think of our own actions in those terms.

And if you want to motivate someone else to do something, describing it in *why* terms will also help persuade them to give it a try. If you want your son to study for his chemistry test, telling him that he should try to do well in chemistry because it will help him get into college is probably more inspiring than telling him he should open up his textbook and start memorizing all the elements on the periodic table. Either way he has to learn that *H* stands for hydrogen, but describing *what* he should do probably won't light a fire under him, and describing *why* he should do it just might.

So is it ever helpful to think about the things we do in nitty-gritty, *what*-am-I-literally-doing ways? Yes. For one thing, it turns out that thinking this way is really useful when you need to do something that is *difficult, unfamiliar, complex*, or just takes *a lot of time to learn*. If you've never operated a vacuum cleaner before, you're actually better off thinking "sucking up crumbs" (*what*) than "keeping things clean" (*why*).

　For example, psychologists Dan Wegner and Robin Vallacher asked experienced coffee drinkers to drink a cup of coffee and then rate how well each of thirty different descriptions fit with what they had just done. (I'll bet you didn't think there even *were* thirty ways to describe drinking a cup of coffee. I know I didn't.) Their choices included relatively abstract, *why*-based descriptions like "promoting my caffeine habit" and "getting energized," along with more concrete, literal, *what*-based descriptions like "drinking a liquid" and "swallowing."

　Half of the people who participated in the study got to drink out of a normal, everyday coffee mug. The other half were given a much more unwieldy mug weighing nearly half a pound. (Some of you are probably thinking that's not really very heavy. So I should point out that this was 1983, and nobody was drinking enormous Starbucks coffees out of containers the size of an oxygen tank back then. A half-pound mug was a *really* heavy mug in 1983.) When they were asked to choose the best descriptions for what they had just done, the people who got to drink out of a typical coffee mug tended to prefer the *why* descriptions over the *what* descriptions. In other words, under normal conditions, people who are used to drinking coffee preferred thinking about drinking coffee in terms of the reason why they were drinking it.[4]

　But the heavy-mug drinkers strongly preferred the more concrete *what* descriptions. They were thinking about the specific actions they were taking, like "raising a cup to my lips." You see, in order to actually manage to drink out of a cup that was *much* heavier than anything they normally used *without spilling*, these people needed to think about the real mechanics of coffee drinking. They needed to concentrate on the *what* of what they were doing (i.e., grasping the handle firmly, raising the cups to their lips, swallowing), rather than the *why*. By focusing on the concrete *what*, they were able to successfully drink from the odd and unfamiliar cup without making a mistake. If they had thought only in abstract *why* terms, "getting energized" might have easily become "getting scalded and wet."

Wegner and Vallacher found the same results in a study where students were asked to eat Cheerios either with their hands or with chopsticks. Those who had to use chopsticks preferred to think of their actions as "putting food in my mouth" and "moving my hands" (*what*) rather than as "reducing hunger" or "getting nutrition" (*why*). Again and again, we find that when actions are difficult to accomplish, it is easier and much more helpful to think about what we are doing in simple, concrete *what* terms rather than lofty, more abstract *why* ones. (At this point, you may be wondering if social psychologists get a particular pleasure out of asking people to do really odd things, like eating Cheerios with chopsticks, or eating raw radishes, or not laughing at Robin Williams. The short answer is yes, we do. It makes up for all those hours spent learning statistics.)

As we gain more experience doing something and it becomes easier for us, we often start to see it in a more abstract *why* way—more in terms of its meaning or purpose. For example, in one study, more inexperienced, underage drinkers tended to describe drinking an alcoholic beverage as "swallowing" or "lifting a glass," while inpatients in an alcoholism treatment program preferred thinking of it as "relieving tension" or "overcoming boredom." The ones who were relatively new to drinking alcohol were, presumably, less personally familiar with the reasons *why* you drink. The alcoholics, on the other hand, knew the reasons all too well.

When people think about what they are doing in *why* terms, they are guided by the big picture—their smaller, everyday actions become a part of something larger and more important. They are more connected to long-term goals. As a result, when people think *why* rather than *what,* they are less impulsive, less vulnerable to temptation, and more likely to plan their actions in advance. (Okay, maybe not when the *why* thinkers in question are alcoholics, but you get my point.) Thinking *why*, they feel more certain of who they are and what they want. And they are much less likely to feel that forces outside of them (like other people, luck, or fate) are controlling what happens to them.

When people think about what they are doing in *what* terms, they are focused on the nitty-gritty—the actual mechanics of getting from Point A to Point B. And while they are sometimes less motivated, and more in danger of not seeing the forest for the trees, they are particularly adept at navigating a rocky road. When what you need to do is particularly difficult to get done, it pays to forget about the bigger picture and focus on the task at hand.

So, since both the "big picture" *why* and "nitty-gritty" *what* modes of thinking have their advantages and disadvantages, the best strategy is to shift your thinking style to match the goal you want to achieve. Sometimes this happens automatically, but not always. It's important to make sure you are using the optimal style, and if not, to shift accordingly. To get motivated and enhance your self-control (or to help someone else do the same), think *why*. Consider the larger meaning or purpose behind what you are doing. If you want to stick to your diet when faced with the allure of the dessert tray, remember *why* you are trying to lose weight. When your employees are doing a lackluster job, remind them of *why* their performance matters—for the company and for themselves.

To tackle a particularly complicated, difficult, or unfamiliar goal, on the other hand, it's best to think *what*. When faced with learning a new routine, break it down into specific steps. Skiing for the first time? Focus on keeping your knees bent and your ski tips together. Forget about impressing everyone with your speed and grace—that's a great way for a novice skier to end up wrapped around a tree.

Complete the exercise below to see how you can do this with goals you already have. (A quick note: Throughout the book, I'll be giving you written exercises to help you learn how to use new strategies to improve your achievement. When you're learning something new, writing it down step by step is an excellent way to help make it a habit. Consider keeping a notebook just for practicing the exercises in this book. Eventually, with practice, your brain will embrace the new strategy and begin to use it automatically, so you won't need to go to the trouble of written exercises. But for the time being, taking the trouble to actually write it all down is really worth your while.)

How to Think "Why"

1. Write down an action you've had trouble taking recently because you haven't felt motivated or you've given in too much to temptation. It can be anything from not ordering dessert to answering all your important e-mails each day.

2. Now, write down *why* you want to take that action. What is the purpose of the action *for you*? What goal does it help you to achieve? How will you benefit from it?

The next time you attempt this action, stop and think about the *why* you just identified. Repeat this over and over again, until it becomes a habit (and it will—with repetition, any relatively simple act will become automatic and effortless. You just have to keep at it.)

How to Think "What"

1. Write down something you want to accomplish that is really complicated, highly difficult, or very unfamiliar or new to you.

Maybe you want to create your own website but aren't experienced with computers, or perhaps you are thinking about starting a new career.

2. Now, write down *what your first step should be*. What is the specific action that you need to take in order to begin to accomplish this goal?

The next time you think about this goal, stop and think about the very next specific action you need to take and focus on that. This too will quickly become a habit.

Now versus Later

If you're going to strike the right balance when it comes to thinking *why* versus *what* in pursuit of your own goals, it will be helpful to know when you might unconsciously be *biased* toward one kind of thinking or the other. That way, you can catch yourself favoring the *why* or *what* and compensate for it. A couple of pages ago, I told you that once a task becomes easy or familiar, most of us start favoring *why* thinking. Another powerful influence on whether you think of an action or a goal in abstract *why* or concrete *what* terms is *time*—specifically, how long it will be before you actually do whatever it is you are planning to do. Are you going to start your new diet tomorrow, or next month? Are you considering taking a vacation next week, or next year? Recent research has shown that most of us are biased to think about more *distant* future plans in higher level, more abstract terms—ones that emphasize the *why*. *Near* future plans, on the other hand, tend to be more concrete—more focused on *what* you will need to do to get it done.

Psychologists Yaacov Trope and Nira Liberman made this discovery when they asked a group of undergraduates to choose the best descriptions for a set of everyday activities. One group was asked to imagine doing each activity in the near future ("tomorrow"), while another group was asked to imagine each activity in the more distant future ("next month"). Trope and Liberman found that the students preferred to describe an activity such as "moving into a new apartment" as "packing and carrying boxes" (a *what* description) when imagining doing it tomorrow, but preferred the more abstract, *why*-based "starting a new life" when imagining the same activity a month from now.[5]

It turns out that these differences have important implications for how we make choices and decisions. And they can lead us into different sorts of trouble. *Why* thinking leads you to pay more attention to what psychologists call *desirability* information. In other words, whether or not taking that action or achieving that goal will result in good things for you. How fun, pleasant, or rewarding will it be? When we consider doing something in the more *distant* future, this is primarily what we're trying to evaluate. Will going to medical school *a few years from now* make me successful and rich? Will speaking at that conference *six months from now* be good for my career and enable me to see old friends? Will having my in-laws over *next Christmas* be wonderful for my kids? If the answers are "yes," then you are likely to adopt that goal (like getting into medical school) or take that action (like inviting your in-laws for the holidays).

More concrete, *what* thinking leads you to place more weight on *feasibility* information—whether or not you can actually *do* whatever needs to be done. How likely are you to succeed? What obstacles stand in the way of your success? When we consider doing something in the *near* future, this is what we spend the most time thinking about. What are the chances I can get into medical school *next* year given my grades? Who will watch my kids if I attend that confer-ence *next week*? Where the heck are all those relatives going to sleep when they arrive *tomorrow*?

Did you ever wonder why you commit yourself so often to some-thing in the future that seems like a good idea at the time but be-comes more and more awful as the day approaches? "Why did I ever agree to this?" we lament. "How did I think I could get into med school with a C in biology?" "Why did I think I had room in my house for a dozen more people?" And now the panic sets in—because when you decided your goal was to become a doctor, when you decided to fill your house with your husband's family, you didn't really spend all that much time thinking about whether or not you could make it work. You were thinking *why*, not *what*, and if it's any consolation, it's a situation most of us fall in again and again. Because we are biased to think about future events more in terms of *why* we want to do them and less in terms of how we'll actually get it done, we adopt goals and plans with potentially rich rewards that are also logistical nightmares.

For more near events, we make the opposite mistake. How many spur-of-the-moment chances to do something fun, interesting, or rewarding have you turned down because they just seemed like too much hassle? I once turned down a free trip to India because I thought it would be too stressful to try to prepare for it adequately in just a few weeks' time (Did I need vaccinations? Could I get my passport renewed? What about a visa? Who would watch my dog?). I didn't go even though I knew that if I had really exerted myself, I probably could have pulled it off. It was a decision I came to regret so much that eventually I did take a trip to India, except instead of being free it cost me many thousands of dollars. (So much for *what* thinking.) Many of us have a hard time being truly spontaneous or seizing unforeseen opportunities in the near future. We focus too much on the *what*, not enough on the *why*—getting so bogged down by the details that we forgo opportunities that might have been really rewarding (or, in my case, significantly cheaper).

Liberman and Trope have illustrated the *why-what* trade-off in a series of clever studies. In one, Tel Aviv University students were given a choice of course assignments. They varied whether the assignment was boring but easy ("history of psychology" readings in Hebrew, the students' native language) or interesting but hard ("romantic love" readings in English, which students could read but with much more difficulty). The researchers also varied *when* the assignment would be due—the students would be given one week to work on it, and it would be due either the following week (in the *near* future) or nine weeks later (in the more *distant* future). Students who had to complete the assignment the next week overwhelmingly preferred the easy but boring option—they were willing to sacrifice interest to keep from having to work too hard. Students who could put off the assignment for nine weeks, on the other hand, chose the harder but more interesting readings hands down. And though in some ways the more noble, and certainly more desirable, choice, there is no doubt that some of these students regretted their decision when grappling with their English-to-Hebrew dictionaries two months later. So when we think about what we want to do in the *distant* future, we sacrifice practical considerations for the potential for reward. And when we think about what we'll do in the *near* future, we tend to be all business, no pleasure. Put differently, about the future, we think like explorers—but when it comes to the here and now, we're more like accountants.

And speaking of accounting, these biases have even been found to apply to decisions involving money. For any gamble, you need to consider two things: the payoff and the odds. The payoff is the *desirability* information—it's *why* you are gambling, the reward you'll (potentially) get from it. The odds are about *feasibility*—it's *what* could actually happen, the probability that this will work out for you. When students were given a choice between a lottery with a high probability of winning $4 or low probability of winning $10, those who were to play *that day* strongly preferred the sure thing with the low payoff, while those who were to play *two months later* usually picked the long shot with the bigger payoff. A similar result was found in a study of raffle preferences—for a raffle being drawn *that day*, people preferred the raffle ticket for a chance to win a Brita filter pitcher (an unpopular item, and therefore one you have a good chance of winning), but when the raffle was *two months from now*, most people preferred the chance to win a new stereo (the very valuable item with the much less favorable odds). In any scenario that involves risks and rewards (and really, when you think about it, that applies to just about anything), it's important to weigh both kinds of information as clearly and objectively as possible. Knowing how your thinking may be affected by *time*—by whether you are deciding about the near or distant future—is crucial if you want to compensate for your natural bias and make the best possible decision.

The differences caused by *why* thinking and *what* thinking go beyond just the choices we make. In another study, Liberman and Trope asked people to plan how much time they would spend on a set of work-related and leisure activities either "next week" or "a week a year from now." When the plans were for the more distant future, an average of eighty-two hours were allotted, compared with an average of sixty-eight hours for the near future. So people tended to think that on average they would have about *fourteen more hours* available each week next year than they do now. It goes without saying that that's probably not realistic, though it does explain why so many of us find ourselves struggling to juggle all the goals and plans we thought we'd have enough time for.

Also, when planning for next week, the amount of time study participants planned for work activities was negatively related to the time spent for leisure activities—in other words, people quite rationally recognized that time spent doing one thing means time *not* spent doing another. Interestingly, this wasn't the case when it came to future planning. In the distant future, participants seemed to consider each activity in isolation, and how much time they would like to spend on it, rather than recognizing the trade-offs they would necessarily have to make.

Thinking *what* when it comes to your goals is an excellent way to not only be more realistic about your time, but also to prevent procrastination. In one study, Liberman, Trope, Sean McCrea, and Steven Sherman asked undergraduates to complete a short survey and return it to them via e-mail within three weeks in order to earn a cash prize.[6] Before receiving the survey, each participant completed a task designed to put them in either a *why*-thinking or *what*-thinking mindset. To encourage *why* thinking, the students were asked to take a list of ten activities like "opening a bank account" or "writing in a diary" and come up with reasons *why* someone might do these things. To create a *what* mind-set, students were given the same list and asked to describe *how* you would actually go about doing each activity. The researchers then recorded how long it took for the students to achieve their goal (by completing the survey and sending it back). Remarkably, the ones who had been encouraged to think *what* sent in their surveys *nearly ten days earlier* on average than those who thought *why* (in another version of this study, the difference was closer to fourteen days). So thinking about your goal with a *what* mind-set leads you to focus on the specific action you need to take, which helps you to act more quickly in achieving your goal. Focusing too much on *why* you want to do something, on the other hand, may lead you to be rather sluggish when it comes to actually doing it.

Psychologists are often asked some form of the question "Is it better if I do A or B?" Is it better to vent your emotions or to distract yourself from what's bothering you? Is it better to focus on your mistakes or to leave the past behind? More often than not, the answer we find ourselves forced to give is, "Well, it depends." So if you ask me if it's better to think in terms of the big picture or the nitty-gritty, you leave me no choice but to say that it depends—in this case, it depends on what kind of goal you are trying to achieve. Big-picture, *why* thinking about your goal is most helpful for getting you motivated and energized, focusing you on the rewards you can gain, and encouraging self-control and persistence. Nitty-gritty, *what* thinking will benefit you most when your goal involves doing something difficult or unfamiliar, focusing you on the practical details of getting the job done, and helping you to avoid procrastination. Greater achievement comes not from choosing one style over the other, but from deciding how to think about your goal to best overcome the specific challenges you are facing (or how to talk about a goal to best meet someone else's challenges).

The Power (and Peril) of Positive Thinking

You are probably already well aware of the importance of "thinking positive" when you are setting a goal for yourself, or working to reach that goal. Believe in yourself, believe you will achieve your goals, and you will succeed. It would be easy to fill a generously sized bookcase with all the self-help books whose central thesis is this relatively simple idea. And it's a popular idea among research psychologists, too.

So the world loves an optimist, and the good news is that optimism comes pretty naturally to most of us. In studies of optimistic beliefs, psychologists routinely find that most of us believe we are much more likely than our peers to have good things happen to us—to have successful careers, own our own homes, make a lot of money, and live past ninety. We believe we are much *less* likely than everyone else to get divorced, have a heart attack, have a drinking problem, or buy a car that turns out to be a lemon. And by and large, this is a good thing. It's "by and large" because there are important limits. You need to be careful with positive thinking and make sure it's directed in the *right* way.

You see, there is more than one way to think positively about the future. Pretend for a moment that you have the goal of losing weight. There are at least two ways in which you could "think positively" about this goal:

1. You could say to yourself: "I have the ability to lose weight, and I am confident I can reach my goal." In other words, you could think positively about your *chances for success.*

2. You could say to yourself: "I will easily be able to avoid temptations like doughnuts and potato chips, and have no problems sticking to my new exercise regimen." In other words, you could think positively about *easily overcoming obstacles to success.*

When most self-help books talk about the importance of being positive when it comes to reaching your goals, they lump both of these kinds of positive thinking together. They tell you to believe that you will win, and believe that you will win easily. Unfortunately, lumping both kinds of thinking together is a BIG mistake. Because one form of positive thinking is a great thing to do, and the other is a total no-no and a recipe for failure.

Let's start with #1—*thinking positively about your chances for success.* Probably the most widely known and universally accepted theory in the study of motivation is something called Expectancy Value Theory. It states, in a nutshell, that people are motivated to do anything as a function of (1) how likely they are to be successful (that's the *expectancy* part) and (2) how much they think they will benefit from it (that's the *value* part). And of course the more motivated you are, the more likely you are to reach your goal. So it's not just pop-psychology feel-good nonsense. Believing you will succeed really *does* make you more likely to succeed. (There is an important exception to this rule, for a particular kind of goal that I'm going to talk about a lot in Chapter 4. But for most goals this is true, so let's keep it simple for now.)

While there are nearly countless examples in psychology studies on this subject, one of my favorite illustrations of this effect is from a recent study of exercise habits. Tara Parker-Pope, a *New York Times* columnist who writes about health and wellness, recently reported on research in the *Annals of Behavioral Medicine* that looked at the use of home-gym equipment.[7] It's pretty hard to find adults who haven't, at some point in their lives, fooled themselves into thinking that if they just had the convenience of owning their own treadmill or stationary bike, they would use it all the time. (For me, it was one of those stair stepper machines. My husband is still chiding me about that one. But until he gets rid of the barbell set I keep tripping over, I really don't think I should have to listen.) So who does actually use their home gym, rather than just let it collect dust? It turns out that the people in the study who *truly believed they could do it* were nearly three times as likely as those who doubted themselves to still be using their equipment a year later. (In my case, I really have to admit that even when I bought it, I knew deep down I probably wouldn't stick with it. I didn't honestly believe I had a high likelihood of success. I actually *hate* stair steppers.)

So if it's a good thing to believe you will succeed, then surely it must be good to *imagine yourself succeeding easily*, and avoiding temptations and overcoming obstacles with the slightest of effort (that's positive thinking type #2). Intuitively, that makes sense. But actually, it's really, really wrong. Psychologist Gabriele Oettingen has extensively studied the motivational impact of believing you will succeed versus believing you will *easily* succeed, and has found time and again that these beliefs have very different effects on achievement.[8] For example, in one study, obese women who wanted to lose weight were enrolled in a comprehensive weight-reduction program. At the start of the program, Oettingen asked the women to tell her about their expectations for successfully losing weight. And after reading everything I just wrote about positive expectations, it shouldn't surprise you to learn that the women who believed they would succeed in losing weight lost an average of twenty-six pounds more than those who believed they would fail.

But Oettingen also asked the women about their fantasies with respect to the weight-loss process—how they *imagined* it would happen. For instance, they were asked whether or not they imagined themselves easily resisting temptations like the box of leftover doughnuts in the lunchroom at work. Women who imagined that the path to weight loss would be easy lost an average of twenty-four pounds *less* than those who imagined themselves having a hard time resisting temptation. Oettingen and her colleagues have found the same pattern when looking at students in search of high-paying jobs after college, at single individuals looking to form lasting romantic relationships, and at seniors recovering from hip replacement surgery. No matter who they are and what they are trying to do, we find that successful people not only have confidence that they will eventually succeed, but are *equally* confident that they will have a tough time getting there.

Why is believing the road will be rocky so important for achieving your goal? For starters, despite being so unpleasant, negative emotions like anxiety and worry are useful. And that's primarily because they can be *very* motivating. They can motivate us to take extra effort or to plan how we will deal with problems before they arise. Psychologist Dan Gilbert, in his book *Stumbling on Happiness,* observed that "we sometimes imagine dark futures just to scare our own pants off."[9] And we do this because it pays.

Oettingen's studies show that people who believe goal pursuit will be difficult plan more, put in more effort, and take more action in pursuit of their goals. They expect to have to work hard, so that's exactly what they do. In contrast, people who believed that getting a good job after college would be easy sent out fewer applications. Those who imagined themselves falling quickly, hopelessly, and mutually in love with a secret crush were less likely to actually talk to that person about their feelings. Students who thought that doing well on an upcoming exam would be a piece of cake studied for far fewer hours. Patients who imagined themselves getting around effortlessly on their brand-new hip didn't work as hard at their rehabilitation exercises. Ultimately, people who think that reaching their goal will be a breeze simply aren't prepared for what lies ahead of them, and they can be devastated when the dreams that they've enjoyed dreaming about so much don't actually come true.

Then what is the best way to set goals so that you will reach them, without getting stuck daydreaming? The optimal strategy to use when setting a goal seems to be to think *positively* about how it will be when you achieve your goal, while thinking *realistically* about what it will take to get there. Oettingen refers to this as *mental contrasting*— first you imagine attaining your goal, and then you reflect on the obstacles that stand in the way. If you want to get a high-paying job after college, start by imagining yourself accepting an offer at a top firm, and then think about what stands between you and that offer—namely, all the other really outstanding candidates that will be applying for jobs. Kind of makes you want to send out a lot of applications, doesn't it? That's called feeling the *necessity to act*—it's a psychological state that is crucial for achieving a goal. Daydreaming about how great it will be to land that job or fall in love with that special someone you've had your eye on can be a lot of fun, but it won't get you anywhere. Mental contrasting turns wishes and daydreams into reality, by bringing into focus what you will need to do to make it happen.

It's worth pointing out that mental contrasting only helps you commit to achieving a goal if the goal is something you really believe you can achieve. (Here, again, we see the importance of believing you can reach your goal.) If you don't believe you'll succeed, mental contrasting will lead you to *dis*engage from the goal. In essence, it will help you to abandon an unattainable fantasy. And this is actually another great thing about using this strategy. Considering both what you want *and* what stands in your way will give you the clarity to make good decisions—when your chances for success are high, it will increase your commitment to your goal, making you more likely to successfully achieve it. When your chances are not so good, it will help you to recognize that and move on.

And while abandoning your fantasy may be painful and disappointing, it's also a very important and necessary thing to do for your own well-being. Only when we have come to recognize that a goal we have *cannot* be attained do we make room in our lives for something we *can* achieve. For instance, it's only when we admit to ourselves that our dysfunctional and hurtful relationship can't be saved and we finally end it that we open ourselves up to the possibility of a healthier and happier relationship with someone else. Giving up your dreams of medical school when you realize they *can't* come true

allows you to step back and think about what other career you might
be best suited for.

Returning to the topic of goals you think you *can* achieve, Oettingen and her colleagues (in this instance I was one of them) have shown
in numerous studies that when people who believe they can succeed
are instructed to use the strategy of mental contrasting when setting
their goals, they routinely outperform those who are equally confident
but whose thoughts are all about imagining the happy ending. In studies of twelve-year-olds learning a foreign language, fifteen-year-olds
doing test prep over a summer break, adults trying to attract a mate,
and nurses trying to improve communication with parents, mental
contrasting led to greater effort, energy, planning, and overall higher
rates of achieving goals.[10]

In a study of the effectiveness of mental contrasting with hospital
human resource personnel, the managers trained to use this strategy
reported two weeks later that they had improved time management
and found it easier to make decisions. They even reported that they
had more completed projects. Interestingly, they also reported that
they had reassigned more projects to other managers compared to the
no-training group. In other words, they were better able to see which
projects they could handle successfully and which would be better
handled by someone else. They behaved more rationally, more effi-
ciently, and were much happier at work because of it. And the price
of all this efficiency and happiness? Taking a few moments to learn a
very simple technique that can be applied to every goal you are pursuing, or are merely thinking of pursuing. Here's how:

Setting Goals through Mental Contrasting

1. Grab your notebook or just a piece of paper, and write down
   a wish or concern you have currently. This can be something

you are *thinking of doing* or something you are *already involved with doing* (like taking a vacation to the Caribbean, or moving to LA to become a screenwriter, or losing ten pounds).

2. Now, think about what a happy ending would look like for this wish or concern. Write down one positive aspect of this happy ending (for example, how great it would be to relax on the beach without checking your e-mail).

3. Next, think about the obstacles that stand in the way between you and your happy ending (for example, my overfondness for cheese tends to stand in the way between me and the thinner me who lives in my weight-loss happy ending).

4. Now list another positive aspect.

5. And another obstacle.

6. And another positive aspect.

7. And another obstacle.

Now, what do you think your chances for success are? Should you pursue this goal? By contrasting the things you have to gain with the obstacles standing in your way, you should now have a better sense of how likely you are to succeed, and how committed you are to that success.

In this chapter, we've talked about the importance of setting specific, difficult goals for increasing motivation. We've looked at how the ways in which we describe those goals, to ourselves or to others, can influence our chances for success. And we've learned how to direct and harness the benefits of positive thinking (and realistic thinking) about the goals we're setting. For some of you, if you stopped reading this book now, you'd already be more successful in reaching your goals than you were when you started.

But don't stop reading now. Instead, move on to the next chapter, and we'll talk about the goals you are already pursuing in your own life. Where did they come from? How did you end up choosing them over other, equally attractive goals? The answers may surprise you. And if you want to choose goals *wisely*, in ways that will make you happier and more successful, then you need to start by getting a handle on what you've been doing right and what you may want to do differently.

What You Can Do

I'm going to end each of the chapters in this book with a short summary of the main points I've tried to get across. That way, you can see at a glance the steps you can take in your own life to improve your ability to reach your goals. I'm giving you a lot to process here, so I hope this helps.

- **Be specific.** When you set yourself a goal, try to be as *specific* as possible. "Lose five pounds" is a better goal than "lose some weight," because it gives you a clear idea of what success looks like. Knowing exactly what you want to achieve keeps you motivated until you get there. Avoid "do your best" goals— they are too vague to be really motivating.

- **Make it hard.** It's also important when you set goals to make them *difficult*, while still being *realistic*. You want to challenge yourself and set the bar high, because challenges really get the motivational juices flowing, while avoiding goals that are more or less impossible. Remember that if you set the bar too low, you may achieve your goal but are unlikely to surpass it—most people tend to slack off once they've reached their original target. Nobody sets out with the goal of losing five pounds and ends up somehow losing twenty.

- **Think *why* or *what*.** Goals can be thought of in relatively abstract, *why*-am-I-doing-this terms or in more concrete, *what*-am-I-actually-doing terms. For example, dealing with the mess in your closets can be thought of as "getting organized" (*why*) or "throwing out clothes I never wear" (*what*). Think about your goals in *why* terms when you want to get energized, stay motivated, or avoid temptations. Think about your goals in *what* terms when you are dealing with something particularly difficult, unfamiliar, or anything that takes a long time to learn.

- **Consider value *and* feasibility.** Remember that we all tend to think more in *why* terms when contemplating our goals in the distant future. This leads us to give more weight to what's desirable or valuable about the goal (like how much fun a trip to Disneyland would be) and too little weight to how feasible it is (as in, "How the heck am I going to afford this trip to Disneyland?"). In the near future, we naturally think in *what* terms, which can lead to too much emphasis on being practical and not enough emphasis on enjoying what life has to offer. The best goals will usually be the ones you've adopted after weighing both desirability and feasibility in an unbiased way.

- **Think positive but don't underestimate.** When you're setting a goal, by all means engage in lots of positive thinking about how likely you are to achieve it. Believing in your ability to succeed is enormously helpful for creating and sustaining your motivation. But whatever you do, *don't* underestimate how difficult it will be to reach your goal. Most goals worth achieving require time, planning, effort, and persistence. Thinking things will come to you easily and effortlessly will leave you ill prepared for the journey ahead, and as a result can be a recipe for failure.

- **Use mental contrasting to set your goals.** When you are thinking about taking on a new goal, make sure you think about *both* the wonderful things that will happen if you succeed *and* the obstacles that stand in your way. This process of *mental contrasting* will not only help you to make a good decision about whether or not to adopt the goal, but it will naturally engage your motivational systems and maximize your commitment to the goals that you do decide to achieve.

CHAPTER 2

Do You Know Where Your Goals Come From?

NOT ALL GOALS ARE CREATED EQUAL. AND EVEN TWO PEOPLE WHO seem to be working toward the same goal, like having a successful career, often have *very* different goals in mind. That's because success at work can be about many things, depending on the person—it can be about gaining security, or validation, or glory, or perhaps even personal growth, just to name a few of the possibilities. Some kinds of goals seem to lead to lasting improvements in happiness and well-being, while for others the changes are fleeting, if they happen at all. When you are coping with great difficulty or something really challenging, there are goals that will naturally lead to hard work and persistence, and others that are often a recipe for helplessness and depression.

Achieving isn't just about knowing how to reach your goals—it's at least as much about pursuing the kinds of goals that will help you to develop your full potential and actually enjoy the process of getting there. But before I tell you in the coming chapters about how and why goals differ, which ones will work best for *you*, and how you can change your goals (or change other people's goals), it's helpful to start by understanding where the goals you *already have* came from. Knowing why you've made the choices you've made in the past makes you better able to reevaluate them honestly and objectively, and frees you to make different choices from now on.

It won't surprise you to learn that your *beliefs* are important influences on the goals you adopt. For instance, you would probably only commit to the goal of improving your math skills if you believe that math skills *can* be improved in the first place—otherwise it just wouldn't make sense to try. Our beliefs determine whether we see a goal as within our reach or as a waste of time and energy. So I'll be focusing on a few of the common beliefs people hold that have a lot of influence on our goals. You'll see how these beliefs may have shaped your own choices in the past. And you'll find out that some of those beliefs—ones you yourself may hold—are, to put it bluntly, just plain wrong.

It probably will surprise you to learn that the other major influence on the goals you adopt is your environment, and that its influence is almost always unconscious. In other words, throughout your day you are actively pursuing goals *you may not even know you have*—goals that have been triggered by signals and cues around you, including the actions of other people. By understanding how these signals and cues affect you, you can learn to recognize and control their influence. And just as important, you can learn to use those signals and cues to shape the goals of your employees, students, and children.

How Believing Shapes Achieving

Beliefs about Intelligence

Your beliefs about your strengths and your weaknesses play a large role in determining the goals you set for yourself. If I believe that I'm good at math and science, then setting myself the goal of becoming an engineer makes sense for me. If I believe that I am uncoordinated and slow, then trying to make the varsity basketball team probably doesn't make so much sense. Our beliefs about our abilities influence what we think is possible—and what we might realistically be able to achieve.

Interestingly, it's not just whether or not you think you have ability that matters. In fact, what seems to be most important is whether or not you think you can *get* ability. In other words, do you think that intelligence (or personality, or athletic prowess) is something that is *fixed*, or something that is *malleable*? Is a person stuck at a certain level of smartness, or can they get smarter? Psychologists call these beliefs *implicit theories*—they are personal beliefs about the kind of thing intelligence is (or personality, or morality, or any other kind of characteristic or quality.) They are called *implicit* because they aren't necessarily something you've thought consciously or deliberately about. But despite the fact that we may not even realize that we hold them, these theories are powerful shapers of the choices we make for ourselves every day.

Let's start with implicit theories of intelligence. Take a moment to complete the following exercise in your notebook.

What Is Intelligence, Anyway?

Take a moment to answer the questions below. Try to be completely honest. (I know they are a little repetitive, but bear with me.)

1. **You have a certain amount of intelligence, and you really can't do much to change it.**

1	2	3	4	5	6
Strongly Disagree					Strongly Agree

2. **Your intelligence is something about you that you can't change very much.**

1	2	3	4	5	6
Strongly Disagree					Strongly Agree

3. **To be honest, you can't really change how intelligent you are.**

1	2	3	4	5	6
Strongly Disagree					Strongly Agree

Now, add up your score.[1]

What makes someone smart? If you believe that smartness is something you are more or less born with, something that is largely genetic, or something that develops in childhood but then is pretty much constant through adulthood, then you are an *entity theorist* when it comes to your intelligence. (And if you scored 10 or higher, then this is the theory for you.) The "entity" theory of intelligence is, in a nutshell, the belief that a person has a certain amount of intelligence and that there isn't anything anyone can do about it (in other words, intelligence is an unchanging *entity*). You are either smart or you're not.

On the other hand, if you believe that smartness is a quality that is developed over time through experience and learning, and that people can get more of it if they apply themselves, then you are an *incremental theorist*. (And if you scored 9 or lower, this is the theory you believe in.) The "incremental" theory of intelligence is the belief that smartness is a malleable quality—people can get smarter at any point in their lives.

Implicit theories can sometimes be more specific, too—focusing on a single trait or attribute. For example, most Americans believe that mathematical aptitude is more of a fixed entity—that you're either good at math or you're not. But when it comes to overall intelligence, it seems to be split down the middle, with just about everybody falling into either the entity or incremental camp. And like most people, you may not have ever thought about which camp you're in until you answered those questions above. But whichever theory sounds right to you, even if you never stopped to consciously think about it before, it has almost certainly shaped your life and the goals you have chosen for yourself in profoundly important ways.

Much of the work that has been done to identify and understand implicit theories comes from the laboratory of Stanford psychologist Carol Dweck. In her book *Mindset,* she elaborates on the many ways in which our beliefs about our own ability to grow and develop (or *in*ability to do so) shape every aspect of our lives. Across dozens of studies, Dweck and her students have shown that people who believe their personal traits, like smartness, are fixed become overly concerned with receiving validation. They want, whenever possible, to receive confirmation that they are smart (or, at the very least, that they are not stupid).[2] They want to feel smart. They want to look smart. And if you think about it, this makes a good deal of sense.

If I only have a fixed amount of smartness, then it's really important for me to have *a lot* of it, since I can't actually get any more. And remember that being smart isn't just a matter of pride or flattering your ego—you want to have high ability so that you can be a successful person and get the things in life you want. So if you are an entity theorist when it comes to intelligence, your primary goal becomes proving to yourself and to everyone else that you *are* quite smart, every chance you get.

Not surprisingly, entity theorists make choices and set goals designed specifically to validate their intelligence. As a rule, they avoid goals that are too challenging, preferring the safer bets. About this

I can speak from personal experience, since I was, until graduate school, very much a die-hard entity theorist. Like a lot of people, I thought that a person was smart when it came to particular subjects because her genes made her that way. Also, like a majority of Americans, I believed in something that psychologists call the *inverse effort rule*—if you have to work hard at something, you aren't good at it. Effort compensates for a lack of ability. So whenever possible, I chose subjects that came easily to me—ones that made me look and feel smart.

When I was twelve, I begged my parents to buy a piano, and I took about a year of piano lessons. Then I realized that I would have to work really, really hard to become even a halfway decent pianist, and I quit. It's a decision that I have always regretted. You see, because I quit, I robbed myself of all the enjoyment and satisfaction I could have gotten from playing the piano, even if I never played particularly well. Entity theorists shortchange themselves in this way all the time by concentrating too much on proving themselves at the expense of experiences that could potentially enrich their lives.

Incremental theorists tend not to make that mistake. When you believe that your ability—any ability—can be grown and developed over time, you focus not so much on proving you are smart, but on cultivating your smartness. Challenges aren't threatening—they are opportunities to acquire new skills. Mistakes don't mean you are stupid—they are full of information that can help you to learn. I often marvel at the number of skills my mother has acquired in her adult life—things that she had little experience with growing up and no formal training in. My mother has taught herself to draw charcoal sketches, quilt elaborate and intricate patterns, design and create her own clothing, and is practically a master gardener. She refinishes furniture. She built a rock wall around her property, with rocks she dug out of that property, *by herself*. And when I was growing up, I don't remember her doing *any* of these things. It's not as if she never makes mistakes. She does—particularly when she's learning something totally new. Her early quilts were overly ambitious and the stitching wasn't perfect. Some of her plants didn't thrive. Sometimes, part of the rock wall would fall down. But even though she found these experiences frustrating, she learned from them, and she never doubted that she would "get the hang of it eventually." And that's because when it comes to drawing, sewing, gardening, painting, and building rock walls, my mom is an incremental theorist.

Looking for evidence that implicit theories do indeed shape our choices, Dweck asked junior high and college students to describe the goals they pursued in the classroom. Those who believed their intelligence was fixed agreed with statements like "Although I hate to admit it, I would rather do well in a class than learn a lot" and "If I knew I wasn't going to do well at a task, I probably wouldn't do it even if I might learn a lot from it." Those students who believed their intelligence could be increased preferred statements like "It's much more important for me to learn things in my classes than it is to get the best grades."

In another study of college students, this time at the University of Hong Kong, Dweck and her colleagues showed how these beliefs can influence important real-life decisions. At the University of Hong Kong, all classes are conducted entirely in English, despite the fact that some of the students are not yet proficient in English when they arrive on campus. So Dweck asked those students whose English could use some improvement if they would be interested in enrolling in a remedial English proficiency course. Only the students who believed that they could get smarter (the incremental theorists) showed any interest in the course—73 percent of these students were willing to enroll. Those who believed their smartness was fixed (the entity theorists) wanted nothing to do with it—only 13 percent of these students expressed a willingness to take the course. Most of them did not think a remedial course could actually help them improve. And just as important, they believed that *taking* a remedial course would publicly expose their lack of ability.[3]

Can a Leopard Change Its Spots?

Implicit theories aren't just about intelligence—they can be about practically anything. You can believe that your personality is fixed—that you are who you are and you can't teach an old dog new tricks. Or you can believe it is malleable—that you can change and improve your personality and turn over a new leaf. And even young children are guided by these beliefs, particularly when it comes to personality and character. For instance, Dweck and her colleagues studied a large group of ten- to twelve-year-old boys and girls and asked them about their friendship goals. Those children who believed that their own personality and character couldn't be changed were more focused than their peers on being popular and avoiding rejection. On Valentine's Day, these children would make valentines for the most popular children, hoping to win their favor. Those more focused on avoiding rejection would make valentines only for the children who they knew would give one in return. On the other hand, the children who believed they could improve and grow as a person tended to choose goals that were more about developing relationships. Their valentines went to children they said they would like to know better, opening the door to friendship.[4]

We find the same patterns outside the classroom as well—even when it comes to choosing a mate. People who believe that their personalities are pretty much fixed tell us that they are looking for a mate who will see them as "perfect" and make them feel good about themselves. They choose partners who they think will feel "lucky to be with me." And they are quick to exit a relationship that becomes too argumentative or critical. Those who believe their personalities can change seem to prefer partners who will challenge them to develop and grow, and are more likely to see a "rough patch" in the relationship as an opportunity to learn about their partner and themselves.

Psychologist Jennifer Beer has shown that shy people even have different theories about their own shyness—theories that influence how they interact with their social world.[5] In one study, Beer offered shy individuals a choice between two encounters involving another person, which she told them would be videotaped. One was a situation in which they would be paired with a very social and charming person, from whom they could learn some valuable social skills. The downside of this choice, they were told, was the fact that they would probably appear awkward on the video compared to the expert charmer. They also had the option of choosing to talk to someone even *more* shy, with even *worse* social skills. They wouldn't learn anything from this experience, but at least they would look good on the video by comparison.

Those people who believed that "I can change aspects of my shyness if I want to" (the ones who thought shyness was malleable) strongly preferred the opportunity to learn, even if it made them look foolish. Those who felt that their "shyness is something about me that I can't change very much" (the ones who believed it was fixed), on the other hand, much preferred the chance to look good by comparison. When we believe that there is something about ourselves we cannot change, we pursue goals that focus exclusively on presenting ourselves to others in the best possible light. Ironically, these are goals that often actively *prevent* change—goals that make it impossible for us to learn and grow.

How We Get Unstuck

How often have you found yourself avoiding challenges and playing it safe, sticking to goals you knew would be easy to reach? Are there things you decided long ago that you could never be good at? Skills you believed you would never possess? If the list is a long one, you are undoubtedly an entity theorist—and your belief that you are "stuck" being exactly as you are has done more to determine the course of your life than you probably ever imagined. Which would be fine, if the entity theory were true. Only it isn't—it's dead wrong.

Let's focus on the example of intelligence (though you can make the same arguments about personality characteristics as well). I'm not trying to suggest that our genes don't play a role in determining how smart we are. And yes, smart parents often have smart kids. But as psychologist Richard Nisbett points out in his excellent book *Intelligence and How to Get It,* smart parents give their children a lot more than just a bunch of chromosomes. They create home environments that are richer in learning opportunities. They talk more to their children. Often, they make more money and so are better able to provide educational opportunities and send their children to better school districts. Smart parents seem to give their children many, many more chances to *develop their intelligence.*[6]

And if you don't believe me, just look at what happens when less privileged children, from educationally impoverished backgrounds, are given the same kinds of chances. They *get smarter.* To take just one example, look at the extraordinary success of the KIPP (Knowledge Is Power Program) charter schools. Like most KIPP schools, the KIPP academy in the South Bronx serves primarily poor, minority students, many of whom receive little guidance, support, or educational encouragement in the home. KIPP provides a rich educational environment as well as explicit instruction in the importance of discipline and hard work. These students go to school from 7:30 a.m. to

5:00 p.m., with additional time on Saturdays and over the summer. Teachers visit students' homes, insist on respectful and courteous behavior at all times, and make themselves available via phone at any time of the day or night. Students put extra time into learning, and teachers provide the care and support that is tragically so often missing in the homes of poorer children.

And what does all this extra time and care and support accomplish? A great deal. More than 80 percent of KIPP students perform at or above their grade level in both mathematics and reading—about *twice* as many as a typical New York City school. According to KIPP, their graduating eighth-graders outperform 74 percent of students *nationwide* on reading and math tests—a remarkable feat considering the fact that a KIPP student usually starts out performing at around the 28 percent level. Given the opportunity, there is no doubt that KIPP students are in fact getting smarter.

Carol Dweck provides yet another example of how students can get smarter in the right environment—in this case, an environment in which they are *explicitly taught* the incremental theory of intelligence. She divided seventh-grade students at several New York public schools into two groups: a control group and a *you-can-get-smarter* theory intervention group. Students met for half an hour a week, for eight weeks, with a member of the research team. The researcher spent those sessions teaching the children about the physiology of the brain and how it learns and grows, through science-based readings, activities, and discussions. The researcher also emphasized how intelligence is malleable and can be developed through experience and hard work. For comparison, the control group of students spent the same amount of time learning about other aspects of the brain, like how memory works. But their lessons did not involve any discussion of the nature of intelligence. And while the control group's math scores worsened over the course of the seventh grade (an unfortunately common finding among students transitioning from grade school to junior high), students in the intervention group showed *improvement* in math scores after receiving the special theory-based training. This suggests that the key to getting smarter is first coming to believe that it is *possible* to get smarter—our beliefs can open (or close) that door.[7]

Nisbett writes that "the degree of heritability of IQ places no constraint on the degree of modifiability that is possible."[8] In other words, even if your genes are playing a role in determining how much intelligence you *start* with (or what kind of personality you start with), that doesn't necessarily mean that they predict what you end up with. In study after study, we find that people who are given opportunities to develop their skills and knowledge, and who are motivated to do so, do indeed get smarter. No matter how you measure it, whether with IQ scores, standardized tests, or GPAs, it's clear that intelligence is profoundly malleable—experience matters *a lot*. And if you've believed up until now that you *couldn't* get smarter—that you just weren't good at math, or writing, or computers, or music, or socializing—then maybe it's time to toss out your entity theory. It's been doing you wrong.

You, on Autopilot

When most of us think about setting goals, we tend to think of it as a very conscious, deliberate affair. We weigh the pros and cons, we assess our chances of success, and if we decide to adopt the goal, we commit ourselves fully to it. It's all very intentional—nothing accidental or thoughtless about it. And it's certainly true that some of the goals we pursue are very much the product of purposeful, conscious intention. But not all of them. If the truth be told, not even most of them. Because the vast majority of goals you are pursuing, every day of your life, operate *entirely without your awareness*.

As creepy as that sounds, there are good reasons why human beings work this way. For one thing, the conscious mind—the part of your mind that handles the stuff you are aware of at any moment—is surprisingly limited. It can handle only so much at once before it gets confused and starts dropping things. The *un*conscious mind is another matter. Its processing power is enormous. Metaphorically speaking, if your unconscious mind can hold information equivalent to a NASA supercomputer, your conscious mind can hold roughly the contents of a Post-it note.

Consequently, we work best when as much of what we are doing can be delegated to the unconscious mind as possible. And typically, the more we do something, the more automatic it becomes—the more it is controlled by our unconscious thought. Most adults have had the experience of driving from work to home at the end of a long day and suddenly realizing they have no memory of how they got there. The entire way home, your conscious mind is preoccupied by something else . . . and then, presto, you're home again. Fortunately for you, your unconscious mind is a pretty decent driver. It even stops at red lights. And even though you weren't consciously thinking to yourself "I want to go home," your unconscious mind knew that was your goal, so it took you there.

But *how* did it know you wanted to go home if you weren't actually thinking "I want to go home"? The answer is that the goal is triggered in your mind by cues in your environment. The setting sun, finishing work for the day, sitting in your car—all these cues tell your unconscious mind that it's time to go home. Cues that get paired with a particular goal again and again can come to activate that goal without you even realizing it, until it's all over and you're sitting in your driveway—sometimes, without you *ever* realizing you were pursuing that goal at all.

The Wonderful Thing about Triggers

What aspects of your environment can trigger the unconscious pursuit of a goal? We are only beginning to identify and understand all the potential sources, but a good short answer would be that *just about anything* can trigger goal pursuit.

For example, words or images that are *related* to the goal can do it. In one study, psychologists John Bargh and Peter Gollwitzer observed people playing what's known as a "resource-dilemma" game.[9] In this case, they were fishing from a computerized version of the village fishing pond. Each player wanted to catch as many fish as possible in order to maximize their own profit and win the game. But, just like in real life, you can take only so many fish without overdepleting the pond, at which point you and everyone else in the village go hungry. So some cooperation is necessary, and every time a player catches a fish they have the choice between keeping the fish (to get the highest possible personal profit) or throwing it back (to benefit the community, and your own longer-term interests).

Before beginning the game, Bargh and Gollwitzer asked some of the participants to construct sentences out of a jumble of words that included *helpful, support, cooperative, fair,* and *share.* Remarkably, simply reading these words seemed to unconsciously trigger the goal to cooperate. Those participants returned 25 percent more fish than the people who hadn't been exposed to the cooperation-triggering words. In fact, they returned the same number of fish as the people who were given the explicit, *conscious* goal of being cooperative! And that's worth taking a moment to think about—a consciously, intentionally chosen goal can give you the same results as a completely unconsciously triggered goal. This is a relatively new discovery in the science of motivation, but it's one we're seeing again and again. Having the goal is what matters—how it got there appears to be much less important.

In another study, Bargh and Gollwitzer asked students to work on a Scrabble-like puzzle, making words out of letters randomly placed together. Each student worked on the puzzle alone in a room with an intercom (and, unbeknownst to them, a video camera). After two minutes a voice came over the intercom, commanding the student to stop working on the puzzle. But before beginning the puzzle, half of the students had been asked to work on *another* puzzle—this one a word search, containing words related to the goal of achievement, such as *win, succeed, strive, master*, and, of course, *achieve*. Bargh and Gollwitzer found that 57 percent of the students who had an achievement goal unconsciously triggered continued working on their Scrabble puzzle even *after* the voice had told them quite clearly to stop (compared to only 22 percent among students who hadn't been triggered).

Maybe now those "motivational" posters you see plastered everywhere with pictures of mountains and rivers and words like "TEAMWORK" and "DETERMINATION" in big, bold letters are starting to seem a little less silly, right? Most people look at those and think, "Yeah, right . . . like I'm going to be more motivated because I'm forced to stare at a poster that says 'SUCCEED' all day. Who cares about a stupid poster?" Well, it turns out your unconscious mind does. And it's already gone to work.

But you don't necessarily need to read goal words to unconsciously trigger goals. Other studies have shown that the mere presence of *means* that could be used to achieve the goal can trigger it. Walking past the gym can trigger the goal of wanting to work out. A plate of fruits and vegetables can trigger the goal of eating healthy. (Strategically walking my husband past the jewelry store just before a birthday or anniversary has paid off for me on more than one occasion.)

Even *other people* can trigger goals—especially people you are close to, who you know want you to pursue a particular goal. Psychologist James Shah interviewed college students to determine how much each student's father valued high achievement.[10] He found that when the students were subliminally (unconsciously) exposed to their own father's name before completing a set of difficult problems, those students who associated Dad with the goal of high achievement worked harder and performed better. Also, the closer the relationship with Dad, the stronger the effects.

But when it was over, they had *no idea* that they had been trying particularly hard. The goal of achieving was triggered by unconscious thoughts of their fathers and was pursued completely without awareness. Interestingly, unconsciously thinking about a loved one who does *not* approve of a goal can also *inhibit* its pursuit—you are less likely to want to get drunk or leave all the dishes in the sink if your unconscious mind is envisioning your mother's wagging finger or disappointed sigh. Under certain circumstances, though, this can backfire—recent research has shown that among more "rebellious" individuals, unconsciously triggered thoughts of an achievement-loving dad can lead to *less* effort and *worse* performance. Evidently, when it comes to rebels, even their unconscious minds don't like being told what to do.

Remarkably, the goals of people you don't even *know* can be goal triggers. Psychologists refer to this as *goal contagion*—because at an unconscious level, goals do appear to be quite contagious.[11] Just seeing someone else pursue a particular goal makes you more likely to start pursuing it yourself. In one of the first studies of goal contagion, for example, a group of Dutch men and women read a short story about Johan, a college student who was planning a vacation with friends. In one version of the story, Johan was going to a farm in his village to work for a month before taking the trip. Though not explicitly stated, this information implied that Johan had the goal of earning money in order to go on his trip. In the other version, Johan was going to spend the month volunteering at a community center. After reading one of the two Johan stories, everyone had the opportunity to earn money by completing a computer task as quickly as possible—the faster their performance, the more money they could earn. Those who had read about the Johan who had the goal of earning money were 10 percent faster than those who read about Johan the volunteer! And once again, the faster participants were completely unaware that anything about Johan had influenced their own behavior. But Johan's moneymaking goal had become contagious, and the people exposed to it worked harder to earn money without ever realizing why.

In another study, a group of male participants read the story of Bas, who was meeting his former college friend Natasha in the local pub. They spend the night catching up, drinking, and dancing. In one version of the story, Bas and Natasha part ways at the end of the evening. In another, Bas walks Natasha home and, upon arrival, asks, "May I come in?" The goal of seeking casual sex is implied (quite strongly) but never actually stated. After reading about either the sex-seeking Bas or the heading-home-alone Bas, each of the male participants in the study found themselves in a position to offer help to an attractive female undergraduate named Ellen. You probably won't be surprised to learn that the men who had read about sex-seeking Bas spent significantly more time and energy helping the beautiful and vulnerable Ellen.

So, at this point, you may be getting worried. Does this mean that anytime I see someone with a particular goal, I'm going to adopt it? No—there are limits on how "contagious" a goal will be for you. For example, Johan's moneymaking goal turned out to only be contagious for men and women who themselves were short on cash—the participants who felt that they had plenty of money did not show any effect at all. A goal must seem *desirable* before your unconscious mind will adopt it.

Okay, but what if the goal is something I shouldn't have? Can *bad* goals be contagious, too? Will watching too much *Sopranos* turn me into a criminal? If my friend cheats on her husband, will I unconsciously adopt that goal, too? Absolutely not. Nothing can trigger a goal that you feel is *wrong* to pursue, no matter how desirable it may seem. In another version of the Bas study, when casual sex-seeking Bas was also described as excited about "the upcoming birth of his child," the results changed dramatically. Because they viewed the goal of seeking causal sex when you are already in a relationship as reprehensible, the men in that version didn't find Bas so contagious and, as a result, were not particularly helpful to poor Ellen.

There are important limits to what the environment can do. The good news is that nothing in your environment is going to trigger in you the goal of being a mass murderer, or robbing a bank, or cheating on your spouse, unless those were goals you already had to begin with. In general, unconsciously operating goals are ones that we either have already consciously adopted (but are just continuing to work in an unconscious way) or are goals we see in a very positive light.

Make Your Unconscious Work for You

Now that you know how cues in your environment can trigger the unconscious pursuit of goals, it's time to take a good look around and see what *your* environment may be triggering. And even more important, take the time to figure out what is *missing*. If there are goals you want to pursue (losing weight, stopping smoking, remembering to call your mother, fixing up the house), are there triggers in your environment that will help your unconscious mind activate those goals? Remember that the triggers can be anything, so long as their meaning is clear to *you*. Leave healthy snacks out where you can see them. Leave a fitness magazine lying on the counter in your kitchen. Keep a to-do list, in big letters, someplace where you see it every day. Put a nice, framed photo of your mom next to the phone. It doesn't matter what kind of cues you use—as long as you fill your environment with them, you can count on your unconscious mind to start giving you a hand in reaching the goals you want to achieve.

Of course the same advice applies to times when you want *someone else* to be more successful in pursuing a goal. Are there cues in your teenagers' rooms that will help them remember to do their homework? (My parents gave me Einstein and Beethoven posters in high school. Very clever of them.) Are there cues in your employees' workspace that will inspire them to work with enthusiasm and efficiency? Are there cues in your home that will encourage your spouse to be more cooperative and supportive? When you think about the kinds of triggers you might add to these environments, remember that the same trigger may lead to very different goals, depending on the person. For example, being in a situation of holding power over others seems to unconsciously trigger social-responsibility goals (like helping others or giving to charity) in people who strongly value community. The same situation triggers more self-interested goals (like getting ahead at work or obtaining financial rewards) in people who are more individualistic.

So tailor the cues you create to the person they are meant for—this may take some creativity on your part, but it will be well worth the effort. Delegating goal pursuit to the unconscious parts of the mind is a great way to free up mental space and energy for all the things that constantly require your attention. It's a great way to keep yourself on track when temptations and distractions arise. And just like when you find yourself pulling into your driveway at the end of a long day, you may find yourself achieving goals without really knowing quite how you got there.

What You Can Do

- **Know what is influencing you.** If you want to make better choices when it comes to setting goals, it's helpful to understand some of the hidden influences on those choices. By bringing them to light, we can evaluate whether they are right or wrong, and if we want to, lessen their influence.

- **Know what you believe about your abilities.** The goals we set for ourselves are shaped in large part by our beliefs about our abilities. If there are goals that appeal to you, but you have avoided setting them in your life, it's time to ask yourself why. How sure are you that your beliefs are correct? Is there another way to look at things?

- **Embrace the potential for change.** Believing you have the ability to reach your goals is important, but so is believing you can *get* the ability. Many of us believe that our intelligence, our personality, and our physical aptitudes are fixed—that no matter what we do, we won't improve. These "entity" beliefs focus us on goals that are all about validating ourselves, rather than about developing and growing. Fortunately, decades of research suggest that this belief is completely wrong— "incremental" beliefs that our characteristics can change over time turn out to be supported by scientific evidence. So if you believe there is something about you that you *cannot* change, and that belief has shaped the goals you've chosen in your life, it's time to toss it. Embracing the (accurate) belief that you *can* change will allow you to make better choices and reach your fullest potential.

- **Set up the right environment.** Another powerful influence on the goals you pursue is your environment, and that influence is almost always unconscious. The words we read, the objects we see, the people we interact with—just about anything we encounter can trigger unconscious goal pursuit. Role models motivate us, in large part, through goal contagion. In other words, we adopt the goals we see other people pursuing, provided we see those people in a positive light.

- **Use triggers to tap your unconscious.** To keep yourself motivated, fill your environment with reminders and triggers that will keep your unconscious mind working toward your goal, even when your conscious mind is distracted by other things.

PART TWO

Get Set

CHAPTER 3

The Goals That Keep You
Moving Forward

At the start of every semester, I stand at the front of a large lecture hall looking at a new group of about 100 to 150 fresh-faced young undergraduates. They sit, with pens and notebooks in hand, just waiting for me to start speaking so that they can feverishly write down everything I say. When I was a graduate student, I had eagerly looked forward to my future career as a professor, imagining how I would inspire and engage my students. In my lectures, I would open the door for them into the fascinating and insightful world of scientific psychology. I would help them to better understand themselves and, in so doing, help them to reach their fullest potential. In my head it was something like *Dead Poets Society*, only with a little less standing on tables and a lot less poetry. So you can imagine my disappointment when I came to understand that in the reality of the college classroom, the question I am asked most often by my students is, "Professor, will this be on the exam?"

You really can't blame the students—I have been fortunate enough to teach at some of this country's finest universities, and these are young people with first-rate minds. But they are also young people who are focused, for the most part, on getting good grades and proving that they are smart. It's not that they are all entity theorists, believing that their intelligence is fixed—though many undoubtedly are. It's mostly that modern college undergraduates don't feel that they have the time (or inclination) to join me on a journey of scientific and self-discovery. They need to get into law school. Or medical school. Or an M.B.A. program. Tell students that they should focus a little less on their grades and a lot more on thinking deeply and meaningfully about what you are trying to teach them, and they will look at you as if you have seven heads. Or worse, you'll get the patronizing eye roll and sigh. "Isn't Professor Grant Halvorson naïve? Focus less on grades? She must think this is *Dead Poets Society*."

But what difference does it make, really? Does it matter if your goal is to prove that you are good at what you do, or if instead it's to grow and improve? Aren't both kinds of goals motivating? Sure, they can be. But that motivation will look and feel *very* different. In the last chapter, I talked about how your beliefs can shape your tendency to focus on goals that are about performance, or goals that are about progress. In this chapter, I'm going to tell you more about how these two kinds of goals differ from one another, in ways that *really* matter.

For example, the kind of goal you end up choosing will affect how interesting and enjoyable your journey to achievement will be. It will influence how prone you are to anxiety and depression, and how you handle it when you get hit with a bad case of the blues. Most important, it will determine not only how strong your motivation is, but how long you'll persist when the going gets tough. You see, some kinds of goals make you much more likely to keep trying and not give up, no matter how discouraged you may get. Others seem to be a perfect setup for failure. It's time we all learned to tell them apart.

So think back to when *you* were a high school or college student—

in your classes, did you care more about developing your ability and learning as much as you could, or were you trying to show your teacher (or your parents, or yourself) that you already *had* a lot of ability? In your current job, do you tend to see a new project or assignment as an opportunity to learn and expand your expertise, or as a chance to prove yourself or impress your boss? When problems arise in your romantic relationships, do you focus on growing as a couple and learning from your mistakes, or on evaluating and judging your partner (and yourself)? In other words, is your goal to *be good* or to *get better*?

Before continuing, take a moment to jot down your answers to the following statements in your notebook or on a piece of paper. Remember to be honest—there are no right or wrong answers.

What Motivates You—Being Good or Getting Better?

Using the scale below, rate how much you agree with each statement. In other words, rate how true this is of you in general.

Not at all true		Somewhat true		Very true
1	2	3	4	5

1. It is very important to me to do well at school or work compared to my classmates or coworkers. 5
2. I like having friends who can teach me something about myself, even if it isn't always positive. 3
3. I am always seeking opportunities to develop new skills and acquire new knowledge. 5
4. I really care about making a good impression on other people. 5
5. It's important to me to show that I am smart and capable. 5

4   6. I strive to have open and honest relationships with my friends
        and acquaintances.

4   7. I strive to constantly learn and improve in school or at work.

5   8. When I am with other people, I think a lot about how I am
        "coming across" to them.

5   9. I feel good about myself when I know that other people
        like me.

4   10. I try to do better than my coworkers or classmates.

5   11. I like to be in relationships that challenge me to change for
        the better.

4   12. In school or at work I am focused on demonstrating my
        ability.

Add up your scores from numbers 1, 4, 5, 8, 9, 10, and 12. Divide
this total by 7.
This is your **be-good** score.

Add up your scores from numbers 2, 3, 6, 7, and 11. Divide this
total by 5.
This is your **get-better** score.

Which score is higher? If you are like most people, you pursue
both kinds of goals to some extent. But which do you pursue *more*?[1]

Understanding who succeeds and who gives up or fails in any
achievement situation—be it in the classroom, on the playing field,
or in the workplace—has been a major concern of scientific psychologists for decades. Most people assume it has a lot to do with
intelligence, but that's surprisingly wrong. How smart you are will
influence the extent to which you experience something as difficult
(for example, how hard a math problem has to be before it stumps

you), but it says *nothing* about how you will deal with difficulty when it happens. It says nothing about whether you will be persistent and determined or feel overwhelmed and helpless.

The *goals* you pursue in the classroom, playing field, and work-place, on the other hand, can tell us quite a lot about how you will cope with difficulty, and whether or not you are likely to ultimately succeed. Psychologists who study achievement have been particularly interested in the differences that arise when people focus on performing well to demonstrate ability (*being good*) versus focusing on progress, growth, and gaining mastery (*getting better*).

When Your Goal Is to Be Good

Psychologists refer to the desire to *be good*—to show that you are smart or talented or capable, or to outperform other people—as having a *performance goal*. When you pursue performance goals, your energy is directed at achieving a particular outcome—like getting an A on a test, reaching a sales target, getting your attractive new neighbor to go out with you, or getting into law school. Though they don't necessarily need to be, the performance goals most of us pursue in our everyday lives are often tied closely to our sense of self-worth. We choose these goals in the first place because we think reaching them will give us a sense of validation—making us look and feel smart, talented, and desirable. And then we judge ourselves according to whether or not we are successful. So not getting an A isn't just disappointing in its own right, but it also means I'm not smart enough, not good enough. Coming up short of my sales goal means I'm not good at my job. When my neighbor doesn't seem interested in me, I'm unattractive and unworthy. When I don't get into law school, I'm a total failure. Performance goals are characterized by an all-or-nothing quality—you either reach the goal or you don't. You win or you lose. As the saying goes, "close only counts in horseshoes and hand grenades"—definitely not when it comes to performance goals. When all you care about is being good, being *almost* good or *mostly* good is really not much consolation.

Performance goals are very motivating, not surprisingly, because there is often so much riding on success. In study after study, we find that people pursuing *be-good* goals work hard to do well and, under the right circumstances, are the highest achievers. Students with strong performance goals often get the highest course grades; employees with strong performance goals often are the most productive. If I told you that I was judging you based on how well you did something— that I was evaluating your intelligence, or your competence, or your athletic ability, or how likable you are, you'd probably be very moti- vated to do it as well as you possibly could. But performance goals have a double-edged-sword quality—those ties to self-worth that make them so motivating are also what make them less adaptive when the going gets tougher.

If you think about it, this makes sense. When my goal is to get an A in a class and prove that I'm smart, and I take the first exam and I *don't* get an A . . . well, then I really can't help but think that maybe I'm not so smart, right? Concluding "maybe I'm not smart" has sev- eral consequences, and none of them are good. First, I'm going to feel terrible—probably anxious and depressed, possibly embarrassed or ashamed. My sense of self-worth and self-esteem are going to suf- fer. My confidence will be shaken, if not completely shattered. And if I'm not smart enough, there's really no point in continuing to try to do well, so I'll probably just give up and not bother working so hard on the remaining exams.

When you pursue the goal of *being good*, you can quite easily become a victim of a tragic self-fulfilling prophecy—believing that you don't have what it takes, you stop trying, which dooms you to fail. Which of course just reinforces the (mistaken) belief that you didn't have what it takes in the first place. (As Thomas Edison once noted, "Many of life's failures are people who did not realize how close they were to success when they gave up.") So it's not surprising that performance goals can also lead to the lowest achievement, along with a heavy dose of disappointment and self-doubt.

When Your Goal Is to Get Better

Not every student is obsessed with getting A's. In each of the classes I've taught over the years, there has always been another group of students—admittedly, a minority—who seemed to care more about what they could learn than what they had to prove. They are easy to spot because their behavior is so very different from the be-gooders. They ask questions—questions that they *know* won't be on my exam. They ask about how the topic I'm currently lecturing on is related to what we talked about in class weeks ago, or how it's related to something they learned in a different course, or to something they saw on the news. They challenge my interpretation of a study—asking if there isn't another way to look at the results. These are the students that hang around after class to ask *more* questions. They're the ones who come to my office hours, midterm exam in hand, wanting to know *why* they got a particular question wrong—not to argue with me, but to understand. To truly master the material I am trying to teach them. To *get better*.

Psychologists refer to the desire to get better—to develop or enhance your skills and abilities—as a *mastery goal*. When people pursue mastery goals, they don't judge themselves as much by whether they achieve a particular outcome—like getting an A or surpassing a sales goal. Instead, they judge themselves in terms of the *progress* they are making. Am I improving? Am I learning? Am I moving forward at a good pace? It's less about any one performance and more about performance over time. These goals are tied to self-worth in a totally different way, because they are about self-improvement rather than self-validation—about becoming the best, most capable person you can be, rather than proving that you already are.

When we pursue mastery (get-better) goals, we are less likely to blame our difficulties and poor performances on a lack of ability, because that wouldn't make sense. Of course I lack ability—I haven't mastered this yet! Instead, we look to other, more controllable causes. Am I putting in enough effort to learn this material? Should I be using a different strategy? Should I ask an expert for help? When people run into trouble in pursuit of get-better goals, they don't get depressed and helpless like the be-gooders—they take action. They ask themselves what they are doing wrong, and they fix it. If I get a C on my first exam, I double my study time and try a different study technique, like using flashcards or outlining. If I fall short of my sales goal, I sit down with the more experienced salespeople in my company and ask them for guidance. If my neighbor doesn't seem interested in me, I think about how I might get him to notice me and how we can get to know each other better. If I don't get into law school on the first try, I seek out advice from law school professors or admissions officers to see what I can do to make myself a more attractive candidate before applying again. Get-better goals can sometimes lead to the greatest achievement, because people who focus on getting better rarely make the mistake of giving up too soon.

In study after study, psychologists have found that the pursuit of be-good performance goals and get-better mastery goals leads people to look, feel, and behave very differently. In the remaining pages of this chapter, I'll highlight some of the most interesting and important differences we've found.

Which Goal Is Best for Me?

I wish there were a simple answer to that question. This is another one of those times where I'm forced to admit that "it depends." As I mentioned earlier, there are times when be-good performance goals seem to be more motivating than get-better mastery goals. People who are trying to prove that they are smart or worthy often approach a task with enormous energy and intensity. This turns out to be particularly true when tangible rewards are at stake. In one study, psychologist Andrew Elliot and his colleagues[2] asked study participants to work on a game very similar to Scrabble, where they would try to make as many words as possible after rolling a set of dice marked with letters, for which they would score points. Those in the be-good goal condition were told that "the purpose of this study is to compare college students with one another in their ability to solve these puzzles." Those in the get-better goal condition were instead told that the purpose of the session was "to learn how to play this game well." Half of the students in each group were also told that if they did well enough, they would get a chance to earn extra credit points in the course they were currently taking. College students *love* extra credit points, so this was a very desirable reward.

When making words didn't earn them any extra credit, students in the be-good and get-better goal conditions scored about the same—right around 120 points. But when the extra credit reward was introduced, those in the be-good goal group scored 180 points—50 percent higher than the still 120-point get-better goal group. It turns out people who are focused on trying to develop a skill are not that impressed by rewards. But when you are trying to demonstrate what you can do, it's that much more motivating when high ability earns you something you really want.

Other studies have shown that the pursuit of be-good goals can lead to higher scores on a wide variety of tasks, like solving math problems or playing pinball, and in some cases they can even lead to higher course grades. But in many of these studies, it's clear that the participants weren't really all that challenged by what they were doing—the problems or games were relatively easy, and the courses were ones in which most students did pretty well. So when you find something relatively easy to do, it's very motivating to focus on giving the best possible performance and validating your goodness, and it will probably pay off for you.

A very different picture emerges, however, when the road gets rockier—when people are dealing with unfamiliar, complex, or difficult tasks, with obstacles, or with setbacks. That's where the advantages of focusing on growth over glory become clear.

Dealing with Difficulty

Laura Gelety and I ran a series of studies specifically looking at how people handle difficulty in pursuit of both be-good and get-better goals.[3] We told participants in our studies that we were interested in problem solving. Half of them were then told that their score on the problems they were about to work on reflected their "conceptual and analytical abilities," and that their goal should be to try to get a high score. In other words, we gave them the goal of trying to *be good*, to demonstrate their smartness. The other half were told instead that the task was a "training tool" that would help them to develop their abilities, and that their goal should be to "take advantage of this valuable learning opportunity." We gave these students the goal of trying to *get better*, by improving their problem-solving skill.

We also varied the difficulty of the problems by introducing challenges for some of the participants. We threw in unsolvable problems, without actually mentioning that they were unsolvable. We interrupted participants while they were working, using up their time even though they knew time would soon be up. Across the studies, we found that the pursuit of get-better mastery goals was unaffected when we ramped up the difficulty factor. No matter what we did to them, participants in the easier and more challenging conditions did equally well. A very different picture emerged when it came to be-good performance goal pursuit. Introducing difficulty or obstacles to be-gooders resulted in significantly fewer problems solved.

Remember a few chapters ago when I said that expectations for success are very important for motivation? That people tend to do well when they *believe* they are going to do well? That's perfectly true. But one of the most interesting findings to emerge from our studies is that it is *more* true for be-good goals than get-better goals. When we introduced challenges and ramped up the difficulty for our participants, their expectations for success very understandably went down. They felt, given how hard the task seemed, that they were less likely to do well. But those people who were pursuing be-good goals seemed to be most affected—their expectations dipped *way* down. And perhaps more important, even when their expectations did dip, those participants pursuing get-better goals were *unaffected* by it. In other words, no matter how poorly they thought they would do on the problems, they remained motivated to try and to learn.

That's worth taking a moment to think about. When you are focused on getting better, rather than on being good, you benefit in two very important ways. First, when things get tough—when you are faced with complexity, time pressure, obstacles, or unexpected challenges—you don't get so discouraged. You're more likely to be-lieve you can still do well if you just keep trying. Second, when you *do* start to have doubts about how well you are doing, you are more likely to stay motivated anyway. Because even if you think succeed-ing will be difficult for you, you can still *learn*. Improvement is still possible. You can still get better. So when a task is difficult, and *per-sistence* is the key to higher achievement, get-better mastery goals have the clear advantage. And there is no better place to see that advantage than in the grueling and dream-crushing ordeal that is the college pre-med experience.

Persistence and the Pre-med

Everyone who wants to go to medical school is required to take a set of core science courses in college, including several courses in chem-istry and biology. Pre-med students approach these courses with, at best, trepidation and, at worst, abject terror. That's because good grades (preferably A's) in pre-med courses are pretty much essential for getting into medical school. And general chemistry, taken during the first semester of a student's freshman year, is the first hurdle to be overcome.

For many students—particularly those at top-tier colleges and universities—this is the first truly difficult course they have ever taken *in their lives*. Students who have been at the top of the honor roll throughout middle and high school find themselves suddenly in a course where typically half of them will get a C or lower. The ones who succeed will have to fight for it—they will have to handle the difficulty with grace and determination, keeping up their effort and motivation in the face of that disappointing first midterm. But who fights for it? Who succeeds, and who gives up and becomes a psy-chology major? (I'm only half kidding. Psychology is one of the most popular majors on most college campuses, and I'd wager that while it's mostly because psychology is fascinating, it's at least partly because psychology seems to be a safe haven for many former pre-med refugees.)

Carol Dweck and I believed that the goals students were pursuing in their chemistry courses might have a lot to do with who fought for success and who gave up too soon. So we asked the freshman chemistry students at Columbia University to tell us about what their main focus and objectives were with respect to chemistry. Just to be clear, *everyone* in that course wanted to get an A. It's not as if some of them didn't care what grade they ended up with—Columbia is a pretty competitive place. But for some of the students, grades seemed to be all they cared about. And more important, they believed that their grades reflected how smart they were—good grades mean you've got it, poor grades mean you don't. They agreed with statements such as "In school I am focused on demonstrating my intellectual ability." Other students told us that they also cared a lot about learning and developing, endorsing a statement such as "I strive to constantly learn and improve in my courses" and "In my classes I focus on developing my abilities and acquiring new ones."

Armed with a sense of the goals these students where pursuing, we looked carefully at their course grades throughout the semester. We found that the students who actively pursued get-better goals not only received higher overall course grades, but that they did so precisely because they *improved* with each exam. In fact, get-better goals didn't actually lead to higher grades on the very first exam—their benefit was felt in subsequent exams, when the students who held them were more likely to keep up or even increase their efforts and stay motivated. We saw the opposite pattern when it came to students who were focused on proving themselves through their grades—their performance actually deteriorated over time, particularly when their first exam grades were less than stellar. So when persistence is what is needed to succeed—when you need to be in it for the long haul and not give up too soon—get-better goals are just what the doctor ordered.[4]

Lest you think that these goals only matter in the classroom, I can assure you that we find these effects everywhere. For example, in one study, psychologist Don VandeWalle and his colleagues observed sales performance among 153 employees of a medical supplies distributor, who were responsible for the sales of over two thousand lines of medical supplies and equipment. Theirs was a challenging job—one that required effort and persistence (often in the face of frequent rejection). At the beginning of the observation period, the salespersons were asked to fill out surveys indicating whether they were primarily performance-goal (be-good) focused ("I very much want my coworkers to consider me good at selling") or mastery-goal (get-better) focused ("Learning how to be a better salesperson is of fundamental importance to me") with respect to their jobs. Vande-Walle found that focusing on be-good performance goals did *not* lead to superior sales. On the other hand, those salespeople with stronger get-better goals set themselves higher sales targets, put more time and effort into their sales, and engaged in better planning. As a result, the stronger their focus on getting better, the more units they sold. So even in the "real world" outside the college classroom, people who pursue getting-better goals are in fact better at getting the difficult jobs done.[5]

Having a Good Time

Many people have no doubt told you that when it comes to your goals, it's important to enjoy "getting there." That you need to love not just the result, but the "process"—the means as well as the end.

They've told you that this is the key to happiness. Good advice, except for the part where they forget to mention *how* exactly you go about doing that. It's not always easy to enjoy getting there, to savor the experiences along the way. For many of us, it just doesn't come naturally to focus on what is interesting and enjoyable about what we're doing when we're in goal-pursuit mode. Many of my students seem so focused on memorizing the material they need to remember for my exams that they barely stop to think about what they are actually learning. And that's because they, like many of us, are trying to achieve be-good, performance goals. Be-good goals are all about the outcome, and so that's what holds all of our attention.

Get-better goals, on the other hand, are all about the journey. In dozens of studies, psychologists have found that when people pursue get-better goals, they find greater interest and enjoyment in what they do. They have a heightened attention to the process, experience a greater sense of involvement and immersion, and personally value what they are learning more. This was true even among our pre-meds— the ones focused on getting better told us that they found the experience of learning chemistry interesting, enjoyable, and engaging. When pursuing the right goals, even the periodic table of elements has a certain charm.

Having more fun pursuing your goals is a good thing in and of itself, but that's not all. Interested students are also more likely to be active, rather than passive, participants in their own learning. Studies show that students who find the material interesting are more likely to generate their own questions and seek the answers to satisfy their curiosity.[6] They use "deeper" processing strategies, like looking for themes, connections, and underlying principles in the material they are learning, instead of the more "surface" processing strategies like rote memorization and cramming so favored by be-gooders. They are less likely to procrastinate.[7] And all that active learning and question asking and not procrastinating leads, not surprisingly, to higher achievement. If you choose get-better goals, you have greater success *because* you enjoy the process of getting better. So sometimes you really can have your cake and eat it, too.

Asking for Help

One of the most important things you can do to reach any difficult goal is know when to ask for and accept help. Seeking help can be a very effective way to cope with obstacles, face challenges, or just navigate unfamiliar terrain. But sometimes—in fact all too often—people avoid asking for help because they don't want to look or feel incompetent. Asking for help means admitting you need it. So if your goal is to *be good*, to show how smart or capable you are, then needing help may feel like an admission of failure. On the other hand, seeking help is a great way to *get better*, and the people who pursue mastery goals instead of performance goals clearly know it.

Psychologist Ruth Butler found this to be the case when she looked at how school teachers' own goals with respect to their teaching predicted their tendencies to seek help. Butler distinguished between two kinds of help that people can seek. "Autonomous" help promotes understanding and learning, so that eventually you can do whatever it is on your own. "Expedient" help refers to those times when you really just want someone to do the work or handle the problem for you. Put differently, expedient help is giving a hungry man a fish, and autonomous help is teaching him *how* to fish.

Among her group of 320 elementary, middle, and high school teachers, Butler found that some pursued mostly get-better goals in the classroom. They said that they felt most successful when they "learned something new about teaching or myself as a teacher" and when they "saw that I was developing professionally and teaching more effectively than in the past." Others focused mainly on be-good goals and felt most successful when "my classes did better than those of other teachers on an exam" or when "the principal commended me for having higher teaching ability than most of my colleagues." It shouldn't surprise you at this point to hear that those teachers who pursued get-better goals were more likely to seek help. Specifically, they sought autonomous learn-to-fish help ("I'd prefer someone to refer me to books that can help me improve my knowledge" and "I'd prefer to be offered a workshop on methods of classroom management") but did not seek expedient give-me-the-fish help ("I'd prefer that the principal or someone else deal with the disruptive students" and "I'd prefer someone to refer me to workbooks that the students can do by themselves").[8]

So far, I've told you that people who focus on improving and developing their abilities have quite a few advantages over people who focus on demonstrating their abilities. Get-better goals lead you to handle difficulty gracefully, persist in the face of challenge, find interest and enjoyment in what you do, use better strategies, and seek the right kind of help when you need it. But even a life chock-full of get-better goals is no guarantee that things will never go wrong. Things *will* go wrong. Sometimes very wrong. And, as it turns out, get-better goals are handy when that happens, too.

When Feeling Down Can Fire You Up

Everybody gets the blues. No matter what your goals are, there will be times when things don't work out for you—when circumstances change, when problems arise unexpectedly, when getting what you wanted was harder than you thought it would be. Bad things happen, and they can be very, very depressing. Of course, for people who focus on growth and progress, as opposed to constantly trying to prove themselves, the depressions that do occur tend to be both less severe and less frequent. When you're striving to get better, you are less likely to blame bad things that happen on something about you that can't be changed, so you don't get quite so depressed. And that's good news because it means that by emphasizing getting better over being good, we can help both ourselves and others to live lives less burdened by emotional pain and its terrible consequences.

But as I said earlier, everybody gets the blues—even if you fill your life with get-better goals, bad things will sometimes happen, and you'll be depressed by them. The really remarkable news is that it turns out depression doesn't work quite the same way for everyone, and how it affects you depends on the goals you pursue. My colleagues Carol Dweck, Allison Baer, and I first noticed this through our interactions with an undergraduate research assistant in our lab at Columbia University who I'll call Robyn. Even though I have worked with hundreds of undergrads in my lab over the years, I still remember Robyn as one of the most relentlessly energetic, motivated, and capable students I've ever known. If you asked her on Monday to have something done by Friday, it was finished on Tuesday. She was always on time, always eager to help and to learn, always 100 percent engaged. So you can imagine our surprise when she told us, several months into her assistantship, that she had been suffering on and off from a painful depression *the entire time we had known her*. You could have knocked me over with a feather. "Nobody who's depressed looks like *that*, do they?" we thought. "Is that possible? Can you run around like that, be that effective, and actually be depressed?"

Understanding Robyn became our new challenge, and since she

was so clearly a mastery-seeking, getting-better kind of person, we wondered if perhaps depression looks very different when it's not coupled with the goal of trying to prove yourself and validate your worth. To find out, we asked a group of just under a hundred undergraduates to fill out a diary every day for three weeks. In it, we asked them to tell us about the worst thing that happened to them each day, how they were feeling about it, and what, if anything, they did in response. We also asked them to check off from a list of daily activities anything they had done that day, including studying, hanging out with friends, and doing household chores, such as washing dishes or laundry.

Before beginning the study, the students filled out a questionnaire that measured whether they were focused mostly on achieving be-good performance goals ("I feel as though my basic worth, competence, and likability are 'on the line' in many situations I find myself in") or get-better mastery goals ("As I see it, the rewards of personal growth and learning something new outweigh the disappointment of failure or rejection").

We weren't at all surprised to find that those students who spent most of their time trying to be good were more likely to experience depression than those who were more focused on getting better. Nor was it surprising that the worse the be-gooders felt, the less likely they were to do something useful about it. Feeling bad made them less likely to try to take any action to try to solve the problem. Feeling bad also made them less likely to function well in other aspects of their lives—their dishes lingered in the sink, their dirty laundry piled up, and their textbooks gathered dust.

But we were surprised to find that when they did experience depression, the getting-better group responded very differently to it. The worse they felt, the *more* likely they were to get up and do something about it. If the problem was something they could fix, they took action. If the source of their depression was something out of their own control, they tried to see the silver lining and grow from the experience. And here's what's really remarkable: the more depressed getting-better people get, the *more* likely they are to keep up with their other goals—the sadder they felt, the quicker they were to tackle the laundry pile and crack those books. So when you are pursuing get-better goals, taking a poor performance "to heart" is actually good for you. Feeling bad seems to fuel the fire, making you that much more motivated to achieve success.

If you focus on growth instead of validation, on making progress instead of proving yourself, you are less likely to get depressed because you won't see setbacks and failures as reflecting your own self-worth. And you are less likely to *stay* depressed, because feeling bad makes you want to work harder and keep striving. You get up off the couch, dust off the potato chip crumbs, and get busy getting better.[9]

It may seem incredible to you that shifting the focus of your goals from being good to getting better can so dramatically affect your life. Think of it this way: goals are like lenses in a pair of glasses. The goals you pursue determine not only what you see but how you see it—the things you notice and how you interpret what happens to you. Failures become feedback on how to improve. Obstacles become surmountable. Feeling bad propels you *off* the couch. Change your goal and you change your glasses—your world becomes a very different place.

What You Can Do

- **Be good or get better?** In this chapter, we focused on the difference between goals that are about proving yourself (*being good*) and goals that are about *im*proving yourself (*getting better*). At work, in school, in your relationships—do you see what you are doing as trying to become the best, or showing everyone (including yourself) that you already are?

- **Be good to perform well.** Wanting to *be good* is very motivating and can lead to excellent performance, provided that things don't get too difficult. Unfortunately, when the road gets rocky, people who are focused on proving themselves tend to conclude that they don't have what it takes—and give up *way* too soon.

- **Get better to improve performance.** When we focus on *getting better*, we take difficulty in stride—using our experiences to fuel our improvement. People who pursue growth often turn in the best performances because they are far more resilient in the face of challenges.

- **Get better to enjoy the ride.** When your goal is to get better rather than to be good, you tend to enjoy what you're doing more and find it more interesting. In other words, you appreciate the journey as much as the destination. You also engage in deeper, more meaningful processing of information and better planning for the future. You are even more likely to ask for help when you need it, and more likely to truly benefit from it.

- **Get better to fight depression.** People whose goals are more about self-growth than they are about self-validation deal with depression and anxiety in more productive ways. Feeling bad makes them get up and take action to solve their problems, rather than just lie around and feel sorry for themselves. Not surprisingly, their depressions tend to be both milder and shorter than those of people who are constantly trying to prove they are capable and worthy.

- **Get better to achieve more.** The bottom line is, whenever possible, try to turn your goals from *being good* to *getting better*. Rather than lament all the ways in which your relationships aren't perfect, focus on all the ways in which they can be improved. At work, focus on expanding your skills and taking on new challenges rather than impressing everyone with how smart and knowledgeable you are. When your emphasis is on what there is to learn rather than what there is to prove, you will be a lot happier and will achieve a lot more.

CHAPTER 4

Goals for Optimists and Goals for Pessimists

AT THE TIME I AM WRITING THIS CHAPTER, MY SON MAX IS JUST OVER a year old. Right around his first birthday, Max took his very first steps. Now he is toddling nonstop (and falling nonstop) all over the house. Even though he is my second child and I've been through this process before, I never quite get used to watching the baby crash into things or fall on his face. Watching him zigzag across a room at high speeds, arms flailing wildly, fills me with anxiety. I want him to learn to walk—in fact, it's my goal as his parent to help him to do that. So I have taken precautions. I bought new plush carpets to cover our hard tile floors. I set up safety gates to block stairs and entrances to rooms with sharp-edged furniture. In the rooms where Max is free to toddle, I've gotten rid of everything pointy. I make him wear little shoes with rubber slip-resistant soles to give him better traction. If I could find a helmet in his size, he'd be wearing it.

My husband also has the goal of helping Max learn to walk, but his approach couldn't be more different from mine. He *encourages* Max to climb the stairs—and just about anything else. He leaves the floor strewn with obstacles and watches to see if Max can navigate around and over them. While I am constantly offering Max my hand to steady him, my husband keeps his hands to himself and waits to see if Max can do it on his own. He isn't particularly concerned when Max falls, and he is thrilled to see him master new challenges. He laughs, loudly, at my zealous childproofing. (Though when I bring home one of my more expensive safety gadgets, he stops laughing.)

We both have the same goal—helping our son to learn to walk—but we think about that goal very differently, and so we approach it in completely different ways. For my husband, helping Max to walk is about helping him to achieve something. Learning to walk is an accomplishment. It's an opportunity to move forward in his development—to gain a new and exciting ability. My husband approaches Max's toddling steps with a sense of eagerness—he can't wait to see what Max will do next, and he feels his job is to facilitate that progress however he can.

For me, helping Max to walk is about keeping him safe while he learns. Learning to walk is fraught with danger. It's an opportunity for your child to really hurt himself. I approach Max's toddling steps with a strong desire to be vigilant—I feel like my job is to keep him safe while he learns, and I can't wait until he masters walking so he can stop falling down so much. I want him out of jeopardy.

According to psychologist Tory Higgins, my husband and I have the same goal but we each have a different *focus*.[1] My husband has what Higgins calls a *promotion* focus with respect to the goal of helping Max to walk. Promotion-focused goals are thought about in terms of achievement and accomplishment. They are about doing something you would *ideally* like to do. In the language of economics, they are about maximizing *gains* (and avoiding missed opportunities). When his father lets Max tackle the stairs, he is trying to give him an opportunity to gain something—a new skill.

I, on the other hand, have a *prevention* focus when it comes to Max's walking. Prevention-focused goals are thought about in terms of safety and danger. They are about fulfilling responsibilities, doing the things you feel you *ought* to do. In economic terms, they are about minimizing *losses*, trying to hang on to what you've got. When I put up the gate that keeps Max off the stairs, I'm trying to avoid a loss—in this case, a serious injury.

Like *being good* and *getting better*, promotion and prevention goals can be the very same goals, just thought about in very different ways. As a professor I've seen these differences countless times among my pre-med students. It's easy to spot the ones who are trying to get into medical school because they've always dreamed of being a doctor (a promotion focus), and the ones who are more worried that if they *don't* get in, they'll let their parents and themselves down (a prevention focus). Both kinds of students will work hard to get in—both will be devastated if they fail. But they will work *differently*. They will use different strategies, be prone to different kinds of mistakes. One group will be motivated by applause, the other by criticism. One group may give up too soon—the other may not know when to quit.

Think back to your high school or college classes once again, and try to remember what it was like when you were trying hard to get a good grade. Did you think of getting an A as an achievement, something you ideally hoped to attain? Or did you think of getting an A as an obligation, something you ought to be able to earn? Do you spend your life pursuing accomplishments and accolades, reaching for the stars? Or are you busy fulfilling your duties and responsibilities, being the person everyone can count on? In most situations, do you think you are focused more on what you have to gain or on what you have to lose?

In this chapter, you'll learn whether or not you see the world, and your goals, in terms of gains or losses. And you'll see how it has shaped your choices, your feelings, and the way you've pursued your goals in the past. Unlike *being good* and *getting better*, I'm not going to be telling you that one goal is better for you than the other. Everyone pursues both kinds of goals to some extent, and each goal has its pros and cons. Since most people have a dominant focus—a way they tend to look at the goals in their own lives—the trick is to be able to identify your focus and then do the things that will work best for *you*. Whether you're pursuing promotion goals or prevention goals, in this chapter you'll learn what you can do to improve your chances of reaching them.

Before continuing, take a moment to jot down your answers to the following statements in your notebook or on a piece of paper. Remember to be honest—there are no right or wrong answers.

What Motivates You?

Complete this exercise as quickly as possible. Use only a word or two for each answer.

1. Write down a quality or characteristic you IDEALLY would like to possess (or possess *more* of).
2. Write down a quality or characteristic you feel you OUGHT to possess (or possess *more* of).
3. Name another IDEAL quality.
4. Name another OUGHT quality.
5. Name another OUGHT quality.
6. Name another IDEAL quality.
7. One more OUGHT quality.
8. One more IDEAL quality.

Most people have a pretty easy time coming up with the first few answers but find that coming up with the third or fourth "ideal" or the third or fourth "ought" is much more difficult. How do you tell if you are promotion- or prevention-minded? Which came more easily to you—ideals or oughts? If ideals came more quickly to you, then you are used to thinking in terms of ideals, so you are more promotion-minded. If oughts came more quickly and easily, you are more prevention-minded.

Being Loved and Staying Safe

Human beings, and mammals more generally, appear to be born with the innate desire to satisfy two essential needs: the needs for nurturance and security. Put a little more simply, we want to be loved and kept safe. Higgins argues that the pursuit of promotion and prevention goals arises in response to these universal needs. In other words, we pursue promotion goals—seeking achievements and accomplishments—in order to *get love*. If I can become the person I *ideally* want to be, then other people will admire me for it, and I will have a life filled with love and a sense of belonging. Similarly, we pursue prevention goals—fulfilling responsibilities and avoiding mistakes—in order to *stay safe*. If I can be the person I *should* be, then no one will get angry with me or disappointed in me. If I don't make any mistakes, I can keep out of trouble and have a life filled with peace and security.

As the old song goes, the key to happiness is to *both* "accentuate the positive" *and* "eliminate the negative." That's promotion and prevention in a nutshell. When you're in promotion mode, you're trying to fill your life with positives—like love, admiration, rewards, and other pleasures. When you're in prevention mode, you're trying to keep your life free of negatives—like danger, guilt, punishment, and other pains. Because we all want both love and safety, to maximize our positives and minimize our negatives, we all pursue both kinds of goals throughout our lives. Sometimes, the situations we find ourselves in will dictate which focus we have at that particular moment. For example, an intimate evening spent with your romantic partner is typically about seeking love (a promotion goal), while an afternoon spent testing your smoke alarms is typically about seeking safety (a prevention goal). A trip to a Las Vegas casino is usually promotion-focused because it's about gambling to *win* money—if all you wanted was to avoid losing money, you'd probably just stay home. A trip to the dentist's chair, on the other hand, is often prevention-focused because it's about trying not to lose something—namely, your teeth. It's very rare (though technically possible) to walk out of that office with more teeth than you had when you went in, but quite common to walk out with fewer.

Even though we all sometimes pursue both types of goals, it's also true that most of us come to have a dominant focus—we tend to think more about being loved than about staying safe, or care more about being safe than about being loved. Why might that be? Recent evidence suggests that it may, at least in part, be due to the ways in which we were rewarded and punished by our parents. You might think that people who end up promotion-minded were rewarded more, and that those who are prevention-minded were punished more, but that's not the case. It's actually that they are rewarded and punished *differently*.

Promotion parenting rewards children by showering them with praise and affection when they do something right, and *withholding love* when they do something wrong. When Susie comes home with an A on her paper, Mom and Dad tell her she is wonderful and beam with pride. When she comes home with a C, Mom and Dad shake their heads and become distant, offering no reassurance. Susie learns quickly that living up to her parents' ideals for her gets her the love she wants, and disappointing them leaves her feeling sad and alone. She comes to think about her goals as opportunities to *gain* something—her parents' love and approval. Over time, this extends beyond her parents to become her view of the world—a place where winners take all.

Prevention parenting involves punishing children for doing something wrong, and rewarding them for doing something right by *not* punishing them. In other words, when you do something right, you stay safe. When Billy comes home with a C on his paper, Mom and Dad hit the roof. They yell at him, telling him this grade is unacceptable, and send him to his room without dinner. Perhaps he is grounded as well. When he comes home with an A, no one yells, Billy gets dinner, and he gets to keep his freedom. Billy learns quickly that if he does the things his parents think he should do, life is peaceful and he stays out of trouble. When he makes mistakes, he anxiously awaits the punishment he knows he'll receive. He comes to think about his goals as opportunities to *avoid losses*—to keep bad things from happening. Over time, this extends beyond his parents to become his view of the world—a place where it's better to be safe than sorry[2]

Parents aren't the only influences on our pursuit of promotion and prevention goals. Because Western cultures tend to value independence and emphasize the importance of the individual, they typically foster promotion goals. The American Dream is a perfect illustration of promotion—it's about reaching for the stars, taking risks, going for the glory. Eastern cultures, in contrast, tend to value interdependence and place the greatest importance on the groups to which we belong, like our families. When people think of themselves and their goals in terms of what is best for their group, it fosters a prevention focus. Just playing a team sport can give you a sense of this—when other people's happiness and well-being are at stake, you feel responsible. You don't want to make any mistakes. You want to be someone everyone can count on, and that is what prevention focus is all about.[3]

But as I mentioned earlier, regardless of the fact that most of us have a dominant focus, it's also true that our focus can change as a result of the particular situation we find ourselves in each day. Some goals seem to inherently have a promotion or prevention focus. Trying to win the lottery, or taking a vacation to the Caribbean, is something that most of us would *ideally* like to do. It's hard to imagine thinking of either goal as a duty or matter of safety and danger. If you don't win the lottery or take the vacation, it's not something you're likely to worry about. On the other hand, taking your child to get vaccinated is pure prevention—it's all about safety and could hardly be construed as an achievement. Getting your child a flu shot is not something you're going to brag to anyone about, and no one's going to love you for it.

At this point, you might be thinking that this is really interesting (and I certainly hope you are), but at the same time you may be wondering how useful it is. Why does it matter if we have one focus or the other, if we see our goals as achievements or as obligations? To really do justice to that question, I probably need a whole book. The difference between promotion-mindedness and prevention-mindedness has been shown to be enormously important in almost every aspect of our lives—it impacts the decisions we make, the strategies we use, our responses to setbacks, and our very sense of well-being. But I've got to do this in just a chapter, so I'll try to touch on what I think might be the most useful bits to know.

Think Positive! (Or, Then Again, Maybe Not)

A couple of chapters ago, I told you about the Expectancy Value Theory of motivation. The gist of it is that when we decide whether or not to pursue a goal, we are motivated both by how likely we are to succeed (the expectancy part) and by how desirable the outcome will be (the value part). What I didn't mention is that these two factors get weighted a little differently depending on your goal's focus. When you are pursuing a promotion goal—something you see as an achievement—you are trying to gain something. When it's about gain, you are going to be motivated both by high value and a high likelihood of success. In fact, the more valuable the goal, the *more* you care about your chances of success. That's because more valuable goals usually mean a bigger investment of your time and effort. If you're going to expend all that energy to reach it, your chances for success had better be good.

But when you are pursuing a prevention goal, you are trying to avoid a loss. It's about being safe, avoiding danger. A high-value prevention goal is one where safety really matters and where failure is particularly dangerous. So the more valuable the goal, the more you will see reaching it as a *necessity*. And consequently, the *less* you care about your chances of success. Think about it this way: if it's a matter of life or death (the ultimate kind of prevention goal), do you care if the odds are against you? If there were a one-in-a-million chance that a treatment would cure your terminal illness, wouldn't you do whatever you had to to get your hands on it anyway?

Even in more mundane, everyday circumstances, we find evidence for differences in how promotion- and prevention-minded people think about expectations for success. For example, in one study, college students were asked to rate how likely they would be to enroll in a particular course. Some of the students were told that a high grade in the course would earn them entrance into an honor society, making the course much more valuable academically. For promotion-minded students, their decision to enroll was based almost entirely on the grade they thought they would get—those who thought they would do well enrolled, and those who thought they'd do poorly didn't.

Among prevention-minded students the more valuable the course was, the less likely they were to base their decision to enroll on the grade they thought they'd get. In other words, they were viewing the course as a necessity, so the odds of doing well in it mattered less. They felt they had to try.[4]

Staying Motivated

You might think that once you've committed to a goal and started pursuing it, having high expectations for success is the most motivating for everyone. So encouragement should always be welcome. But actually, it isn't. When you're trying to reach the goal you've set for yourself, promotion and prevention focuses continue to create very different reactions to the positive (or negative) feedback you might receive along the way.

The kind of motivation you have when you are trying to reach a promotion goal—an achievement or accomplishment—feels like *eagerness,* an enthusiastic desire to really go for it. Not surprisingly this eagerness is heightened by positive feedback—in other words, the more you seem to be succeeding, the more motivated you become. Increasing confidence heightens your energy and intensity. Negative feedback, on the other hand, dampens your eagerness. Feeling like you might fail saps your motivation. Doubting yourself takes the wind right out of your sails.

In pursuit of prevention goals—seeking safety and security—the motivation you have feels like *vigilance*, a desire to stay clear of danger. Vigilance actually *increases* in response to negative feedback or doubting yourself. There's nothing like the looming possibility of failure, the very real likelihood of danger, to get your prevention juices flowing.

I saw this difference firsthand in a study I conducted with Jens

Förster, Lorraine Chen Idson, and Tory Higgins.[5] We gave participants a set of difficult multiple-solution anagrams to work on (e.g.,
NELMO, which, provided you don't have to use all five letters, can
be elm, one, mole, omen, lemon, melon, etc.). All the participants
were told that if they performed well, they could earn more money.
But we also manipulated their goal's focus—those in the promotion
condition were told that they would be paid $4 and could earn an
extra dollar if they performed above the 70 percent level, while those
in the prevention condition were told that they would be paid $5 but
could lose a dollar if they performed below 70 percent. It's important
to note that in *both* cases, the participants were paid $4 for scoring
below 70 percent, and $5 for scoring above 70 percent. In *both* cases,
participants had the same goal—to earn $5 rather than $4. But the
focus was different—in one case, it was on *gaining* $1, and in the
other, it was on *not losing* $1. In one case, it's getting the dollar you
want, and in the other, it's keeping the dollar you ought not to lose.

About halfway through the task, we gave everyone feedback. We
told them that so far they were performing either above or below
their target level of 70 percent. So they were led to believe that they
were either well on their way to succeeding or possibly in danger of
failing. Following feedback, we asked them to tell us how likely it
was that they would reach their goal and also measured their motivation. Two sets of remarkably different reactions occurred. After positive feedback, expectations for success in the promotion group
soared, and so did their motivation. But when the prevention group
was told they were doing well, their expectations didn't change at all,
and their motivation actually *decreased*.

After negative feedback, expectations for success in the promotion
group went down a bit as you might expect, and so did motivation.
But in the prevention group, expectations dropped dramatically. These
participants were quite sure they were going to fail. Despite that

drop, or more accurately *because* of it, motivation surged! So the next time you are tempted to give your prevention-minded friend or colleague a few words of encouragement, you actually might want to reconsider. You may be doing more harm than good.

Before continuing, take a moment to jot down your answers to the following questions in your notebook or on a piece of paper. Remember to be honest—there are no right or wrong answers.

Which Goals Are You Good at Reaching?[6]

Answer the following questions using this scale:

1	2	3	4	5
Never or		Sometimes		Very Often
Seldom				

1. How often have you accomplished things that got you "psyched" to work even harder?
2. How often did you obey the rules and regulations that were established by your parents?
3. Do you often do well at different things you try?
4. I feel like I have made progress toward being successful in my life.
5. Growing up, did you avoid "crossing the line," avoid doing things your parents would not tolerate?
6. Not being careful enough has gotten me into trouble at times.

To calculate your promotion success score: Q1 + Q3 + Q4 = ?
To calculate your prevention success score: Q2 + Q5 + (6–Q6) = ?

How Optimists and Pessimists Are Made

Why are some people optimistic? One rather obvious answer is that some of them have good reason to be. They have been successful in achieving their goals in the past, and their past successes give them confidence when it comes to the future. It's also true that some people are really good at reaching promotion-focused goals in particular, while others excel at prevention. The questions you just answered were taken from a measure Higgins and his colleagues have designed to capture those differences. It identifies people with a history of success in promotion or prevention—what Higgins calls promotion and prevention *pride*. Both kinds of people have good reason to be optimistic, and therefore you might expect both kinds of pride to predict higher levels of optimism. But you would be wrong.

Successful prevention goal pursuit requires us to dampen or suppress our optimism in the service of our motivation. When you need to be vigilant, you can't afford to be confident—no matter how successful you've been in the past. People with a history of reaching their prevention goals seem to know this intuitively. In a study I conducted with Tory Higgins, we asked participants who were high in either promotion or prevention pride to complete measures of optimism and well-being. We found that only a history of reaching promotion goals predicted optimism—people who were good at prevention were happy to tell us about their past successes, but when it came to predicting success in the future, they wanted nothing to do with it.

An interesting difference emerged with respect to well-being, too. Our measures tapped into two senses of personal well-being—positive views of yourself ("I'm great") and feelings of mastery and competence ("I've gotten things done"). People who are good at promotion told us that they were high in both kinds of well-being. People who are good at prevention only claimed the latter—they admitted that they had gotten things done in the past, but they were uncomfortable being too positive about themselves. Too much self-admiration, it seems, feels dangerous to them. It is a luxury they believe they cannot afford. And they are perfectly right—if you are pursuing a prevention goal, the strategy of "defensive pessimism" can be enormously useful. In her book *The Positive Power of Negative Thinking*, psychologist Julie Norem points out that:

> Defensive pessimism is more than just pessimism. Setting low expectations—thinking that things might turn out badly—kicks off a reflective process of mentally playing through the possible outcomes.[7]

By thinking about everything that could go wrong, defensive pessimists are better prepared to handle the obstacles that get thrown in their path. In pursuit of prevention goals, it is also a recipe for the greatest vigilance, and therefore the strongest motivation.

So the next time you are trying to light a fire under someone with a prevention focus and really get them motivated, think carefully about the role models you hold up for them to emulate. Typically, when we want to inspire someone, we point to the achievements of famous individuals, risk takers who "believed in themselves," such as Michael Jordan, Bill Gates, and Barack Obama. For a prevention-minded person, being regaled with stories of successful people with can-do attitudes may have the opposite effect you are looking for. For example, in one study, college students were presented with one of two different role models. The positive role model was a recent graduate in their own major who won a scholarship to graduate school, was offered several attractive job positions, and reported that he was "extremely happy with life and where it is going." The negative role model was also a recent grad in their major but with a very different story. He wasn't able to find a job after graduation and had been working in fast-food places in order to earn a living. "Right now," he said, "I'm down about things, not sure where to go from here."

The researchers found that while the promotion-minded students were more motivated by the traditional positive role model, those students who viewed their goals in terms of prevention were more inspired by the negative role model. In the weeks after reading about the unfortunate graduate, they studied harder for quizzes and exams, kept up more with reading assignments, and procrastinated less.[8] So while some people may be motivated by the accomplishments of their heroes, others appear more influenced by a compelling cautionary tale.

In her excellent book *Bright-Sided: How the Relentless Promotion of Positive Thinking Has Undermined America*, author Barbara Ehrenreich offers a vigorous critique of the American culture of illusory optimism. "Positivity," she writes, "is not so much our condition or our mood as it is part of our ideology—the way we explain the world and think we ought to function within it." The banishment of negative thinking, or even *realistic* thinking, Ehrenreich argues, has played an influential role in bringing about many of our current troubles—from the pervasive need for prescription antidepressants to the subprime mortgage-induced financial crisis. "A vigilant realism," she concludes, "does not foreclose the pursuit of happiness; in fact, it makes it possible. How can we expect to improve our situation without addressing the actual circumstance we find ourselves in?"

As heartening as Ehrenreich's message is to those of us who are uncomfortable with too much positive thinking, it's easy to end up feeling a bit confused. Are all those books that tout optimism and the importance of self-confidence really wrong? Is there really no benefit to positive thinking? It seems like sometimes optimism is a good thing, while at other times it is reckless and counterproductive. Well, now that you understand the difference between promotion and pre-vention goals, you can better navigate the confusing sea of self-help advice. Optimism is indeed a good thing, particularly in pursuit of achievements, accolades, and big gains. A more pessimistic realism, on the other hand, is invaluable in pursuit of security or avoiding disastrous losses. The greatest motivation, and consequently the best performance, is the result of matching your outlook to the nature of the task at hand.

Promotion, Prevention, and Priorities

When you see the world in terms of achievement or safety, different things matter to you. You even find different kinds of products appeal-ing. You literally shop differently. For example, psychologists Lioba Werth and Jens Förster found that promotion-minded people tend to prefer products that are advertised as luxurious or comfortable. In one study, when choosing among sunglasses and wristwatches, promotion-minded participants were excited by features like "fashion-able earpieces" and "time-zone settings"—attributes that are hardly necessary but convey a sense of coolness or sophistication. Prevention-minded people, on other hand, are drawn to products advertised as safe and reliable. They preferred sunglasses with a "long guarantee period" and wristwatches with "secure buckles." In another study, prevention-minded participants preferred washing machines adver-tised with the slogans "established for many years" and "consumer tests prove: safe and reliable." Those with a promotion mind-set pre-ferred instead to have "the newest technology available" and "lots of new functions."[9]

It's important to remember that your focus can change from mo-ment to moment, depending on the situation you're in, and so too will your preferences. For example, *what* you are buying can trigger a particular focus—if you want a product that will keep your children from getting into poisonous cleaning products, you will have a prevention focus while making your choice, because that is a decision that is inherently about safety and danger. You will want the established and reliable cabinet lock and won't care much about how hip and trendy it may be. Similarly, promotion-minded persons may buy themselves a flashy red sports car with lots of high-tech toys, but when it comes to buying their teenager *her* first car, chances are they will be thinking about antilock brakes and air bags.

Your Focus and Your Feelings

When you set a goal for yourself and reach it, you feel good. That much is obvious. But what does "good" feel like? The answer is in large part determined by your goal's focus.[10] When your goal is an achievement, a gain, you feel *happy*—joyful, cheerful, excited, or, in the vernacular of a typical teenager, totally stoked. It's a high-energy kind of good feeling to reach a promotion goal. It's a very different kind of good to reach a prevention goal. When you are trying to be safe and secure, to avoid losing something, and you succeed, you feel *relaxed*—calm, at ease, peaceful. You breathe the sweet sigh of relief. This is a much more low-energy kind of good feeling, but not any less rewarding.

The focus of your goal also determines the particular kind of bad you feel when things go wrong. In fact, Higgins first discovered the difference between promotion and prevention when he was trying to explain why some people reacted to their failures with anxiety, while others reacted by sinking into depression. When you are going for gain, trying to accomplish something important to you, and you fail, you tend to feel *sadness*—dejected, depressed, despondent. As a teen might put it, totally bummed. It's the low-energy kind of bad feeling—the kind that makes you want to lay on the couch all day with a bag of chips. But failing to reach a prevention goal means danger, so in response you feel the high-energy kinds of bad feeling— anxiety, panic, nervousness, and fear. You freak out. Both kinds of feelings are awful, but very differently so. And the strategies you use to get rid of those feelings (or to help someone else get rid of them) will be very different, too.

The Strategies That Fit Your Focus

Imagine for a moment that you are a hunter, concealed in the bushes deep in the forest, awaiting the appearance of an unsuspecting deer. You hear a rustling and see a flash of brown in the brush some distance away—too far to know for certain if it is a deer, some other less edible or trophy-worthy animal, or simply the wind and your eyes playing tricks on you. You have a choice—shoot or don't shoot. Consequently, there are four possible outcomes, depending on the choice you make. You could shoot and be right that it was a deer, or shoot and be wrong, wasting your ammunition and scaring off any actual deer in the vicinity. You could *not* shoot and judge correctly that there was no deer, or not shoot and be wrong, missing an opportunity to bring home a trophy buck.

Psychologists refer to these kinds of scenarios as examples of *signal detection*, where the object is to successfully distinguish the "signal" from the "noise." In other words, did you see the deer or didn't you? Was it really there (the signal), or was it just the wind in the bushes (the noise)? If you say "yes" and you are correct, that's called (appropriately, given my hunting story) a *hit*. If you say "yes" and you are wrong, that's a *false alarm*. If you say "no," and if you're right, that's a *correct rejection*, but if you're wrong, it's a *miss*.

When we pursue promotion goals, we are particularly sensitive to the potential for hits—we want to really go for it. "Nothing ventured, nothing gained" is a very promotion-focused philosophy. There is nothing worse, in the eyes of someone pursuing a promotion goal, than a miss (not shooting when the deer really was there) because it represents an opportunity for a hit that was squandered. So people who are promotion-minded have a habit of saying "yes" in these sorts of situations. They shoot. They have what psychologists call a *risky bias*—and as a result they will end up with not only a lot more hits, but also a lot more false alarms. They may be a bit more likely to take down a deer, but they are also more likely to scare them all away by shooting at unsuspecting bushes.

Prevention-minded people, on the other hand, are cautious. They want to be *sure* they saw the deer before they shoot, rather than risk making a mistake. They really hate false alarms, or taking a chance and having it turn out to be wrong. So in pursuit of prevention goals, they tend to say "no" more, or have what psychologists call a *conservative bias*. They don't shoot—they keep waiting. They won't scare away the deer or waste any ammunition, but they may come home empty-handed a little more often.[11]

These risky and conservative biases manifest themselves in all kinds of ways. For example, people with prevention goals are more reluctant to disengage from one activity to try another, vastly preferring the devil they know to the one they don't.[12] But their conservative nature also makes them less likely than their risk-loving peers to procrastinate, for fear that they won't have time to get the job done.[13]

When people have promotion goals, they feel free to be more exploratory and abstract in their thinking. They brainstorm. They generate lots of options and possibilities to reach their ideals. They are much more creative. They are also particularly good at picking up on connecting themes or synthesizing information. In pursuit of prevention goals, such abstraction and creativity are reckless and time-consuming. If you want to stay out of danger, you need to take action. Prevention-focused thinking is concrete. You pick a plan and stick to it. You attend to the specifics. Consequently, people who are prevention-minded are great with details and have better memory for what they've seen and what still needs to be done.[14]

People who are promotion- or prevention-minded even use different strategies in their social relationships. Promotion focus leads us to see our friendships in terms of gain, so we use *eager* strategies for friendship that keep things positive—like being supportive to your friends or making plans to have fun together. Prevention, on the other hand, leads us to see relationships in terms of potential losses, so we use *vigilant* strategies to maintain them—like staying in touch and not losing contact. These differences can also emerge when things in our social world go wrong.

Unfortunately, everyone has had the experience at one time or another of being rejected or feeling left out. Interestingly, the *way* you are excluded can determine whether you respond with promotion or prevention strategies. Psychologist Dan Molden and his colleagues conducted a study in which people were told they would be forming friends over the Internet.[15] Each participant believed that he or she was communicating via computer with two other people who were hidden from view in neighboring cubicles. Molden then varied the form in which the participant was socially excluded in the online interaction—participants were either explicitly rejected by their new computer friends or just simply ignored. In the rejection condition, other members of the discussion responded to the participant's opinions with statements like "Are you for real?" "Really, you're kidding, right?" and "I don't understand people like you." In the ignoring condition, the other two struck up a conversation after discovering that they live in adjacent living complexes, leaving the participant completely out.

Molden found that when people are rejected (social exclusion that is explicit, active, and direct) they feel a sense of *loss* that leads to prevention-focused responses. These people feel anxious, withdraw from the situation, and feel regret about things they said or actions they took. When people are simply ignored (social exclusion that is implicit, passive, and indirect) they feel a failure to achieve a social *gain*, a missed opportunity, which leads them to more promotion-focused responses. They feel sad and dejected but are more likely to attempt reengagement and to regret things they *didn't* say and actions they *didn't* take.

Use the Strategies That Fit

So promotion and prevention focuses predispose us to use different kinds of strategies to pursue our goals. If you see your goal in terms of promotion, you are more likely to seek ways to advance and use riskier strategies, ones that really go for "hits" and involve actions that get you closer to your goal. If you see in terms of prevention, you are more likely to be careful and use conservative strategies, ones that avoid "false alarms" and involve actions that help you to avoid making dangerous mistakes. But that's not the whole story. Because it turns out that making sure you use the strategy that *fits* your focus is really important.

Using prevention strategies to reach prevention goals, and promotion strategies to reach promotion goals, gives your motivation an added boost. Tory Higgins argues that, in general, using the appropriate, best-fitting means to reach a goal adds extra value to the goal. It just feels right. As the saying goes, it's not whether you win or lose but how you play the game. "Playing the game" well means doing it the way that feels good and right to you. Dozens of studies by Higgins and his colleagues have shown that when we match our strategies to our goals, using the ones that "feel right," we are more engaged, involved, and persist more.[16] We are more likely to succeed in reaching them, and more likely to enjoy the process along the way.

One example of the importance of matching can be seen in a study Tory Higgins and I conducted, along with Allison Baer and Niles Bolger, looking at how promotion and prevention-minded people cope with the challenges in their daily lives. We asked participants in our study to fill out daily diaries for three weeks, telling us about how they coped with their most difficult problem each day. We gave them a list of promotion-focused coping strategies, such as "I looked for additional means to advance my goals," "I focused on doing things I knew I would like," and "I made the day better in other ways in order to make up for the incident." Prevention-focused strategies included "I was careful not to make any more mistakes" and "I avoided any other negative events that day."

Even though both ways of dealing with problems can be successful, we found that on days when participants used coping strategies that *matched* their typical goal focus, they were significantly happier and less distressed. Mismatched coping strategies, on the other hand, led to less happiness and greater distress. So it's not enough to take action when you encounter a problem or set a goal. Not every kind of coping will work for every person. You need to take the action that fits your goal, and understanding how promotion and prevention work can help you make the best choice—the one that feels right.[17]

When One Goal's Strength Is Another's Weakness

Because promotion and prevention goals lead us to use different strategies, there can be times when one kind of goal is more effective than the other. In other words, there are things that we are really good at (or really lousy at) when we are focused on either promotion or prevention.

Executing any modestly complicated task, like reading a book or painting a room, involves what psychologists call a *speed-accuracy trade-off*. The faster you go, the more mistakes you make. But going slow has costs too—particularly if time is valuable and you are in a hurry to get the job done. It shouldn't surprise you to learn that promotion- and prevention-minded people end up on opposite sides of this particular trade-off. In pursuit of promotion goals, we tend to favor speed over accuracy. It's better to get the whole house painted even if it's a little patchy and there's quite a bit of paint on the floor. If I don't understand what I've just read, I'll just keep reading and probably catch on eventually, because I really want to finish this book.[18]

When our goals are about prevention, however, we much prefer to go slowly and get the job done flawlessly. Of course, it's going to take forever, but that's a price the prevention-minded will willingly pay. And when they come across a written passage they can't understand, studies show that prevention-minded people frequently engage in rereading, going over and over the material until they've grasped it. They are slower readers, but they don't miss a thing.[19] (Interestingly, research has uncovered one instance in which prevention leads people to be reliably faster than promotion. Prevention-minded drivers judge high-traffic situations as more dangerous and are quicker to hit the brakes.[20])

There is also evidence that the two kinds of focus lead to different rates of success over time. Promotion-focused goals lead to energetic and enthusiastic motivation in the shorter term but can be less adaptive when in long-term maintenance. Prevention-focused goals, on the other hand, remind us that slow and steady can sometimes win the race. For example, in two studies that looked at success rates in programs for smoking cessation and weight loss, promotion-minded people had higher quit rates and more weight loss in the first six months, but prevention-minded people were better able to not light up and keep off the weight over the following year. The best strategy might be to approach a difficult goal with a promotion focus, concentrating on what you have to gain by quitting smoking (or losing weight, or landing a new job), and then once you have achieved it, tackle maintenance with a prevention focus so that your hard-earned gain doesn't slip away.[21]

When you have a prevention focus, you are on the lookout for trouble. Because prevention focus leads us to be particularly sensitive to obstacles that might derail us from our goals, we are better at resisting temptations and distractions when we think about our goals in terms of what we have to lose. Surprisingly, research shows that we actually enjoy the pursuit of prevention goals more when there are distractions to be resisted![22] In one study, when a math task was disrupted by video clips of previews of upcoming films and humorous animated commercials, participants with a prevention focus not only performed better than those with a promotion focus, but they even performed better than prevention-focused participants who had *no* distractions. In pursuit of prevention goals, the presence of temptations or obstacles increases the motivation to be vigilant, leading to even greater achievement.

For one final example, let's look at the effect of promotion and prevention on the art of negotiation. When two parties haggle over price, the buyer needs to balance his desire to negotiate the lowest possible price with the knowledge that if he bids too low, the negotiation may fail and the seller will walk away. In one study, psychologist Adam Galinsky and his colleagues divided fifty-four M.B.A. students into pairs and asked them to take part in a mock negotiation involving the sale of a pharmaceutical plant.[23] One student was assigned the role of "seller" and the other "buyer," and both were given detailed information about the circumstances of the sale, including the fact that the "bargaining zone" would range from $17 million to $25 million. Galinsky then manipulated the goal focus of the buyers. Before the negotiation began, half were told to take a couple of minutes and write down "the negotiation behaviors and outcomes you *hope* to achieve . . . think about how you could *promote* these behaviors and outcomes," giving them a promotion focus. The other half were told to write down the behaviors and outcomes "you seek to *avoid*" and how they "could *prevent*" them, giving them a prevention focus.

Each pair began their negotiation with an opening bid from the buyer. Promotion-minded buyers opened with a bid an average of nearly $4 million *less* than prevention-minded buyers. They were willing to take the greater risk and bid aggressively low, and it paid off. In the end, promotion buyers purchased the plant for an average of $21.24 million, while prevention buyers paid $24.07 million. Why? Galinsky argues that a promotion goal leads the negotiator to stay focused on their (ideal) price target. Prevention goals, however, seem to lead to too much worrying about a negotiation failure or impasse, leaving the buyer more susceptible to less advantageous agreements. This is another one of those things that's worth taking a moment to think about—two negotiators, each armed with *identical* information, facing similar opponents, and yet one overpays by nearly $4 million. The only difference was that one was thinking about what he had to gain, while the other was thinking about what he had to lose.

Armed with an understanding of promotion and prevention, so much of what we do (and what our friends and family members do) makes much more sense. Perhaps now you see why you've always been a risk taker, or why you've always avoided risks like the plague. It's clear why you are uncomfortable with being too optimistic, or why you are known for your unshakeable confidence. You get why some things have always been hard for you, while others came easily.

Along with this understanding of your past, you now know how to make the most of your future—how to embrace your promotion- or prevention-mindedness and do the things that will increase your motivation and help you achieve your goals. You'll feel better ignoring the well-meaning advice and input from others when it conflicts with your goal's focus. You'll know how important it is to trust when something "feels right," and to use that feeling to guide you from now on.

What You Can Do

- **Promotion is for gain, prevention is for avoiding loss.** In this chapter, I told you about the difference between goals that are *promotion*-focused and those that are *prevention*-focused. When your goal has a promotion focus, you are thinking of it as an achievement or an accomplishment—something you would ideally like to reach. When your goal has a prevention focus, you are thinking more in terms of safety and danger—it's something you feel you ought to do. More generally, promotion goals are about maximizing *gains*, and prevention goals are about avoiding *losses*.

- **Optimism works if you are promotion-minded.** If you are a promotion-minded person (or if you happen to be pursuing a promotion-focused goal), having confidence in yourself and thinking positively will help you to achieve your goals. Optimism is very motivating in pursuit of promotion goals—it enhances the eagerness and intensity with which we tackle the obstacles in our path.

- **Optimism fails if you are prevention-minded.** If you are prevention-minded, or trying to avoid a loss, too much optimism is a bad idea. Confidence reduces your motivation and dampens your vigilance. In fact, a touch of pessimism is probably what will serve you best—there is nothing like the very real possibility of danger to get your prevention juices flowing.

- **Promotion goals give us a rush, prevention goals give us relief.** In pursuit of promotion goals, we feel happy or joyful when we succeed ("Woohoo! I am awesome!"), and sad and depressed when we fail ("Ugh, I'm such a loser."). When goals are about prevention, we tend to feel more calm and relaxed when we succeed ("Phew, I dodged a bullet there."), and more anxious or nervous when we fail ("Oh *no*! Now I'm really in trouble!").

- **Promotion loves risk.** Promotion goals create a *risky bias*. They make us say "yes!" to everything, make us hate missing an opportunity. They lead to greater creativity and exploratory thinking. Promotion-minded people love to generate new ideas, come up with new options. They prefer speed over accuracy. They negotiate well because they aren't afraid to make a bold opening move. They see the big picture and seize the moment.

- **Prevention loves caution.** Prevention goals lead to a *conservative bias*—making us more likely to say "no" in fear of making a mistake. They make us less likely to try new things or use new methods to reach our goals, but also help us avoid procrastination through better planning. Prevention-minded people are detail-oriented. They value accuracy over speed. They perform better in the face of distractions and temptations. They don't let things slip through the cracks.

- **Use the right strategy.** Both promotion and prevention can lead to success—the important thing is to identify your focus and use the strategies that *fit* with your focus. Strategies that fit your goal will not only lead to greater achievement, but they also *feel right*—making your journey to success a happier and more satisfying one.

- **Examine the situation.** Remember, even though most of us have a tendency to see our goals in terms of either promotion or prevention, sometimes the situation you find yourself in will determine your focus. So you'll need to stay aware of that and change your strategies from time to time to fit your goal.

CHAPTER 5

Goals Can Make You Happy

I GOT UP THIS MORNING AROUND FIVE. MY SON IS AN EARLY RISER, so I dragged myself out of bed, made some coffee, and settled down on the couch with Max and his bottle to watch the local New York news. Today a woman named Deborah Koenigsberger was being honored as "New Yorker of the Week" for her work as founder of Hearts of Gold, a charity that raises millions of dollars each year in private donations to feed, clothe, shelter, and care for homeless mothers and their children. They provide job training and education for both the moms and the kids. They throw monthly parties, sponsor art classes, and organize outings. Moms with job interviews get new professional wardrobes. Even after they have found new homes, they continue to be supported and nurtured, remaining an active part of the Hearts of Gold family.

Here's the thing—Deborah Koenigsberger is quite clearly a *very* happy woman. She simply glows. When the reporter for NY1 asked her about her work with Hearts of Gold, it was obvious that despite all the hard work and dedication it takes to pull it all off, she wouldn't have it any other way. Her eyes sparkled. She smiled from ear to ear.

Hearing her story snapped me right out of my morning stupor. It inspired me—and not only because the mission of Hearts of Gold is so critical, and the plight of the women and children it serves so moving. I looked at Deborah Koenigsberger's face and thought to myself, "I want to be happy *like that.*"

Achieving any goal will generally give you at least a moment of happiness. But there is happiness—that pleasant but often fleeting sensation of goodness, and then there is *happiness*—the head-to-toe feeling of lasting warmth and well-being that comes from pursuing certain kinds of goals. I have that kind of happiness in my life from time to time, and you almost certainly do, too. When we fall in love, when we spend special times with close friends and family, when we accomplish an act of personal growth, when we give selflessly of our time or resources to people who need our help—whether it's a co-worker, a neighbor, or a stranger at the soup kitchen, we feel really and truly *happy.* As I've gotten older and learned more about myself, both as a psychologist and a person, I have made choices that have brought more of that kind of happiness into my life. But I certainly could use even more of it, and I'm guessing you could, too.

Forming meaningful relationships, growing and developing as a person, giving back to your community—these all seem like very admirable goals to pursue. But their value lies in more than just their nobility. Seeking fame, wealth, and adoration, on the other hand, is decidedly less noble. It's perfectly understandable, and all too common (particularly, it seems, in the age of "reality" television), but not really very admirable. As it turns out, it's also not very good for you. People whose goals are all about image maintenance and financial gain tend to have far less *happiness* in their lives, even if they succeed in becoming rich and famous. But why is that? Shouldn't reaching your goals, no matter what they are, make you not just happy, but *happy*?

Actually, no. It turns out that some goals are much better for us than others, because they nourish our essential needs as human beings. They make our inner lives richer, enhancing our own sense of self-worth instead of leaving us to seek worth and validation in the eyes of others. And to be truly *happy* (and optimally motivated), it's not only the *content* of your goal that matters—it's also the *source*. Are you enduring the pressures and stresses of medical school because you want to, or because your parents want you to? Are you working hard on that project because you want it to succeed, or because your boss told you to? People who pursue goals because of external pressures, even noble and worthwhile goals, not only don't work as hard, but they don't work as *well*—they use strategies that are superficial, ones that will just "get them by." These are the many students in my classes who never open the book all semester and then cram the night before the exam. They might pass my course, but a few months later they won't remember a thing they learned in it.

Achieving a goal isn't everything—*what* you want and *why* you want it matter just as much in the long run. In this chapter, you'll learn whether the goals you've been pursuing in your life are really good for you. And you'll see how external pressures—including *rewards*—can sometimes undermine your happiness and the happiness of those you care about.

What We Really Need

Throughout the history of our science, psychologists have enjoyed arguing about the nature and number of fundamental human needs—the motivations that all human beings have and must satisfy in order to have psychological well-being. This is something we are apt to do even in bars or at parties. (Beware of inviting psychologists to your parties.)

Some have proposed a mere handful of needs, while others have come up with as many as forty. But while there are areas of lively debate, most psychologists agree on the importance of the three innate needs proposed by Edward Deci and Richard Ryan in their Self-Determination Theory.[1] According to Deci and Ryan, all human beings seek *relatedness, competence,* and *autonomy.*

Relatedness is the desire to feel connected to and care for others— to love and be loved. It's the reason we form friendships and intimate relationships throughout our lives. It's why we feel pain and sadness when those relationships end, and lonely when we seek but can't find them. It's why we join clubs, post our profiles on Match.com, and spend way too much time on Facebook. Goals that have to do with making connections—getting to know new people, nurturing and strengthening the bonds you already have with the people in your life, contributing to your community—these goals feed your need for relatedness in much the same way that water quenches your thirst or food diminishes your hunger. But while you can clearly eat or drink too much, there doesn't seem to be such a thing as "too much relatedness"—we can always benefit from new or deeper connections, from a greater sense of belonging.

The desire for competence is about being able to have an effect on your environment and being able to get the things you want out of it. Intelligence is a kind of competence, but by no means the only one. Being good at just about anything can give you a sense of competence. Social, physical, emotional, artistic, organizational, and creative skills can be just as important as smartness when it comes to making things in life go your way. The need for competence drives our curiosity, our innate motivation to learn, the pride we feel when we accomplish something difficult. It's why we often think of ourselves in terms of the things we are good at (as in "I'm clever," "I'm funny," or "I'm a good listener"). Goals that are about increasing your ability to make things happen in your life—developing a skill, learning something new, growing as a person—these are the goals that feed your need for competence. And like relatedness, there doesn't seem to be a downside to competence. You really can never be *too good* at anything.

The last basic need, autonomy, is about freedom. Specifically, it's about choosing and organizing your own experiences. It's about being able to do things because you find them interesting or appealing, because they speak to something about your own nature. Autonomy is feeling like you are, to paraphrase our former president, the decider. It's knowing you are the chess *player*, not the pawn. When we are motivated by our own desires, freely engaging in some activity out of interest rather than feeling pressured by anything or anyone, psychologists call that *intrinsic motivation*. It is, by far, the very best kind of motivation to have (and I'll have more to say on that later). And while you may not have been surprised to learn that people need other people, or that people need to be good at things, you've probably never fully appreciated just how much people need freedom, or how a lack of freedom may be robbing you of your *happiness*.

What We Really *Don't* Need

As I mentioned earlier, not all goals lead to lasting feelings of true satisfaction and well-being, and that's because not all goals satisfy our needs for relatedness, competence, and autonomy. Which ones do? In general, goals that are about making, supporting, or strengthening relationships do. So do goals that focus on personal growth, physical health, or self-acceptance—addressing your shortcomings or, if they can't be helped, simply coming to terms with them. Goals that have to do with contributing to your community or helping others also fulfill these needs.

Here are the goals that *aren't* going to help you achieve lasting well-being: becoming famous, seeking power over others, or polishing your public image. Any goal that is related to obtaining other people's validation and approval or external signs of self-worth isn't going to do it for you, either. Accumulating wealth for its own sake also won't lead to real happiness (this is not to say you shouldn't care about money at all, just that being rich isn't a sure ticket to a happy life). But why do we pursue these goals so frequently if they won't really make us happy?

Well, one reason is that we tend to believe they *will* make us happy. Many of us labor under the delusion that rich and famous people don't have real problems, despite the fact that giving this even a moment of serious thought would force us to admit that if anything, the opposite is true. Rich and famous people have *tons* of problems. For every happy, well-adjusted, and successful celebrity you can think of, I bet you can name five more who suffer from various addictions, a string of failed relationships, and what appears to be an abundance of insecurity and self-loathing.

Psychologists Deci and Ryan argue that we turn to these superficial goals, these external sources of self-worth, when our needs for autonomy, relatedness, and competence are thwarted again and again. This can happen when we find ourselves trapped in situations that are too controlling (robbing us of our sense of personal freedom), overchallenging (robbing us of our sense of competence), or rejecting (robbing us of our sense of relatedness). In other words, when we are under too much pressure or denied choices, when we feel we can't do anything right, and when we are lonely and lack meaningful relationships with others, we turn to goals that aren't very good for us as a kind of defensive strategy. "If I can't get the love I need in my life, then I'll become rich and famous and people will love me for that." The irony, and tragedy, of this strategy is that the pursuit of fame, wealth, and popularity pretty much *guarantees* that your basic needs aren't going to be met. These goals are lousy substitutes for the goals we really should be pursuing. They'll keep you busy but never make you truly happy.

Whose Goal Is This, Anyway?

Until quite recently, my nephew Harrison loved to read. His mother would often find him curled up with one of the books from his book-shelf, happily thumbing through the pages of a story about pirates or wizards. For the last few Christmases, his gift wish from me has been a gift card to Borders or Barnes & Noble, so he could spend an afternoon carefully selecting new volumes to add to his collection. But in the last year, Harrison has rarely picked up a book unless he had to. Ironically, he often *does* have to—this year, one of his fifth-grade teachers assigned all his students to read for a minimum of thirty minutes every school night. Each student needs a parent to sign a paper every night, testifying that the required reading was completed. My sister-in-law, Paula, noticed that soon after the mandatory read-ings began, Harrison started looking up from his book and impatiently watching the clock, eager for the thirty minutes to be over. The same boy who would read on his own for hours without rewards or prod-ding is now anxious to do anything *but* read. In his mind, reading has become something you do because you have to.

When Paula told me about this mandatory reading assignment, I hit the ceiling. I'm sure his teacher means well—obviously I un-derstand how important (and difficult) it is to get kids to read, and assigning a whole lot of reading is one way to do that. But at what cost? In this instance, the cost was my nephew's natural and innate motivation to read—a motivation that would serve him well throughout his lifetime if it had been protected and allowed to flourish.

You see, in addition to choosing the kinds of goals that can lead to lasting well-being, or what psychologist Martin Seligman calls "authentic" happiness,[2] we find the greatest motivation and most personal satisfaction from those goals that we choose *for ourselves*. In fact, as I mentioned earlier, self-chosen goals create a special kind of motivation called *intrinsic motivation*—the desire to do something for its own sake. When people are intrinsically motivated, they enjoy what they are doing more. They find it more interesting. They find that they are more creative, and they process information more deeply. They persist more in the face of difficulty. They perform better. Intrinsic motivation is awesome in its power to get and keep us going.

Intrinsic motivation is enhanced whenever we are allowed to make our own choices and determine our own course of action. In fact, just *feeling like* you are making your own choices, regardless of whether or not you are *actually* making them, will usually do the trick. Deci and Ryan refer to situations where people have choices, or just the illusion of choices, as "autonomy-supportive." This is a very helpful piece of information for parents, teachers, coaches, employers, and pretty much anyone else who has to motivate someone, regardless of age or circumstances. For example, in one study of nearly three hundred eighth- to tenth-grade boys and girls, those who rated their gym teacher as more autonomy-supportive (agreeing with statements such as "I feel my physical education teacher provides me with choices and options" and "I feel that my P.E. teacher accepts me") reported greater enjoyment of exercise. They were even more likely to do physical activity outside of school in their own free time.[3] Believing that you are exercising in gym because *you want to*, because of choices *you* have made, creates positive feelings about exercise, as well as a sense of personal control. And if you feel good about exercising, then it makes sense that you would choose to do it outside of gym class, too.

Again and again, research has shown that when people feel they have choices, and that they are an integral part of creating their own destiny, they are more motivated and successful. Obese participants in a weight-loss study who felt that the staff was autonomy-supportive lost more weight, exercised more regularly, and maintained better weight loss at a twenty-three-month follow-up than those who felt controlled by the staff's decisions.[4] Similar results have been shown for participants in diabetes-management and smoking cessation programs,[5] as well as for patients in alcohol treatment and methadone maintenance.[6] People are even better at keeping their New Year's resolutions when they feel that the resolutions reflect their own personal desires and values.[7]

Autonomy is particularly critical when it comes to creating and maintaining student motivation. Students perceive their teachers to be autonomy-supportive when those teachers focus on the students' needs, ask about and foster students' interests by providing resources, and are flexible and accessible. Autonomy-supportive teachers give students choices and create opportunities for shared decision making. They help students to understand and personally embrace the school's values and agenda. In contrast, "controlling" teachers use incentives that have nothing to do with what is being learned—like rewards and punishments—to motivate students. They make all the decisions and rarely offer explanations. They expect students to be passive learners of whatever it is they've decided to teach. In dozens of studies, psychologists have shown that students with autonomy-supportive teachers are more likely to stay in school, get better grades, demonstrate enhanced creativity and a preference for challenges, and experience greater interest and enjoyment in the classroom.[8] When students' basic need for autonomy is satisfied, they like learning, and they learn a lot more.

On the other hand, when the need for autonomy is thwarted, the opposite pattern emerges. Students who once loved learning for its own sake, who were *intrinsically motivated* like my nephew Harrison, will abandon these pursuits when they feel too controlled. Intrinsic motivation is, unfortunately, a somewhat fragile creature. This was nicely illustrated by one of the earliest studies on the effects of rewards on children's spontaneous motivation to play. Psychologists Mark Lepper, David Green, and Richard Nisbett observed how often and for how long a group of three- to five-year-old preschoolers chose to play with sets of special markers during their free playtime, when many other toys were also available. Next, they told some of the children that they could earn a fancy "Good Player Award" for drawing pictures with the markers (the other children were not offered the reward). Not surprisingly, those offered the award played with the markers for even longer than they did when no reward had been given. So you might think that the rewards were motivating, and in a sense you would be right. The really interesting part came several weeks later, though, when the psychologists returned with the special markers and found that those who had been given a reward to play with markers were now no longer interested in them at all when no prize was involved. Their intrinsic motivation to play with the markers was destroyed by the reward—markers became something you play with only when you get something in return. Their behavior became, in a sense, controlled by the reward. The children who had *never* been rewarded, on the other hand, continued to play with markers for their own sake, just as they had before. Their intrinsic motivation had been left intact—markers remained something you play with because *you choose to.*

Lest you think that rewards are always bad and will always destroy motivation, let me take a moment to reassure you. Some rewards seem to be okay. Rewards that are unexpected are fine, as are those that aren't contingent on performance. So when the preschoolers were surprised by a reward at the end of play, or when they were rewarded no matter what they chose to play with, their innate love of markers remained unharmed. Verbal rewards, like saying *good job* or *nice work,* also don't appear to be to undermining. And of course, rewards remain an excellent way to motivate someone when intrinsic motivation isn't an issue—when, for example, the task is boring or tedious and there is no innate interest and enjoyment to destroy.

Rewards aren't the only things that can undermine intrinsic motivation, either. Threats, surveillance, deadlines, and other pressures also do the trick, because we experience them as controlling and no longer feel we are completely in charge. Unfortunately, most work environments are filled with these undermining influences—eating away little by little at people's sense of personal investment in what they do. Providing a feeling of choice and acknowledging people's inner experience shifts their sense of control back—it makes them feel like they are the origin of their own actions, and returns to them their sense of autonomy. So, since rewards, threats, deadlines, and other consequences of our actions are a fact of life, it's essential that we learn how to create autonomy-supportive environments and protect our intrinsic motivation. Here's how.

How to Create the *Feeling* of Choice

Intrinsic motivation thrives when people are allowed to make their own choices and decide for themselves what actions they will take and which goals they will pursue. Unfortunately, letting everyone make *all* their own choices *all* the time just isn't possible. Sometimes you need people to do what you tell them to do. Students and employees need to be given assignments. Children lack both life experience and fully developed brains, so they often need their parents' guidance to make the best decisions. How can we dole out assignments and encourage the adoption of particular goals without destroying whatever intrinsic motivation may already exist? It turns out that it isn't so much *actual* freedom of choice that matters but the *feeling* of choice. Choice provides a sense of self-determination, even when choice is trivial or illusory. Fortunately, the feeling of choice can be created fairly easily.

Take for example one study in which psychologists Diana Cordova and Mark Lepper gave young children the feeling of choice in a learning game.[9] This particular intervention was specifically aimed at children because research shows that intrinsic motivation goes down steadily in school from third grade to high school. Young children love to learn, but this innate love of learning disappears slowly throughout adolescence. Figuring out how this trend can be halted, or even reversed, is critically important. To that end, Cordova and Lepper gave students a computer math learning program with a science-fiction theme. The program was designed to teach them about mathematical order of operations (e.g., when someone gives you a problem like $6 + 4 \times 5 - 3 = ?$ you are supposed to do the multiplication before the addition and subtraction). So in this instance, as is usually the case with most classroom activities, *what* was learned was determined for the child, without any freedom of choice. However, some students were offered choices over "instructionally irrelevant" aspects of the learning activity. In the feeling-of-choice condition, students got to choose the icon that represented them in the computer game from a set of four options. They got to name their spaceship. They were also able to choose the icon representing their alien enemy and to name the alien's spaceship. The students in the no-choice condition played the same game, except the icons and names were chosen for them by the computer.

Cordova and Lepper found that in the feeling-of-choice condition, students liked the game much more and were far more likely to be willing to stay after class to continue playing, even though it meant giving up valuable recess time. The children who experienced choice, even though the choice was *completely irrelevant* to what they were learning, also used more strategic moves and scored significantly higher on a subsequent math test measuring what they had learned. They reported greater confidence in their own ability and said that they would enjoy a more challenging version of the game in the future. Creating a feeling of choice, even when the choices aren't particularly meaningful, satisfies our need for autonomy and nurtures our intrinsic motivation, creating both a far better experience and a far superior performance.

Creating a feeling of choice isn't simply a way to increase motivation. In fact, evidence suggests that satisfying our need for autonomy is vital to our psychological well-being. Perhaps the best illustration of this comes from the landmark study conducted in the early 1970s by psychologists Ellen Langer and Judy Rodin.[10] Langer and Rodin believed that the rapidly deteriorating mental and physical health of many of the elderly residing in nursing homes was at least in part a consequence of living in a totally "decision-free" environment. At the time, most nursing home residents experienced very little choice on a day-to-day basis. Everything from their meals to their leisure activities and even personal grooming and room cleaning was scheduled and carried out with almost no input or effort from the resident. Even in homes where the elderly were lovingly cared for and attended to, the lack of autonomy was striking.

The intervention designed by Langer and Rodin was simple. Some of the residents were gathered together by the chief administrator and told that they should feel free to decide how they wanted their rooms arranged, choose how to spend their time from a wide variety of activities available, and make their complaints known to the staff so that anything they didn't like could be changed. They were also given the option of caring for a plant, entirely on their own and without assistance from staff. The administrator empha-sized that the choices, and the responsibilities, were those of each individual resident's.

The comparison group technically had the same options, but they were described in terms of "permissions," rather than free choices (as in, "You are permitted to visit people on other floors" rather than "You can choose to visit people on other floors if you want to"). Res-idents in this group were reminded how the staff had worked hard to make things nice for them, and how the staff felt it was *their* responsibility to make the residents happy. Instead of "let us know what you want to change" it was "let us know how we can help you." Plants given to residents were watered and cared for by the nurses, rather than their owners.

The results of the intervention were dramatic. Those in the feeling-of-choice group reported that they were happier and felt more active than those who had their choices obviously made for them. They were rated by the nurses as more alert and as having mental and physical *improvement*, while the health of the no-choice group deteriorated. The choice group spent more time visiting other patients, visiting non-residents, and talking to staff. At a follow-up eighteen months later, nurses rated this group as happier, more actively interested, more sociable, self-initiating, and vigorous. Perhaps the most remarkable result—in the intervening eighteen months, 15 percent of the choice group died, compared to 30 percent of the no-choice group. The mor-tality rate was effectively cut in half, simply by letting people water their own plants and decide for themselves how they wanted their furniture arranged, and if they wanted to play bingo or watch a movie. As I said before, most of us underestimate the role that freedom of choice plays in our well-being and happiness, but we feel its consequences regardless.

How the Goals You Are Given Become Your Own

The other great thing about giving people a sense of choice and autonomy when you assign them a goal is that it is by far the best way to get them to eventually *freely* adopt the goal as their own. Psychologists refer to this process as *internalization*. It is what happens when people take externally based rules and requests and come to personally endorse them as values. It's what happens when children embrace the ideals and advice of their parents as their own. It's what happened to me, when I went from being someone whose mother had to yell at her about tracking mud in the house to someone who yells at her own daughter for tracking mud in the house. Along the way, I internalized my mother's reverence for cleanliness and her goal of keeping a clean house. (Well, not completely. I still don't live up to my mother's standards. But she's German, and in my experience Germans take cleanliness to a whole other level. There was no surface in our house you couldn't eat off of—not that you were actually allowed to eat anywhere other than the table. I don't think I even knew what dust looked like until I went to college. But I digress.)

Internalization is facilitated when our basic needs are supported. It occurs when we are experiencing feelings of relatedness to others—be they our parents, our friends, or our employers. It also requires that you feel competent with respect to the value being internalized—that it is something you can live up to. The main reason that my cleanliness standards aren't quite as high as my mother's is probably that I can't actually pull it off. (I suspect there is magic involved.) Feelings of relatedness *and* competence are greatly enhanced when we are able to understand the rationale behind the value—in other words, when someone explains *why* the goal is so important. Understanding is absolutely critical for internalization. Excessive controls or pressures can disrupt this process, robbing individuals of their sense of autonomy and ensuring that the goal remains something they pursue only if they have to. In my case, my mother not only went to great lengths to explain to me the value and importance of cleanliness (including many references to "what people will think"), but she also made me responsible for cleaning my room entirely on my own. Keeping my room looking nice was something I came to be proud of because I had done it all by myself, until eventually it had nothing to do with Mom, and everything to do with me.

Does that matter? You bet it does. Obviously, if a goal is internalized, you get all the benefits that go along with increased intrinsic motivation (i.e., creativity, deeper processing, better performance, enjoyment, increased desire to work). You also avoid the hassle of having to provide rewards, punishments, or constant monitoring to bring about the behavior you are after. But internalization has another important benefit—we achieve greater well-being, greater *happiness*, from the goals we embrace as our own. One interesting example of this comes from a study by Richard Ryan and his colleagues in which he asked people from a variety of Christian denominations how often they engaged in religious behaviors, such as going to church or praying regularly.[11] He also asked the participants in the study *why* they did these things. Ryan found that those people who engaged in religious behaviors for internalized reasons enjoyed greater psychological well-being, but those who did them for externalized reasons did not. So the religious behaviors themselves aren't going to increase your happiness, unless you do them because you genuinely want to.

I want to say one more thing about autonomy because I think it's very easy to confuse autonomy with independence or, worse, selfishness, and so I want to be very clear about it. Fulfilling our basic human need for autonomy is *not* the same thing as wanting to do everything on your own, or disregarding the welfare or feelings of others. If being autonomous meant being entirely independent of everyone else, and not giving a damn about anyone but yourself, it would completely undermine your other, just-as-important basic need for relatedness. Autonomy is about experiencing a feeling of volition, of authenticity, of choice. It's believing that *you* are the origin of your own actions—that they reflect your beliefs and values. But that is not at all in conflict with *inter*dependence—feeling connected to, caring for, and working in collaboration with others. A goal that is shared with members of your family or your team, or a goal that is pursued for the benefit of others rather than for yourself, is not any less authentically *yours*. In fact, those goals will probably bring you more *happiness* than any other goal you choose to pursue.

What You Can Do

- **There are three basic human needs.** Not all goals will bring you lasting happiness and well-being, even if you are successful in reaching them. The ones that will are those that satisfy your basic human needs for relatedness, competence, and autonomy.

- **Relatedness strengthens your relationships.** You satisfy your need for relatedness by pursuing goals that are about creating and strengthening relationships, or giving to your community. Do you have goals like this in your life?

- **Competence develops new skills.** You satisfy your need for competence by pursuing goals that are about personal growth, learning from your experience, and developing new skills. Are you pursuing goals that would satisfy this need?

- **Autonomy reflects your passions.** You satisfy your need for autonomy by pursuing goals that *you* choose to pursue, because you find them interesting and enjoyable, or because they reflect your own nature and core values. Does this describe the goals you spend most of your time pursuing? Are you doing what *you* want to do?

- **All that glitters isn't gold.** Goals that are all about obtaining external validation of self-worth—like being popular, famous, or rich—not only won't make you truly happy, but will actively diminish your sense of well-being, by interfering with the pursuit of goals that will really benefit you. If you have goals like these in your life, it's time to rid yourself of them.

- **Intrinsic motivation lights the biggest fire.** Goals that are freely chosen create intrinsic motivation, a special kind of motivation that leads to greater enjoyment, longer persistence, enhanced creativity, and better performance. This motivation is destroyed by anything we experience as controlling—including rewards, punishments, deadlines, and excessive monitoring. When you are trying to motivate others, be very careful when it comes to using incentives.

- **Autonomy fuels motivation.** Intrinsic motivation can be protected or even restored when we perceive our environment as autonomy-supportive. When we feel our inner experience is acknowledged and we are offered choices, even trivial or illusory choices, our need for autonomy is satisfied and our motivation and well-being are enhanced. Try introducing these elements when you assign a goal to your child, your student, or your employee. This is also the best way to help facilitate the internalization of goals, because the greatest achievement comes from the goals we ultimately feel to be our own.

CHAPTER 6

The Right Goal for You

In the last few chapters, you've learned about the kinds of goals people pursue. Now you will be able to use what you know about different goals to decide which goals you should adopt for yourself and which goals to assign to (or maybe simply encourage in) your employees, students, or children. But with so many kinds of goals to choose from, you may be finding your options a little overwhelming. Should you pursue promotion or prevention goals? *Being good* or *getting better*? Thinking *why* or thinking *what*?

Before you decide, it really helps to consider what, specifically, you are trying to accomplish. Are you facing a particularly difficult challenge? Will it require persistence? Will succeeding mean resisting temptation or making sacrifices? Is it important to you to not only reach your goal, but also enjoy doing it? Do you need to be creative? Work quickly? Work flawlessly? Unfortunately, there is no single perfect goal for all situations. Each kind of goal has its strengths and also its weaknesses. Choosing the right goal means finding the one that works best in your particular situation, and this choice is an important one because it is one of the keys to success.

In this chapter, I've identified some of the most common situations we find ourselves in when it comes to achieving our goals. For every problem or challenge, you'll find the goals that are best suited to help you tackle it.

When It's Going to Be a Piece of Cake

Some of the goals we set for ourselves are, frankly, not all that hard to attain. Maybe the task you need to perform to reach the goal is relatively simple and easy, or at least simple and easy for *you*. Perhaps you are very familiar with it—you've been down this road before and know exactly what you have to do. Or maybe you already have the ability needed to succeed. When achieving your goal means doing something easy, straightforward, or familiar, you are probably better off focusing on a *be good*, performance goal. As I mentioned in Chapter 3, there is something highly motivating about an opportunity to show off how smart, talented, or capable you are, particularly when there are rewards involved. Feeling like there is something important on the line, that a lot rides on how well you perform, generates feelings of energy and intensity—exactly what you need to do your best when you are in your element.

Another way to achieve your relatively easy goals is to think of them in **promotion**-focused terms. Just knowing that a task is easy gives us a feeling of confidence and optimism, and promotion goals are most motivating when we are confident that we will succeed. (Prevention goals, on the other hand, should be avoided. Too much confidence can lead to apathy when you are prevention-minded.) To give your goal a promotion focus, ask yourself what you have to *gain* by reaching this goal. How is it related to your hopes, dreams, and aspirations?

When You Need a Kick in the Pants

Did you ever feel like there was a goal you really wanted to reach but somehow you just couldn't get yourself motivated to start working on it? Time goes by, days turn into weeks turn into months, but you don't seem to be any closer to your goal? This is a very common experience. For example, it perfectly describes my attempts to exercise regularly for most of my adult life. I really wanted to do it—it just never happened. (Well, until more recently, that is. I've changed my approach—but I'll come back to that later.) Progress can "just not happen" for a variety of reasons. Some of the ways we think about our goals can make low motivation and procrastination more likely, and some can make it less so.

One way to light a fire under yourself is to engage in a whole lot of *why* thinking. Back in Chapter 1, you learned about how we can think of our goals either in terms of the reasons *why* we are pursuing them or in terms of *what* we are literally doing in order to pursue them. The goal to exercise more can be thought of as "wanting to be healthier and more attractive" (why) or it can be thought of as "going to the gym to jog on the treadmill three times a week" (what). Research shows that *why* thinking about our goals is far more motivating and energizing, and it's not hard to see why that's the case. When we think about our goals in big-picture terms, we remember why reaching them matters so much.

Another way to avoid procrastination is to be **prevention**-focused when it comes to the goal. I know this won't sound like a lot of fun, but there is probably no better way to stop dawdling than to give some serious thought to all the dire consequences of potential failure. Prevention-minded people almost never procrastinate—it drives them crazy. Their thinking is that the only way to get out of danger is to take immediate action. So if procrastination is your problem, try thinking about everything you will lose if you fail. I realize that's an unpleasant thing to do, but great achievement does come with a price.

When the Road Looks Very Rocky

Goals can be difficult to achieve for any number of reasons. Sometimes you can be working in an area that is completely new and unfamiliar to you, doing something you've never done before, like being a first-time parent, or starting a brand-new career. Or maybe the task at hand is really challenging or complicated, like running your own business or handling tough negotiations. Perhaps there are many obstacles standing in your way, ones that can be difficult to totally anticipate and avoid. For example, dieters must deal with the constant availability and temptation of calorie-rich foods. They seem to pop up everywhere. (Doesn't every workplace have that one person who insists on leaving home-baked cookies or brownies in the conference room? I think this qualifies as a form of torture.)

There are times when the key to ultimately reaching your goal is resilience in the face of failure. This is particularly true when failure is the rule rather than the exception. Just think of what an actor must go through in the course of his or her career. Even well-known actors have experienced more than their fair share of rejections and bad reviews. Yet somehow, the successful ones figure out how to pick themselves up, dust themselves off, and keep on trying. Politicians lose elections, inventors make gadgets that don't work, lawyers lose cases, and doctors lose patients despite their best efforts. There aren't many highly successful people out there who couldn't tell you a story or two about their darker days. The good news is, when it comes to achieving difficult goals (no matter *why* they are difficult), and learning to persist in the face of failure, there are a few things you can do that should help you *a lot.*

First, you should be **specific** about what it is you want to achieve. Back in Chapter 1, I told you about how the most motivating goals are those that are challenging (but possible) and as clearly articulated as you can make them. "Lose ten pounds" is a better goal than "lose some weight" because you will have a clearer idea of whether or not the goal has been achieved, or if you have to keep on working at it. When we are too vague, it's easy to let ourselves off the hook too soon, particularly when the goal is difficult to reach and the work is hard.

You would probably also benefit from changing your thinking from *why* to *what.* Literal what-do-I-need-to-do-to-reach-this goal thinking is enormously helpful when we are pursuing challenging goals. Staying focused on the actions you need to take makes you more efficient and better able to handle the curveballs that get thrown at you.

Just as easy goals leave us with a sense of optimism and confidence, difficult goals often make us begin to doubt ourselves and our chances for success. When in doubt (literally), your best bet is to give your goal a **prevention** focus. When we pursue prevention goals, we actually thrive on pessimism. Feeling like things might not work out fuels our sense of vigilance, increasing our motivation to reach the goal no matter what it takes. We are far less likely to give up on a goal, even a really difficult one, when we're thinking about what we may lose rather than what we could gain.

My favorite piece of advice by far for dealing with difficulty is to make sure you think about your goal in terms of *getting better*, rather than *being good.* As you'll recall from Chapter 3, when we are focused on personal growth and development, on making progress rather than on proving ourselves, we deal with difficulty far more gracefully. We tend to see setbacks as informative, rather than as signs of personal failure. We don't worry as much about the likelihood of success because we know that even if we never do it perfectly, we will certainly improve. (And getting better is, after all, the goal.)

When my first child, my daughter Annika, was born, my goals as a first-time parent were definitely of the *be-good* variety. Of course I read all the parenting books and watched many parenting shows. As a psychologist, I knew tons about forming "secure attachments" and engaging in "responsive parenting." I was going to be the World's Greatest Mom to my little girl and flawlessly handle all the ups and downs. Right.

What a shock reality turned out to be. From the beginning, Annika was what our family called a "fussy" baby (though I've been told the more politically correct term for it now is "high need"). She screamed from the day she was born until she was about eighteen months old, stopping only to eat and (infrequently) sleep. Because I had been so set on being the World's Greatest Mom, I took her endless demands and irritability as signs of my incompetence and failure as a mother. I blamed myself for all of it. I fluctuated between anxiousness and depression every day. I dreamed of getting in a car and just driving off into the sunset, to escape both the racket and my serious doubts about my capabilities.

Then, something really great happened. At the edge of despair, and curled up on the floor in a corner of my bathroom, I took an honest look at myself and I realized that my thinking about this had been all wrong because my goal had been all wrong from the very start. (We psychologists, it turns out, can be pretty dense when it comes to our own problems—which is more than a little embarrassing.) *No one* is a perfect parent, and it is foolish to believe that anyone can tackle a task as complex and challenging as parenthood and do every single thing right from the get-go. Every child is different, and you can't anticipate what you're going to have to deal with when you welcome your baby into the world.

So I lightened up. I decided to accept the fact that I didn't know everything and that I couldn't possibly do everything right. I made my goal as a parent to *get better*, rather than to *be good*. Instead of proving that I was the World's Greatest Mom, my goal became to be a better mother to my daughter, to try to learn the skills and patience I would need to handle her particular needs. The depression and anxiety lessened as I learned.

I am, I think, a much better mother now than I was then. I am certainly more patient, and every crisis is no longer of epic proportions. According to my husband, I am a lot more fun to be around. I spend a lot less time hiding in the bathroom. In the meantime, my daughter has blossomed from an incredibly difficult baby (her nickname was "Crabcake," with emphasis on the first syllable) into a sweet, sociable, and relatively easygoing little girl. I don't know how much of that is due to the fact that I changed my parenting goals, or if it's simply due to normal childhood development. But whether it helped her or not, it made a world of difference to me.

When You Just Can't Resist

Reaching any worthwhile goal usually means having to resist the allure of temptation. Doing well on an exam means keeping your nose in the books, resisting the temptation to watch TV or join your friends at the party. Moving up the ladder at work means making a good impression and resisting the temptation to tell your boss that he's an idiot. Some goals, like losing weight or quitting smoking, are pretty much *all* about resisting something—the lure of the doughnut or the Marlboro Light.

Overcoming temptation is hard. It usually requires a lot of self-control (something I'll talk more about again later in the book), and most of us need all the help we can get. So it's a good idea to choose goals, whenever you can, that do a better job of handling temptation and distraction.

First, this is another one of those instances where it pays to think of your goals in terms of *why* rather than *what*. As I mentioned in Chapter 1, thinking about why you are pursuing a particular goal—remembering the big picture—is enormously helpful when it comes to resisting temptations. The benefits of consuming a strawberry milk-shake (mainly, a fleeting sensation of yumminess) pale in comparison to the benefits of being healthy and more attractive. The more you keep the reasons for your diet in mind, the more likely you are to be able to stick to it.

Giving your goal a **prevention** focus is also an excellent way to beef up your resistance. As I mentioned in Chapter 4, it's not just that we perform better in the face of temptation and distraction when we are focused on avoiding losses rather than on making gains. We actually seem to *thrive* on it—prevention-minded people perform better *with* temptation than without it! I know that sounds impossibly odd, but it's true. If you are thinking in terms of prevention, temptations and distractions will make you feel the need to be even *more* vigilant. When a prevention-focused dieter eyes that dessert cart piled high with tempting goodies, what she tends to see is a great big pile of danger—like little grenades covered in powdered sugar and chocolate sauce. They are potent reminders of the possibility of failure, and, as a result, the sight of that dessert cart actually heightens your motivation to stick to your diet.

You may have noticed how people seem to get more serious about their health *after* their first heart attack? Former president Clinton has rarely been spotted near a McDonald's since his bypass surgery, and he has never looked more physically fit. Though he didn't suffer a heart attack, my father recently decided to take his health a lot more seriously when he quit smoking—immediately after he tried to go for a run and found himself winded within a few blocks. President Clinton's weakness for french fries and my father's fondness for smoking have both been significantly diminished. Fast foods and cigarettes lost much of their allure once both men were forced to come face-to-face with the dire consequences of giving in to temptation. Generally, in the wake of a health scare or some other frightening experience, our goals become prevention-focused. So long as we sustain that focus, temptations are easily defeated.

When You Need It Done Yesterday

Sometimes, you really need to get something done quickly. Sometimes, quantity matters more than quality. Maybe your house is a mess and you've got company coming in ten minutes. Maybe it's Christmas Eve and you still have to buy presents for everyone on your list. Perhaps you have a book report due tomorrow on a four-hundred-page book you haven't even opened yet. You recognize the need for speed—which goal do you choose?

Here the answer is a simple one (though the task may not be)—give your goal a **promotion** focus. Many studies have shown that when people focus on maximizing gains rather than on avoiding losses, they respond by picking up the pace. They work faster, they take bigger risks, they skim, glossing over the details to just get a sense of the important points. They may make a mistake here and there, but they get results, and they get them quickly.

When You Need It Done Perfectly

On the other hand, sometimes you really need something done right. You don't care so much how long it takes, as long as it's done correctly. When that's the case, you want to give your goals a **prevention** focus instead. When people think about their goals in terms of what they have to lose, they respond by slowing down to avoid mistakes. They work deliberately, they avoid risks, and take the conservative approach. They read every single word, often rereading sentences again and again, to make sure they don't miss a thing. They may keep you waiting a bit longer, but their work will be flawless.

(A quick aside: When I gave this chapter to my mother, who is perhaps the planet's most thoroughly prevention-minded individual, she almost had a panic attack just *reading* about people waiting until the last minute to clean the house for company or shop for Christmas presents. She even suggested I change the examples, because "no one would actually do those things.")

When You Need Those Creative Juices Flowing

Which kinds of goals work best when you want to be inspired? When you want to brainstorm, come up with new and bold ideas, and think outside the box? It won't surprise you to learn that giving your goal a **promotion** focus can heighten your creative powers. Thinking about potential gains rather than losses evokes optimism, more abstract thinking, deeper processing of information, and a willingness to embrace risks. Each of these can fuel the creative process and foster innovative thinking.

So, too, can goals that are of our own making—goals that fulfill our basic need for **autonomy**. The intrinsic motivation associated with autonomously chosen goals, the desire to do something for its own sake, is associated with greater creativity and spontaneity. When we feel too controlled, on the other hand, it tends to dampen our ability to think abstractly or innovatively. Time pressures, punishments, surveillance—even becoming preoccupied with potential rewards—can seriously interfere with the creative process.

Some people seem to pick up on this intuitively and make efforts to try to protect their motivation to create. One of my classmates in graduate school had been a double major as an undergraduate, in both psychology and creative writing. He devoted most of his free time in grad school to poetry and writing courses, and seemed to me to be much more interested in poetry than psychology. One day I finally asked him why he chose to become a psychologist instead of a poet. He replied that he wanted to always love poetry, and he knew that if he had to write for a living, it would destroy his interest and stifle his talent. To protect his writing from the controlling influences of deadlines and public scrutiny, he became a psychologist instead. Poetry remained his own, authentically self-chosen pursuit.

When You Want to Enjoy the Ride

Is it really enough to be successful, if getting there is a total drag? Sometimes reaching our goals means doing things we find stressful, unpleasant, or dull. Nearly everyone who does well in the classroom, by necessity, reads quite a lot—but not everyone actually enjoys reading. Many of the most successful people in your company may in fact hate coming to work each day. Almost every parent loves their children, but many find that *being a parent* is a lot tougher than they had imagined. But it doesn't have to be that way . . . not if you choose goals that will make the journey more interesting, more enjoyable, and more engaging.

If you want to have fun along the way, try focusing on *getting bet-*

ter, rather than on *being good*. In dozens of studies, people who pursue goals that are about learning, growing, and developing skills report they like their classes more, they like their jobs more, and, in general, they enjoy their lives more. In the study of freshman chemistry students I mentioned back in Chapter 3, those students whose primary focus was acquiring knowledge (rather then showing off their ability) found chemistry more interesting and found their lectures more stimulating and enjoyable. We were amazed to find that this effect of *get-better* goals was totally independent of their course grade—in other words, regardless of how well they were doing in the class, they liked chemistry more. Getting-better goals help us to get the most out of an experience, no matter how well we perform.

In general, goals that are **autonomously** chosen are much more interesting and enjoyable to pursue than those that are chosen for us. Controlling influences like rewards and punishments can also take our focus off of what we are doing, making us far less engaged. It's hard to enjoy your job when you are obsessing over your annual review. You're not likely to appreciate the beauty of the music you're creating when your music lessons are forced on you by your well-intentioned parents. Competition is an integral part of playing almost any sport, but when the pressures of competition become too burdensome, when the coach only cares about winning, the experience may become very stressful, rather than a source of pleasure and pride. To maximize the joy of getting there, whenever possible, make the choice to pursue a goal that is authentically your own.

When You Want to Be Really, Truly Happy

When it comes to motivation, all roads don't actually lead to Rome. Not all goals give you the life filled with satisfaction and well-being that we're all looking for, even if you achieve them. Most people assume that, when it comes to happiness, being successful is all that matters. In truth, there are boatloads of very successful, very unhappy people all around us. That's because they have successfully pursued goals that don't actually fulfill their basic needs as human beings—the needs for *relatedness*, *competence*, and *autonomy*.

Remember that we satisfy our need for relatedness by choosing goals that are about creating and nurturing relationships with others, while we satisfy our need for competence by pursuing goals that focus on personal growth (*get-better* goals, incidentally, are ideal for fulfilling this need). Your sense of autonomy will be enhanced every time you pursue a goal that *you* choose, because it speaks to something about you—your interests, your abilities, or the values you cherish.

Goals to avoid are those that we pursue to receive validation from others, like seeking fame, prestige, or great wealth. Anytime you're allowing someone or something else to determine your own sense of self-worth, that's a bad idea. Even if you achieve these goals, your happiness will be fleeting because your true needs will remain unmet. In fact, they tend to make us even more miserable because they keep us too preoccupied to pursue the goals we really ought to be pursuing.

Spend any time with preschoolers, and you'll notice that they couldn't care less about being famous or popular, and that their only interest in money lies in trying occasionally to swallow some. What do they care about? They care about being nurtured by and playing with their caregivers (relatedness). They care about learning to do things, like walk and climb and put the round peg in the round hole (competence). And they care, a lot, about doing *what they want to do*. Trying to exert a controlling influence on a toddler is notoriously difficult—they are fierce defenders of their own autonomy. I've often found it annoying when people talk about the "wisdom of children," because, really, we grown-ups are usually a lot smarter. I don't eat loose change, for example. But I've got to admit that, motivationally, young children get it right. They pursue goals that fulfill their genuine needs, and don't bother with the ones that won't. Which may, at least in part, explain why they are usually so much happier than we are.

What You Can Do

Remember, whenever possible, to choose goals that are better suited to the kind of task you are tackling.

- **When it's easy, choose *be-good* goals.** Focus on demonstrating your ability, and *promotion* goals, focusing on what you have to gain.

- **When you can't seem to get going, choose to think in big-picture terms.** Remember *why* the goal is important to you. Also, choose *prevention* goals, focusing on what you could lose if you fail.

- **When it's hard (or unfamiliar), be *specific* about what you want to achieve.** Think in nitty-gritty, *what* terms about exactly what needs to be done. Choose *prevention* goals, as well as *getting-better* goals, focusing on improvement rather than on giving a perfect performance.

- **When you are tempted, think about your goal in *why* terms.** Choose loss-focused *prevention* goals. Both of these strategies will help you to resist even the most powerful temptations.

- **When you need speed, choose gain-focused *promotion* goals.**

- **When you need accuracy, choose loss-focused *prevention* goals.**

- **When you want to be creative, choose *promotion* goals.** You should also make sure that your goals are authentically self-chosen. Feelings of *autonomy* fuel creativity.

- **When you want to have fun, choose *getting-better* goals, along with *autonomous*, self-chosen goals.** We enjoy ourselves more when we focus on the process and when we are intrinsically motivated.

- **When you want real, lasting happiness, choose goals that satisfy your basic need for *relatedness*, *competence*, and *autonomy*.** Avoid focusing too much on fame, prestige, and wealth—even if you get what you want, it won't make you happy for long.

CHAPTER 7

The Right Goals for Them

So far, the advice you've been given in this book has been about choosing the best possible goals for yourself, to maximize both your success and your happiness. There are times, however, when it's not your own goals that you're concerned about changing, but someone else's. If you are a manager, a coach, a teacher, or a parent, part of your job is to motivate other people. You are responsible for someone else's welfare or, at the very least, their productivity. You want to help them set goals in a way that will lead them to their own greatest success (possibly while also benefiting the team or the company). This of course is much easier said than done.

Most of us resist being told outright what our goals should be. Tell a student that she should focus more on learning than on proving that she is smart (something I have actually tried, by the way), and she will rightly point out that she is being graded for her work, so she *has* to care about how well she performs. Tell an employee that he should see his job as an opportunity for personal growth rather than for financial gain, and once you are out of earshot he will probably tell you exactly where you can stick your "personal growth."

Getting another person to change his goal is hard, but luckily, it's something social psychologists have gotten pretty good at. We had to—in order to really study what different goals do, you need to be able to manipulate them in the laboratory and see what happens. And the good news is that the techniques that work in the lab also seem to work in the classroom, at the office, on the playing field, and around your dinner table. In this chapter, you'll learn how to talk to your employees, students, and children in ways that encourage the adoption of particular goals. *You* will provide the signals and cues that allow them to, often unconsciously, home in on the right motivation. I'll tell you about some of my own research on goal interventions in the classroom, and you'll see how simple, easy-to-use, and powerful these techniques can be.

The Direct Approach

Most managers and leaders have, on a regular basis, the unenviable task of trying to get other people to adopt the goals assigned to them. Companies have agendas, and employees need to support those agendas if the company is to succeed. Teachers, too, struggle to motivate students to want to learn everything that the school board, state officials, and federal government require them to learn (and if possible, even more). While the direct approach—simply telling someone what his goal should be—is problematic, there's just no avoiding it entirely. So when you are doling out goals to your employees and your students, how can you do it in a way that actually promotes acceptance? How can we get people to adopt *for themselves* the goals we tell them to adopt, and stay motivated to actually achieve them? After all, just because a goal looks good to you doesn't mean it will look good to them.

There are several strategies that you can use to increase goal acceptance. For one thing, try giving your employee or student a sense of **personal control**, because doing so restores the feelings of autonomy that being *assigned* a goal diminishes. This can be accomplished in a number of ways. First, it helps when people can choose from several options—even a choice between two goals is still a choice. Or, if the goal has to be predetermined, allowing others to decide *how* they will reach the goal for themselves can also create the feeling of choice. For example, in my social psychology course, the students have no choice but to do well on my exams to get a good grade. So the goal is predetermined by me, but I allow them to choose the *kind* of exam they will take—either multiple choice or essay. This gives the students control over how they will reach their goal, allowing them to tailor their approach to their preferences and abilities. When people can make choices for themselves in the workplace or classroom, they are not only more motivated but also less stressed and anxious, because they have a heightened sense of control over the situation they find themselves in.

Participating in decision making, whether it's about which goal to adopt or how to get there, doesn't just give people a feeling of choice. It also helps them to understand the rationale behind the goal. Why is this goal worth pursuing? Why is it important? How will I benefit from it? Remember that people are motivated to achieve a goal only when they feel it has value. When the value is clear, you'll have far fewer problems getting people on board and fully committed to succeed.

Sometimes, unfortunately, joint decision making just isn't possible, and you need to find another way to increase commitment to an assigned goal. When that's the case, **creating contracts** can be a very useful alternative strategy. Contracts are explicit, often written commitments to engage in particular goal-directed behaviors. They are promises made publicly, and sometimes you actually sign your name to them. Even when initial motivation is low, the act of making the commitment publicly increases the value of the goal. After all, no one wants to fail at something they've promised other people they would do. It's embarrassing, and it makes you feel like you're a person who can't be counted on. Contracts have been shown to increase motivation to reach assigned goals in studies of drug addiction, weight control, smoking cessation, and even marital discord. That's right—even warring spouses can learn to behave themselves a bit better when they've put it in writing.

Recently I caught a few episodes of the television show *The Biggest Loser*, and it's a great example of the motivational power of public commitment. If you haven't seen it, it's a competition in which obese individuals are provided with exercise trainers and given a strict diet. Each week, a person from the team that has lost the least amount of weight is booted off the ranch. The physical work these contestants do each week is grueling, to put it mildly. Once the show begins, they are told how much they can eat, which exercises to do, and how many calories they need to burn doing it. How is it possible to motivate people, who for years couldn't psych themselves up to do so much as a sit-up, to work out for up to *six hours* a day? The answer, in no small part, is that once you're chosen as a contestant on *The Biggest Loser*, you make a commitment to do whatever it takes to lose the weight and to fight to keep your place in the contest. You do all this with the cameras rolling, knowing that millions of people will be judging you based on how well you accomplish the goal you've publicly committed yourself to. But public commitment is an enormously effective motivator, as anyone who's seen the show can attest to.

Given the nature of contracts, however, it's not surprising to hear that some former contestants gain back their weight once the show is over. The contract is broken once the cameras and trainers disappear, so unless the goal to be healthy has been truly internalized so that it becomes *self-chosen*, the commitment to *staying* healthy evaporates over time.

Using Cues

Back in Chapter 2, I told you that most of the goals we pursue in the course of a day are pursued unconsciously. In other words, we don't stop to think, "I'm trying to reach my goal right now." We just do it. If a goal is triggered in our unconscious mind, we go for it—often never realizing that it ever was triggered in the first place.

Goals are triggered by cues in your environment, and those cues can be just about anything that reminds you of the goal. After all, the unconscious mind can be a terrific ally: it's constantly working, it notices everything, and it can keep track of a lot more things at once than your conscious mind can. The goal to perform well on an exam can be triggered by reading achievement-related words (like *win, achieve, succeed,* or *compete*), by meeting a high achiever, or by just thinking about the parent who always pushes you to do your best. Even something as simple as holding a No. 2 pencil, the writing implement of choice for all standardized tests, can be the trigger that kicks your goal into gear.

In one study that demonstrated the power of objects to trigger goals, participants got to give electric shocks to someone who had just insulted them. They gave longer shocks and used higher voltage when there happened to be a gun lying on a nearby table than they did when the gun was replaced with a badminton racket. They had *no idea*, however, that their behavior had been in any way influenced by the gun. (Incidentally, they weren't *really* giving shocks—but they thought they were, and that's what matters.) So just being in the room with a weapon can trigger the goal to be more aggressive, and you almost certainly wouldn't realize it if it happened to you. I know it's odd to think that the sight of some object might affect you this way, but really, it's happening all the time.

In Chapter 2, I also gave you the advice to surround yourself as much as possible with cues that would help you to achieve the goals you want to reach. Now you can take that same piece of advice and apply it to triggering goals in other people. You supply the cues, and the motivation you're looking for in your child, student, or employee will probably follow.

What kinds of cues? Using the right words is a great place to start. Psychologist Tanya Chartrand and her colleagues[1] were able to trigger either the goal of being frugal and thrifty or the goal of enjoying luxury and prestige by exposing people to words associated with either prestige or frugality in a word game. Next, they were given a choice between socks, both worth roughly $6: one pair of Tommy Hilfiger socks or three pairs of Hanes socks. Those who had seen prestige words chose to receive the single pair of Tommy Hilfiger socks rather than three pairs of Hanes socks more than 60 percent of the time, compared to only 20 percent of those who had seen frugal words. The same pattern of preferences emerged when people were subliminally exposed to either prestige brand names (Tiffany & Co., Neiman Marcus, Nordstrom) or thrift brand names (Wal-Mart, Kmart, Dollar Store). So if your spouse, like mine, tends to cling tightly to his wallet, and you'd like to soften him up for a big purchase, try strolling him past a few high-end shops to trigger a goal more compatible with spending. Tip: You may not want to overuse this strategy—after your fifth trip down Madison Avenue for no obvious reason, your spouse may begin to get suspicious.

Words and brands are just some of the cues available to you. Goals can be triggered by the means you use to reach them or by an opportunity to act on them. Gyms can trigger the goal to exercise, farmer's markets can trigger the goal to eat healthy with locally grown food, computers can trigger the goal to start working (or play games, or post on Facebook—it all depends on how you normally use it). Really, anything can be a goal trigger. Just remember two important caveats if you want your cue to work. First, make sure the cue has the same meaning to the other person that it does to you. I have often heard parents justify the purchase of a fancy new computer for their child by saying, "We figure it will make him want to do his homework." The odds are good he'll want to use it for anything but.

Second, remember that you can only trigger a goal that is already seen by the other person in a positive light. In other words, you can't trick someone into a pursuing a goal he thinks is pointless, harmful, or immoral, just because you throw a few cues at him. Achievement cues will only work on someone who already thinks achievement is a good thing. You'll never get your spouse to rein in his spending if he doesn't value frugality, no matter how many times you drive him past the dollar store.

Here's the Picture, You Choose the Frame

One of the most common ways that experimental psychologists manipulate goals is through *framing*. Every time people are given the chance to do something, they ask themselves (often unconsciously), "What kind of opportunity is this? What is this all about?" Just like an actor, we want to know: "What's my motivation?" In real life, you usually need to figure this out on your own, but in a psychology experiment, we provide the answer for you, by creating the frame. Basically, all we are doing is presenting participants with a task and then talking about it in a way that elicits a particular goal.

For example, Tory Higgins and his colleagues often create a promotion or prevention goal simply by giving subjects something to do and then telling them what they could gain if they do well (promotion) or lose if they do poorly (prevention). You can create the same frames by assigning a task and then having people list strategies to make sure everything goes right (promotion) or strategies that make sure nothing goes wrong (prevention).

In my own work, I have usually created a focus on *getting better* by telling my participants that whatever they'd be working on (anagrams, puzzles, math problems, etc.) was an "opportunity to learn a valuable skill" and that it was something on which they would "improve over time." *Be-good* goals are remarkably easy to create—just tell individuals that you're going to compare their performance to other people, or that their performance will be indicative of a valued ability (like creativity, intelligence, or athleticism), and you'll be all set. Most of us are quick to snap into *be-good* goals whenever we feel we are being judged.

It turns out that *how* we are judged can also impact the goals we adopt. Psychologist Ruth Butler found that when we are evaluated compared to *others,* we respond by adopting *be-good* goals, but when instead we are evaluated relative to task requirements or our own progress, we see it as a chance to pursue *get-better* goals. In her study, middle school boys and girls were given a set of ten reasoning problems and told that either they would be given a score relative to their peers' performance (e.g., scoring at the 90 percent level means scoring higher than 90 percent of other students in their grade) or they would receive scores indicating that their own performance was improving, staying the same, or getting worse over time. Before beginning, Butler asked the students to describe their own goals with respect to the task. Those students who believed that they would receive scores relative to their peers agreed most with statements such as "I want to show I have high ability" and "I want to avoid failing on these problems," while those who expected progress scores preferred statements such as "I want to exercise my brain" and "I want to improve my problem solving." (In fact, only the *get-better* group significantly improved their performance over time. They also reported that they enjoyed the experience more than the peer-comparison *be-good* group.) So just knowing that you will be evaluated in a certain way provides a frame. It tells you what this task is "about"—competing with others or making progress. The corresponding goals just naturally follow.

Notice that when psychologists use these techniques, we're not ever saying, "Your goal should be to _____." Framing is much more subtle than that—it creates conditions ripe for people to adopt the goal *on their own*, without feeling pressured or controlled, and as a result they avoid all the problems we associate with goals that are simply assigned.

Catching a Contagious Goal

Like the common cold, goals are remarkably contagious. The sight of someone pursuing a particular goal is one of the more potent triggers of unconscious goal pursuit psychologists have discovered. You don't even have to know the guy doing the pursuing. All that matters is that he and his goal are seen positively. Unappealing people, and unappealing goals, make lousy triggers.

I have used goal contagion in several studies, as part of a research program designed to help college students focus more on personal growth and development and less on proving their abilities. It's a *getting-better* intervention, and it is sorely needed. Studies suggest that on any given day during the academic year, as much as 50 percent of the college student population is depressed to the point of warranting professional treatment. At no point in the history of the American higher educational system have students been more focused on making the grade and being the best, and less focused on acquiring knowledge and developing as scholars and as individuals. It is impossible to not feel desperately sorry for them—they're killing themselves to get ahead. The ones who aren't have often given up altogether. College dropout rates are at an alarming high. Young people need to focus a lot more on *getting better* and a lot less on *being good*.

Unfortunately, simply telling students that they should view their college experience as an opportunity to learn is almost pointless—it meets with a staggering amount of resistance. Students are, after all, very much aware that they are going to be graded and that those grades have important consequences. To chastise someone for caring too much about being evaluated when *you* are doling out the evaluations looks, and feels, hypocritical. So what can we do? Well, for one thing, we can try exposing them to someone with a *get-better* goal, then wait for the infection to spread.

The good news is that it does spread—quickly. The first time I tried this approach was in an introductory psychology class taught by one of my colleagues at Lehigh University. Thirty students in my intervention were given a packet of surveys to fill out, and in the middle of the packet were three brief biographical stories of famous psychologists. Each story emphasized the crucial role that hard work, persistence, and thirst for knowledge played in bringing about the psychologist's success (emphasizing a *get-better* orientation toward psychology). Here's an example of one of the stories I created:

Alfred Adler was born in Vienna, Austria, on February 7, 1870. He is responsible in many ways for much of the present-day philosophy behind psychotherapy practice and the understanding of mental illness. He focused on looking at the person as a whole, rather than as a collection of drives and instincts, thus changing the nature of psychological theory. Interestingly, Adler's academic career did not initially seem promising. A childhood recollection that stood out in his memory, which he liked to tell children having difficulty with their schoolwork, was an occasion when a teacher told his father to take Alfred out of school and apprentice him as a cobbler, since he would never graduate anyway. Having lost interest in school, Adler had failed mathematics. He now decided to show the teacher what he could do: in a short time he became the first in his class in mathematics and never again wavered in his dedication to his studies.

In this biographical sketch, Adler is described as someone who made progress over time. His early academic work was far from impressive—so bad, in fact, that he was considered a lost cause. That he could, with determination and hard work, become one of the most important figures in the history of psychology is an excellent illustration of *getting better.* Had Adler instead focused on *being good,* he might have agreed with his teacher that he lacked the ability to succeed, and spent his life mending shoes rather than troubled minds.

Now let's get back to the study. Another group of thirty students received the same packet, but without the famous psychologists stories, to serve as a comparison. At the end of the semester, I found that the students in the intervention group not only had developed more *get-better* goals in psychology, but actually got higher course grades—more than a third of a grade higher (that's the difference between a B+ and an A–).

Next, I tried the same technique in Lehigh's general chemistry course (substituting famous chemists for famous psychologists). Here's an example of a biography I used:

> Ernest Rutherford was born in New Zealand as one of twelve siblings in a relatively poor farming family. Despite his humble beginnings, he is widely regarded as one of the world's most remarkable thinkers—his contributions to chemistry include the fundamental research that led to our understanding of radioactivity, as well as to the discovery of the structure of the atom (a solid nucleus and orbiting electron shells, as opposed to the prevailing "Plum Pudding" model of J. J. Thomson). In addition, many of his students (Niels Bohr, Hans Geiger, Robert Oppenheimer) went on to be Nobel Prize–winning chemists themselves. Ironically, Rutherford had failed in his first attempt at a career—he was turned down three times when he applied to be a schoolteacher in New Zealand. Success in chemistry did not come quickly or easily—he received several scholarships only because the first-place winners were unable to accept them, having come in second (or lower) each time. Perhaps Rutherford's greatest asset was not his intellect but his hard work and determination, which allowed him to overcome the many obstacles and difficulties he experienced throughout his long career as a chemist.

Again, I found amazing changes among the students in the *get-better* goal intervention group. They reported finding chemistry more interesting. They were more motivated to study and more confident in their chemistry skills. They were more likely to seek help and less likely to think that doing well in chemistry was due to an innate, fixed ability. They were more focused on *getting better* than on *being good*, and somewhat ironically, this led to higher course grades. My *get-better* group showed improved performance with each exam, while the control group's performance got worse each time. In the end, students in the *get-better* group scored on average 10 percent higher on the final exam than those in the control group—a difference of more than a full letter grade.

Recently, I have taken the contagious-goal approach and tried to apply it more broadly, not just to one course but to a student's entire college experience. Recent research in educational psychology suggests that adjustment to college—both academically and socially—is the key to retention. When students feel they are getting the hang of things, they don't drop out. In my study, I wanted to see if a little *get-better* contagion might affect a student's ability to adjust to the difficulties encountered. Again I used biographies, only this time they were about fellow students who had focused on *getting better* and had successfully navigated the ups and downs at Lehigh. Here is an example:

> Ellen is a junior from a small town in Indiana. Even though she was excited to move halfway across the country and go to college, upon arriving Ellen quickly began to feel overwhelmed. Like most first-year students, she was not used to cooking all her own meals, paying her own bills, and doing her own laundry. Back at home she felt like she knew everyone, but here at college everyone was a stranger. And academically, there was just so much more work. Professors assigned whole books to read in a matter of days. She had multiple tests and papers due within the first month of classes. More than once in those first few weeks, she was tempted to pack up and head home. But she never did

give up. Over time, she learned to plan ahead and budget time for her coursework and for taking care of herself. She found that this became easier and easier with practice— within a year she was no longer constantly falling behind in her classes, and she was able to keep her life in order. Of course, there are still occasionally times when things get overwhelming, but Ellen has realized that that's something that happens to everyone, and that there isn't anything she can't manage if she just keeps trying.

I gave these stories to incoming first-year students at Lehigh and checked in with them in the spring semester to see how they were doing and if they had been affected by exposure to the students with *get-better* goals. I danced around my lab for a good ten minutes when I looked at the data and realized that the intervention group not only reported having more *get-better* goals, but also said that they were better academically and socially adjusted to college compared to a control group. They were less likely to believe their performance in college was based on innate ability. They believed more in the value of effort, were more confident, and even had higher GPAs.

How can you use goal contagion to give your children, students, or employees the kinds of goals you'd like them to pursue? You can start by finding role models—stories of people who pursued the goal you'd like them to adopt. Whenever possible, use people they actually know and admire. It's not essential (I doubt any of my chemistry students had posters of Ernest Rutherford in their dorm rooms), but it does increase the likelihood of contagion. Of course, you can provide the role model by pursuing the goals yourself. As a parent, teacher, coach, or manager, you are in an ideal position to inspire the people around you and shape their goals, even if they never quite realize exactly how you do it.

What You Can Do

- **Help make the choice personal.** When you really can't avoid assigning a goal, try to give your employee, student, or child as much choice as possible about *how* to accomplish the goal. Feelings of personal choice are highly motivating. In addition, being a part of the decision making will help the person to see why the goal is worth pursuing—a great way to enhance commitment.

- **Commit in a public way.** When personal choice isn't an option, try using contracts. Asking someone to commit publicly to reaching a goal will increase their motivation—no one feels good about breaking a promise. But remember this technique is only motivating while the contract still holds—once it's over, motivation will diminish unless the person has internalized the goal for himself.

- **Use the right triggers.** Many of the goals we pursue are triggered unconsciously—we aren't even aware that we're working to reach them. You can use just about anything to trigger someone else's goal unconsciously (even words or physical objects), so long as you use something that *they* associate with the goal.

- **Frame the picture.** Careful framing of a situation will shape what people think it is about and influence the goals they adopt. When faced with an opportunity to improve, we adopt *get-better* goals. When we are being evaluated compared to others, we choose *be-good* goals. A chance to gain creates a promotion goal, while the risk of loss creates a prevention goal. By framing what a task is all about, you can create circumstances ripe for adopting the right goal.

- **Make it contagious.** Goals are highly contagious. Whenever we see someone pursuing a goal, it can serve as a powerful trigger, activating the same goal in our unconscious minds. By using the right role models (including yourself!), you can take advantage of this process and use it to spread any goal around, so long as the role model and the goal are seen in a positive light.

PART THREE

Go

CHAPTER 8

Conquer the Goal Saboteurs

LET'S SAY YOU'VE CAREFULLY CHOSEN THE GOAL THAT WILL WORK BEST for you, and you've done everything I recommended earlier in the book when setting your goal to maximize your motivation and commitment. Now you ought to be totally confident that you will succeed, right? Well, not exactly. The possibility still exists that you might not reach your goal. That's because there are still plenty of mistakes you can make that could sabotage your chances for success.

Many people think that the most common mistake we make is not knowing the correct actions to take in order to reach our goals, but that turns out to be wrong. CEOs' strategic plans don't usually fail because no one knew what needed to be done to implement them. Students don't usually fail because they never realized that they should study and do their homework. Your teenager's room isn't a mess because he doesn't know how to clean it.

The problem is much more often in the *execution* of the action needed for the task. We miss opportunities to seize moments because we're too busy to notice them. We use strategies that don't fit well with the kind of goal we're pursuing. We allow other competing goals and temptations to interfere. We procrastinate. We lose confidence. We give up way too soon.

In this chapter, I'll describe in detail the pitfalls that we most often encounter while pursuing our goals, and I'll tell you why they occur. You will no doubt recognize a few from your own past experience and hopefully understand the challenges you'll face in the future much more clearly. But it's not enough just to know what our problems are—we need to know what to do about them. That's why, in the chapters that follow, I'll take you step by step through solutions for dealing with these common saboteurs.

Seizing the Moment

I doubt that anyone reading this book actually needs to be told that reaching your goals requires commitment. We all know that if you aren't motivated to achieve something, that if you don't have serious intentions, it's probably not going to happen. What may surprise you, however, is learning that a strong commitment doesn't buy you nearly as much as you may think it does. It's true that the intention is critical and that you need to *really* want it if you're going to succeed, but it's not nearly enough. Across studies, intentions account for about 20 to 30 percent of the variability in goal achievement—that's a fancy way of saying that about 70 to 80 percent of the time we have plenty of commitment, but we screw it up along the way. I don't know if the road to hell is paved with good intentions, but the road to failure surely is.

There are plenty of different mistakes we can make, but the one most frequently responsible for our troubles is that we miss opportunities to act in a timely manner. Imagine yourself getting up in the morning, eating your breakfast, and sending the kids off to school. You look at the clock and realize that you have about twenty minutes before you have to leave for work. What do you do with the time? There are lots of ways you could use it—many different goals you could work on during those twenty minutes. You could use the time to exercise, pay your bills, organize your closet, or return a phone call. You could check your e-mail, clean your house, or fold some laundry. Which goal should you work on? Probably not an easy choice, since they all may be important to you. So you think it over for a while, and once you decide which goal to work on, you move on to figuring out *how* to work on it. Should you exercise by taking a short walk, doing a few sit-ups, or throwing your yoga video in the DVD player? Should you clean your house by taking on the dishes in the kitchen sink, the ring around the bathroom tub, or maybe all the toys scattered around the family room? By the time you've decided what to do *and* how to do it, half of your time is gone. At this point, you probably say to yourself "never mind, there isn't enough time" and flop down on the couch to catch a few minutes of *Good Morning America.*

Throughout the day, you are given, whether you realize it or not, opportunities to act on your goals. You are constantly making choices about what to do in these moments (again, whether you realize it or not). But given how many goals we are all juggling, and how distracted we often are, it's not surprising that opportunities slip away from us. *Which* goal should I work on in this situation? Is this a *good* situation for that goal? Which *action* should I take? What do I *feel* like doing? Having to decide when, where, and how to act on your goal is hard to do swiftly, and opportunities may pass while you're trying to figure it all out. (Don't worry—an effective solution for this dilemma is coming in the next chapter.)

Another problem is that not every goal is fun to work on, and it's pretty tempting to let the opportunity pass you by when what you need to do is something unpleasant. This has been a clear pattern in my own life when it comes to hitting the gym. Even though I have always wanted to be the type of person who works out regularly, I have to admit that I absolutely loathe exercising. My older brother Dan was the kind of athlete that people in our high school still talk about twenty-five years later—that gene missed me completely. I might have been a halfway decent athlete if I'd tried, but I never did try, because I have never enjoyed running around, jumping, sweating, or lifting anything heavy.

Regardless, I know that I should work out. I know that it's important for my health and, frankly, for my appearance. Exercising more has been a goal of mine for as long as I can remember, but for most of my life, I never actually managed to do it. My past is littered with unused gym memberships, dust-gathering exercise equipment, and cool workout clothes with the price tags still on. Like many of you, I made excuses for my failure, and my favorite one to trot out was, "I'm too busy. I didn't have time today." It felt like it was honest, but looking back, it clearly wasn't. It wasn't literally true that I didn't have any opportunities to exercise. What is true is that every time one arose, I chose to do something else, like sleep in, take a long lunch, stay late at work, or unwind with a drink in the evening with friends. Every time I could have acted on my goal, I decided to act on another goal. These decisions weren't usually conscious—I just (conveniently) forgot about exercising until it was too late. The other, less important but far more pleasurable goal pursuits got all my energy and attention. (Yes, I would much rather work late than exercise. That's how much I hate exercise.)

It's also easy to miss chances to make progress on goals we don't even mind pursuing. Spend too much time on one project or activity, and suddenly you find you don't have enough time for everything else you'd hoped to do that day. Whatever your circumstances, the challenge is to seize these opportunities before they slip through your fingers, and to not let preoccupation, distraction, or indecision keep you from realizing your goal.

Shields Up

Goal pursuit, even when motivation is strong, requires protection. Distractions and temptations can interrupt an otherwise successful endeavor and throw it off course. This is where self-control comes in, warding off these troublemakers like a brawny bouncer at an upscale bar whose job is to keep the riffraff out. Unfortunately, as everyone knows, your self-control can sometimes fail you. You may not have enough of it at the critical moment. When that happens, your brain has some other built-in mechanisms for providing the protection we need, and psychologists refer to these as *goal shielding*. But shields fail too, as any fan of *Star Trek* can tell you. They strain, they weaken, and you wind up with a gaping hole big enough for the riffraff to waltz in.

The good news is that there are things you can do to build up your self-control and strengthen your goal shields (more on that in the coming chapters). The tougher challenge comes when you find yourself in a situation where the shields are working fine but end up protecting the wrong thing. This tends to happen most often when two competing goals are duking it out for control.

Almost all our goals are in competition with each other at one time or another because time spent working on one goal is usually time *not* spent working on your other goals. For instance, time spent writing this book is time I could be spending with my children or (gasp!) working out. However, this is not an insurmountable problem. The goals of being an author, a mother, and a healthy person are not in any sense mutually exclusive. It takes some juggling, but it is possible to find time for all three pursuits, and even more. The real challenge is when you hold two goals that *do* fundamentally conflict with one another—when reaching one goal by definition means sacrificing the other one. You can't live in the lap of luxury and be frugal, you can't travel the world while sticking close to the comforts of home, and you can't enjoy lots of rich and tasty foods while trying to lose weight. That last conflict constitutes one of the fundamental problems dieters encounter, and explains in part why so many diets fail.

According to the goal conflict model of eating, all dieters have, by necessity, two incompatible goals—to enjoy food (something all humans are essentially wired to do) and to control their weight. Encountering a slice of chocolate cake or a large plate of fries is a cue that triggers both goals—to eat and to *not* eat. When competing goals get activated in your brain, it responds by inhibiting one of them, thus providing a goal shield. In other words, the losing goal doesn't just get ignored—it gets completely deactivated. (This is not the same thing as thought suppression—like being told "not to think about white bears," which ironically leads you to constantly think about white bears. Suppression is a *conscious* attempt to ignore an idea that is active in your mind, and it usually doesn't work—inhibition is an *unconscious* attempt to render the idea inactive, and it works very well.) To successfully control your weight, you need to inhibit the goal of wanting to eat too many delicious foods. Unfortunately, our environment is rich with reminders that these foods are all too easily available—in TV commercials, magazine ads, and on the dessert cart rolling past your table—and they're just waiting for you to take a bite. These cues are designed to activate your food enjoyment goal, which in turn inhibits (and deactivates) your weight control goal. The shield protects your desire to eat instead of your desire to lose weight, and temptation wins. (Help for this is on the way—just keep reading.)

One study by psychologist Wolfgang Stroebe and colleagues demonstrated the power of this inhibition without using any actual food. In their experiment, dieting and nondieting participants were subliminally exposed to words related to eating enjoyment, like *tasty* and *appetizing*. Later, they were asked to look at strings of letters flashed on a computer screen and decide whether or not the letters formed a word (like *paper*) or were just gibberish (like *psper*). After exposure to the food enjoyment words, dieters were slower to recognize real words that had to do with dieting, like *slim, weight loss*, and, of course, *diet*. This slowness is a classic effect of inhibition—your brain not only shuts off your weight-loss goal, but everything in your mind related to weight loss, including the words themselves. It's a perfect shield, but unfortunately it's shielding the wrong thing. (Interestingly, nondieters don't show this effect. Their brains don't see the conflict because they haven't personally experienced the goal of weight control and the tension between simultaneously wanting to eat and not eat.)

Conflict between two opposing goals is one of the more intractable problems in motivation, particularly when you can't resolve the dilemma by just giving one of them up. The solution is careful planning—in giving each goal its time and place in the driver's seat (more on this in the next chapter).

How Am I Doin'?

It is practically impossible to reach a goal when you don't have any sense of how well you are doing. Should you speed up? Slow down? Step up your efforts or try a new approach? You have no idea, because you're flying blind. I suppose you might reach your goal by accident, but that is very unlikely, since without feedback your motivational system basically shuts down. When it comes to goals, your brain works on a very simple principle: *reduce discrepancies*. That's how psychologists refer to the difference between where you want to be (at your goal) and where you actually are. When your brain detects a discrepancy between them, it wants to take action to close the gap. But if there is no feedback—no information about how well you are currently doing—then there is no discrepancy to detect. So nothing happens.

Sometimes the feedback you need comes from the outside world—like the grades from your teacher, the evaluations from your boss, or the number of people visiting your website. Often, however, that feedback is something that has to be self-generated. In other words, *you* have to figure out how well you are doing. Psychologists call this *self-monitoring*, and it is an absolutely essential part of reaching any difficult goal. It's also something that we all too often neglect to do, for several reasons.

For one thing, some effort is required. Once you are moving along in pursuit of a goal, it can be hard to apply the brakes in order to get the information you need to evaluate your performance. It's like the motivational equivalent of pulling over to ask for directions when you're lost and in a hurry—even though it's the smart thing to do, it feels somehow counterproductive to stop the car. So to override that impulse to just keep things moving takes a real act of will. It would certainly be easier to go on driving, even though that literally won't get you anywhere.

Another challenge to self-monitoring is dealing with the possibility of negative feedback. Maybe you aren't doing so well, and having to face that fact is psychologically painful. It's a blow to your self-esteem. On the other hand, it is essential information you'll need if you are to actually achieve your goal. If the only way you can succeed requires a change of course, that's not going to happen if you don't know you're performing poorly.

Like most people who struggle to maintain their ideal weight, I get a little anxious every time I step on the scale. In the past, my method of dealing with this anxiety was to just not bother stepping on the scale. This was particularly true when I knew I had been eating rather recklessly. The more I gave in to temptation, the less I wanted to step on the scale. Of course, stepping on the scale doesn't *cause* weight gain, but I could fool myself much more easily if I didn't actually know how much I weighed. (Sound familiar? For some of you reading this, just substitute the words *cholesterol* or *credit card debt* for *weight* and you'll know immediately what I'm talking about.)

I have learned the hard way to do a lot more self-monitoring when it comes to my weight. Now I get on the scale every single day, so that any gains can be immediately countered with better eating and some (gasp!) exercise before they get too out of hand and I need to change clothes sizes again. This is what is so brilliant and effective about Weight Watchers—mandatory weekly weigh-ins and a detailed accounting of everything you eat each day, though somewhat time-consuming, keep you fully aware at all times of how well you are doing each week as you work toward your goal. Weight Watchers and programs like it are essentially lessons in the power of self-monitoring.

Too Little of What You Need, Too Much of What You Don't

Most of the mistakes you can make on the way to achieving your goal fall into two broad categories of wrongs. The first is what psychologists call *underregulation,*[1] not doing enough of something you need to do for success. So far the mistakes I've talked about in this chapter, missing opportunities and not self-monitoring, are examples of this kind of error. Lacking the self-control to avoid temptation and control your impulses is another kind of underregulation. Many of the strategies I'll be sharing with you in the remaining chapters are effective for dealing with this kind of saboteur, because underregulation is by far the most common problem.

The second kind of wrong is called *misregulation*, and just like the name suggests, it is choosing an ineffective strategy to reach your goal. You can be working as hard as you can, practically killing yourself to succeed, yet success will elude you because you're going about it the wrong way. Maybe you're working too quickly when it's vital to be careful and accurate. Perhaps you are trying to fight temptation by suppressing thoughts about food, and it's backfiring. (Incidentally, thought suppression almost never works. Whatever you're suppressing usually just pops up later with an even greater force.) Maybe you're overthinking something you usually do naturally and expertly, and it's causing you to choke under pressure.

It's hard to give good advice when it comes to misregulation because a strategy that works with one goal may not be good for another, so making generalizations that will be true across goals is difficult. Probably the best advice I can give here is to make sure you are self-monitoring, because evaluating your performance is the best way to discover that you need a new strategy, long before it's too late to make a change.

Too often, people blame their goal failures on the wrong things. I hope that after reading this chapter you will take some time to reconsider some of your own past disappointments. Perhaps you thought you lacked ability, when really you just used the wrong strategy. Or you thought you didn't have the time to work on a goal, when really you just let the opportunities you had slip through your fingers. Maybe you were operating in the dark, without the feedback you needed to keep yourself motivated and on the right track. Now that I've told you where your problems may really lie, it's time to start focusing on solutions.

What You Can Do

Many of the solutions for conquering the goal saboteurs will be coming in the following chapters, but here are a few things from this chapter to keep in mind.

- **It's about execution.** Most of the time, we know what needs to be done to reach a goal—we just don't manage to actually do it. Focusing on execution is essential for success.

- **Seize the moment.** Given how busy most of us are, and how many goals we are pursuing at once, it's not surprising that we routinely miss opportunities to act on a goal because we simply fail to notice them. Achieving your goal means grabbing hold of these opportunities before they slip through your fingers.

- **Know what to do.** Once you've seized the moment, you've got to figure out exactly what you're going to do with it. When you can't act swiftly, you risk wasting the opportunity.

- **Put your shields up.** Goals require protection—distractions, temptations, and competing goals can steal your attention and your energy, and sap your motivation.

- **Know how you are doing.** Achieving a goal also requires careful monitoring. If you don't know how well you are doing, you can't adjust your behavior or your strategies accordingly. Check your progress frequently.

CHAPTER 9

Make a Simple Plan

By failing to prepare, you are preparing to fail.

—Benjamin Franklin

PLANNING IS GENERALLY REGARDED AS A USEFUL THING TO DO. DO A quick Google search of "planning quotes" and you will be up to your ears in examples of famous politicians, writers, business leaders, and Founding Fathers who have sung the praises of making a good plan. Management consultant David Allen, in his highly acclaimed book *Getting Things Done,* writes that one of the key objectives of the organizational techniques he teaches is "disciplining yourself to make front-end decisions about all the 'inputs' you let into your life so that you will always have a plan for 'next actions'." In fact, you'd be hard-pressed to find a public figure advising anyone in earnest that the road to success lies in "just winging it."

The scientific evidence from studies of motivation suggests that these enthusiastic planning advocates are perfectly correct. There is no strategy more effective for fighting off those pesky goal saboteurs than doing a little advance planning. If you took just one piece of advice from me, if you could remember only one thing you read in this entire book, I would want it to be this one: make a plan for how you will achieve your goal.

There is one important thing to keep in mind: some kinds of plans don't work very well. This, incidentally, is why planning is sometimes the subject of some humor. (That same Google search will give you a quote attributed to Woody Allen: "If you want to make God laugh, tell him about your plans." And then there's the famous John Lennon line, "Life is just what happens to you while you're busy making other plans.") There is a good reason why some plans don't work, which I think I can best illustrate with an example. A typical person with the goal of losing weight will create a plan for herself that looks something like this:

Step 1: Eat less
Step 2: Work out more

It *looks* like a plan at any rate. It has steps, doesn't it? I suppose technically it is a plan, but it is a *terrible* plan. Studies show that this sort of planning is basically pointless—it does nothing whatsoever to help people reach their goals. People who plan this way (and as it happens, most people plan this way) *feel* like they are making a plan. But all they are really doing is listing the actions that need to be taken in a very general way. They have left all the important details completely out of the plan. *When* will you work out more, and *where*, and *how*? *What* specifically are you going to eat less of, and *how much* less?

Just like goals, not all plans are created equal. An effective plan is one that spells out exactly what will be done, and where, and how. In this chapter I'll show you how to create these simple plans and share with you some truly amazing studies that show how powerful this particular form of planning can be.

The Christmas Essay

In 1997, I sat in the audience during a symposium on motivation presented at the Association for Psychological Science's annual conference in Washington, D.C. I was a second-year graduate student, and to me the psychologists sitting on the dais were like rock stars. One of them was Peter Gollwitzer, a well-known social psychologist from the University of Konstanz, Germany. At this point in my graduate career, I wasn't exactly sure what area I wanted to specialize in. I can say without exaggeration that the talk Peter gave that day changed my life.

He described an experiment he and his students had conducted on the Konstanz campus. Shortly before Christmas break, they approached students on their way to their final exams and asked if they would participate in a study of how people spend their holidays in modern times. Those who agreed were told that they had to write an essay while home on vacation, describing in detail how they spent their Christmas. This essay had to be written and mailed in within forty-eight hours of Christmas Day. Half of the students were given one additional instruction: to decide exactly *when* and *where* they would write the essay. They wrote down this information on a piece of paper, handed it to the researcher, and went off to take their final exams.

A few days after Christmas, the essays started arriving in the mail. Gollwitzer found that 32 percent of the students who made no particular plan for when and where to write it had sent their essay in. Astoundingly, 71 percent of the ones who did make a plan completed their essays—more than *twice* the number of nonplanners. Upon hearing this, I think my mouth practically dropped to the floor. Goal completion *doubled* as the result of the simplest intervention I had ever heard of. The study of human behavior is such a complicated, messy enterprise that, to be perfectly honest, social psychologists are thrilled when their interventions have *any* kind of effect on people's actions, even very small effects. The effect of this kind of planning was HUGE in comparison to most of the studies I'd seen, and it was something you could teach anyone to do. (It was in this moment that I decided that studying goals and motivation was definitely the way I would go.)

The Power of If-Then

The beauty of these plans lies in their simplicity. You take a goal you want to achieve, and you spell out exactly when, where, and how you will achieve it. For example, take the weight-loss goal I mentioned earlier. Step 1, "Eat less," becomes "I will eat no more than 1,500 calories a day." Step 2, "Work out more," turns into "I will work out for an hour at the gym on Mondays, Wednesdays, and Fridays before work." Gollwitzer refers to this kind of planning as forming *implementation intentions*, which is kind of a mouthful. Really it's just a form of *if-then* planning: *if* I am in this situation, *then* I will take this action. If I have eaten 1,500 calories today, then I will stop eating. If it's Monday morning, then I will hit the gym before work.

Years after first hearing the story of the Christmas essay, I had the opportunity to work with Peter and his wife, Gabriele Oettingen, as a postdoctoral researcher at NYU. With our colleague Angela Duckworth from the University of Pennsylvania, we decided to really put implementation intentions to the test, by using them on a group of people notorious for the lack of discipline and self-control: tenth-graders on summer break. These were students who were going to be taking the PSAT test in the fall, and they all had the goal of studying for it over their summer months. In May, we gave the students a book of ten PSAT practice tests and told them that we would collect the book back when they returned to school in September. Half of the students were also asked to decide when and where they would work on the practice problems over the summer (e.g., "After breakfast on weekdays in my room.") The students did not get any reminders of any kind from us over the summer—they didn't even get to keep the piece of paper they had written their plan on. After collecting the books from them in September, we found that nonplanners completed an average of 100 practice problems. Planners, on the other hand, completed a staggering 250 problems! Once again performance more than doubled, even though that performance was stretched out over the course of an entire summer. All this from an intervention that took little more than a moment of the student's time.

That's Not All . . .

Plans like these have enormous value when it comes to reaching our health goals as well. Let's face it—being healthy usually either means doing something unpleasant (like getting screened for a disease) or forgoing something you really want (like a doughnut or a cigarette). So when it comes to reaching our health goals, most of us need all the help we can get. *If-then* plans are perhaps just what the doctor ordered.

In one study, over two hundred men and women in northern England were invited to adopt the goal of reducing their fat intake over the course of a month. Half of the participants were also instructed to make *if-then* plans for how they would eat less fat, and in what situations they would take these actions. Only the group that had made plans was successful in reducing both their overall fat intake and saturated fat intake—those without plans actually slightly *increased* the fat in their diet.[1] A similar study used *if-then* planning to help people quit smoking. Over the course of two months, planners not only smoked significantly fewer cigarettes than nonplanners, but 12 percent of planners had quit completely, compared to only 2 percent of nonplanners.[2]

Yet another study looked at breast self-examination, an important health check that most women intend to perform but far fewer actually remember to do with any regularity. Researchers found that 100 percent of the women who were told to plan where and when they would perform self-exams actually did so in the following month, compared to only 53 percent of the nonplanning group (even though the commitment to perform self-exams was equally strong in both groups). Similar results have been shown for cervical cancer screenings (92 percent of planners, 60 percent of nonplanners) and adherence to an exercise program (91 percent of planners, 39 percent of nonplanners).

Gollwitzer and his colleague Paschal Sheeran recently reviewed the results from ninety-four studies that measured the effects of *if-then* planning and found significantly higher rates of goal attainment for just about every goal you can think of: using public transportation more frequently, buying organic foods, helping others, driving more carefully, not drinking, not starting smoking, remembering to recycle, following through on New Year's resolutions, negotiating fairly, avoiding stereotypical and prejudicial thoughts, doing math problems . . . you name the goal, and these simple plans will help you reach it.

In fact, *if-then* planning works in even the most unlikely of circumstances. In one study, a group of patients in an in-hospital treatment program for heroin addicts—patients who were still in the painful stage of withdrawal—were asked to write up a short résumé by 5 p.m. that day. This résumé would help hospital counselors locate employment for each patient when they were ready to leave the hospital. After receiving their assignment that morning, half of the patients were also asked to decide when and where they would write the résumé. At 5 p.m., the researchers found that none of the nonplanners had remembered to complete the résumé—not a single person. Remarkably, 80 percent of the planners successfully handed theirs in! Subsequent studies of *if-then* planning with schizophrenic individuals and frontal lobe brain injury patients, two groups that have well-documented difficulty pursuing their goals, show similar results. If people with problems of this severity can be successful using these plans, just imagine what they can do for you.

It really doesn't seem to matter in the least what the goal is or who is doing the pursuing. Planning when, where, and how you will take the actions needed to reach your goal is probably the single most effective thing you can do to increase your chances of success. The only question left to ask is, why? How can such a simple strategy be so powerful?

But *Why* Does It Work?

In the last chapter, I told you that the most common problem we run into when trying to achieve a goal is missing opportunities to take action. This can happen because we are preoccupied by other goals or simply so distracted that we either forget about our goal entirely or don't notice the opportunity when it arises. It can also happen because we are reluctant to do whatever is required to reach our goal, because it is difficult or just no fun at all. Whatever the reason, we are constantly letting opportunities to achieve our goals slip through our fingers. If we want to succeed, we literally need to learn how to seize the moment. This is precisely what *if-then* plans are designed to do.

An amazing thing happens in your brain when you decide when and where you will act on your goal. The act of planning creates a link between the situation or cue (the *if*) and the behavior that should follow (the *then*). Let's say your mother has been giving you a hard time about not keeping in touch, so you set yourself the goal to call your mom once a week. After a while, you find that despite your genuine desire to be better about calling, you just keep forgetting to do it. Mom is getting madder by the minute. So you make an *if-then* plan: If it is *Sunday after dinner*, then I will *phone Mom*. Now the situation "Sunday after dinner" is wired in your brain directly to the action "phone Mom."

The second thing that happens is that the situation or cue (*Sunday after dinner*) becomes highly activated in your brain. It's like when a teacher asks if anyone knows the capital of Vermont, and there's that one kid who immediately starts jumping around in his seat and frantically waving his raised hand, saying, "Ooh, ooh, I know, I know, pick me!" When a situation is highly activated in your mind, it is just dying to get noticed. Completely below your awareness, your brain starts scanning the environment, searching for the situation in the "if" part of your plan. As a result, the situation is easily detected, even when you are busy doing other things.

The third thing that happens is what really clinches it. Once the "if" part of your plan actually occurs, the "then" part follows *automatically*, without any conscious intent. In other words, your brain already knows what to do because you already decided what to do when you made your plan. Now, your brain can just execute the plan without any further deliberation. When you've finished cleaning your dishes after Sunday night's pot roast, your unconscious mind walks you over to the phone and you start dialing because you already told it that this is the time to call Mom. (Sometimes this is conscious, and you do actually realize you are following through on your plan. The point is it doesn't *have* to be conscious, which means your plans can get carried out when you are preoccupied with other things, and that is incredibly useful.)

When we think of behaviors that we engage in unconsciously, we usually think of things like habits (chewing your fingernails, singing in the shower) or well-practiced skills developed over hundreds of hours (how a pianist moves his fingers over the piano, or how an expert pool player lines up a shot). Peter Gollwitzer has described *if-then* plans as creating "instant habits"—making a plan is the deliberate creation of an "automatic" routine.[3] However, unlike most of our habits, these instant habits help us *reach* our goals, rather than get in the way of them.

Another benefit of *if-then* planning is that it conserves our most precious motivational resource: our self-control strength. Anytime our unconscious mind can take over, detecting situations and directing our behavior without conscious effort, it is far less taxing and requires less willpower. These plans enable us to conserve our self-control strength in case it's needed later (and it often is). As a result, studies show that *if-then* planners are more likely to be tenacious in the face of even unexpected obstacles. If at first it is blocked, they will try and try again until their action can be taken. Also, because they have conserved self-control strength, they have more of it to use to overcome those obstacles.[4]

If-then plans aren't just good for seizing opportunities. They are also great for suppressing unwanted behaviors (like giving in to temptation) or for dealing with the disruptive thoughts and feelings that can throw our goal pursuit off track. In a study that used *if-then* planning to try to conquer food cravings, dieting women were asked about their favorite high-fat snack food. They were then told that their goal would be to cut their consumption of the snack by 50 percent during the following week. Half of the dieters were also told to create a plan: "And when I think about this snack food, I will not eat it!" (They repeated this to themselves three times.) A week later, the nonplanners had eaten less of their favorite snack (going from four portions per week to three) but didn't succeed in cutting their consumption by half. The planners, on the other hand, went from four portions per week to two! They not only reached their goal, but were *twice* as effective on average as nonplanners.[5]

In another study, competitive tennis players were told to make plans for how to deal with feelings of anxiety and exhaustion that could interfere with their performance during the next match (e.g., "If I am feeling anxious, then I will calm myself and pretend it's just a practice," or "If I am feeling nervous, I will breathe deeply"). Those who made plans played significantly better in a subsequent match, according to evaluations from their coaches and teammates, than players who didn't plan how to deal with their disruptive feelings.

For tackling the problems of missed opportunities and goal shielding, you'd be hard-pressed to find a simpler, more effective strategy than forming an *if-then* plan. I've often thought that I'd like to create a little pamphlet explaining how and why you should make these plans, and then stick it inside every diet, motivational, and self-help book and DVD on the market. I'd also like to leave them lying around in doctors' offices and teachers' lounges. I might send a few to my Congressman. No matter what you are trying to accomplish, whatever weight-loss plan you're trying to stick to, whatever program of self-improvement you've embarked on, whatever challenging goal you've set for yourself, you are far more likely to succeed if you start out with a simple plan.

What You Can Do

- **Make a plan.** Many of the problems we face when trying to reach a goal can be solved by creating simple *if-then* plans. Whether you're trying to seize an opportunity, resist temptation, cope with anxiety and self-doubt, or persist when the going gets tough, these plans can help you do it.

- **Decide what you will do.** Start by deciding what specific actions need to be taken to reach your goal. Avoid vague statements like "eat less" and "study more"—be clear and precise. "Study for at least four hours each night" leaves no room for doubt about what you need to do and whether or not you've actually done it.

- **Decide when and where to do it.** Next, decide *when* and *where* you will take each action. Again, be as specific as possible. This will help your brain to detect and seize the opportunity when it arises, even if your conscious mind is too busy to notice.

- **Formulate your *if-then* plan.** Put it all together in an *if-then* statement. "If it is a weeknight, I will go to my room and study for at least four hours." You can write these plans down in a notebook, if you prefer, or simply repeat them to yourself a few times to let them really sink in.

- **Target the obstacles.** Think about the obstacles and temptations that are likely to arise while you are pursuing your goal. How will you deal with them? Make an *if-then* plan for each. ("If my friends call to ask me to go out on a weeknight, I'll say 'no thanks' and see them on the weekend.") This will allow you to make the best possible decisions well in advance, keeping you on track to succeed no matter what comes your way.

CHAPTER 10

Build the Self-Control Muscle

THE YEAR 2003 WAS NOT A GOOD YEAR FOR ME. IT WAS THE YEAR THAT I turned thirty, separated from my first husband, and lived in near-constant dread of not finding a job before my postdoctoral funding ran out. I coped badly with the end of my marriage and the uncertainty of my career. I ate whatever I wanted, gave up completely on exercising, and rapidly packed on the pounds. I went out most nights to bars with friends and drank a bit too much. Some days I slept until noon. My apartment was a mess. My work suffered. I spent money impulsively, thinking new clothes and dinner at fancy restaurants would make me feel better, and blew right through my savings. It was the lowest point in my life, and I was miserable.

Eventually, having hit bottom, I began the slow crawl back up again. Oddly enough, that change began when I brought home a ten-week-old puppy. Lucy is a miniature schnauzer, and anyone familiar with the breed, or with terriers in general, knows that the little buggers are *very* demanding dogs. If Woody Allen had said, "If you want to make God laugh, tell him you plan *to train a schnauzer*," he would have been right on the nose. Lucy required a lot of me—regular walks, housebreaking, grooming, feeding, playing, and eternal vigilance to prevent the destruction of yet another of my prized possessions when I wasn't looking (Lucy is a chewer—my shoes, books, and coffee table were her favorites). Since I was living in an apartment in New York City, she had to be walked several times a day in order to do her doggie business. This typically started at around 5 a.m.—quite a change from my usual habit of sleeping until lunchtime.

The long and short of it is, I was exercising *a lot* of self-control in order to care for this dog. It took effort, it took planning, and it took a whole lot of patience. The first few weeks were incredibly difficult, mostly because I had grown so unaccustomed to being responsible for anything. But as time passed, it started getting easier. I got used to my new routines, and after a while getting up at 5 a.m. didn't seem nearly so hard. The funny thing is, other aspects of my life started improving as well. I stopped going out so much, started eating better, and rejoined the gym. My apartment was looking cleaner (despite Lucy's best efforts to redecorate), my laundry pile was shrinking, and my bank statements grew less terrifying. I clipped coupons; I looked for sales. My work improved—I was publishing papers again, generating new ideas, speaking at conferences. I interviewed for and was offered a professorship at Lehigh University. And shortly after my thirty-first birthday, I met my future husband (okay, that one I can't really take credit for, other than for recognizing a good thing when I see it).

I'm telling you all this because I think that year in my life nicely illustrates something about the nature of self-control. In the beginning of this book, I introduced you to the idea of the self-control muscle. Just like the muscles in your body, your capacity for self-control dwindles when you don't exercise it. When I turned thirty and my first marriage fell apart, I basically put my self-control on bed rest, and it atrophied. When the time came and I needed to rely on my self-control again to care for a new puppy, it was much like re-turning to the gym after a years-long absence—it hurt like hell and I was easily winded. Then, as I exercised my self-control each day, by sticking to my new routines, it started getting stronger. With that new strength, I found I could start tackling my other challenges and get my life back on track.

I am not, for the record, recommending that if you're having trou-ble reaching your goals, you run out and buy a dog. There are lots of ways to strengthen your self-control muscle, and I'll share with you some of the ones psychologists have tested in this chapter. It's also important to remember that, like your bicep or tricep, your self-control muscle can get tired from exercise, leaving you vulnerable immediately after you've given it a workout. So you'll need to know how you can help your self-control to bounce back after you've done something really taxing. You may also benefit from learning a few other strategies you can use to compensate in those moments when you've used up all your strength and can't afford to wait for your second wind.

Pumping Up

Self-control is enormously important when it comes to achieving our goals—so much so that it is actually better at predicting school grades, attendance, and even standardized test scores than that Holy Grail of ability measures, the IQ test.[1] We rely on our capacity for self-control constantly. When most people hear "self-control," they think of resisting temptation or delaying gratification, but self-control is also needed when we try to make a good impression, and even when we make decisions.[2] (Have you ever felt exhausted after a day of shopping? This is why.) The good news, in fact the *great* news, is that it is within your power to have more self-control than you do right now, and that you can accomplish this in a variety of ways.

Do you have a sweet tooth? Try giving up candy, even if weight loss and cavity prevention are not your goals. Hate exerting yourself physically? Go out and buy one of those handgrips you see the muscle men with at the gym—even if your goal is to pay your bills on time. Psychologist Mark Muraven asked a group of adult men and women in one study to either avoid sweets or use a handgrip over two weeks. The "avoid sweets" group was told to eat as little cake, cookies, candy, and other dessert foods as possible. In the handgrip condition, people were given handgrips to take home and asked to hold them twice a day for as long as possible. Both tasks require self-control—either to resist temptation or to overcome physical discomfort—so both function as a kind of self-control workout. At the end of two weeks of sweets abstinence and hand gripping, Muraven found that participants had significantly improved on a difficult computerized concentration task—having nothing to do with either giving up sweets or using a handgrip—that required lots of self-control.[3] Just by working their willpower muscle regularly, their self-control strength had increased measurably in a matter of weeks!

In another, even more compelling self-control training study, participants were given a free gym membership and individually tailored exercise programs (designed by trainers) that included aerobics, free weights, and resistance training. After exercising regularly over the course of two months, these men and women had not only increased their ability to do a variety of laboratory self-control tasks, but also reported that many other areas of their life had improved as well. They smoked fewer cigarettes, drank fewer alcoholic beverages, and ate less junk food. They said they were better able to control their tempers and less apt to spend money impulsively. They didn't leave their dishes in the sink, didn't put things off until later, missed fewer appointments, and developed better study habits.[4] In fact, every aspect of their lives that involved using some self-control seemed to have improved dramatically. When you exercise, it turns out that it's not just your physical muscles you're building.

As I mentioned back in the introduction, self-control training studies have used many different approaches—directing people to refrain from cursing, or to use their nondominant hand to open doors and brush their teeth. Just sitting up straight every time it occurs to you can help you build up self-control strength. What all these different methods have in common is that each one forces you to do something you'd rather not do—to fight the urge to give in, give up, or just not bother. Pick an activity that fits with your life and your goals—anything that requires you to override an impulse or desire again and again, and make a plan (see Chapter 8) to add this activity to your daily routine. It will be hard in the beginning, particularly if you aren't used to working your self-control muscle that much. I can promise you with complete confidence that it *will* get easier over time if you hang in there, because your capacity for self-control *will* grow. When it does, it can impact every aspect of your life for the better.

Bouncing Back

Even Arnold Schwarzenegger's muscles get tired, and I don't mean because he's now a middle-aged governor instead of a young action hero. Back in the days of Conan the Barbarian, he still found himself on occasion to be too pooped to "pump." Whatever their size, muscles need their rest after they've been taxed too much, in order to bounce back to their original strength. (Even weight-training programs require rest to allow muscles to grow bigger.) The same is true

of your self-control muscle—no matter how strong it becomes, there
will still be times when its energy is spent and you need to let it re-
cover before you ask too much of it. Ideally, you would refrain from
doing anything that requires self-control, and give it the rest it needs.
But life is far from ideal, and we can't always decide when we'll need
to rely on our self-control again to keep us on track to achieving our
goals.

How can we speed up our self-control recovery, or give it a boost
when reserves are low? There are several strategies you can use when
rest is not an option. One approach would be to take advantage once
again of *contagion*. Just as we can "catch" a goal simply from observing someone else pursuing it, it turns out that we can "catch" self-
control by thinking about people we know who seem to have boatloads
of it. People who were asked to think about a friend with good self-
control, for example, held on to a handgrip much longer than people
who thought about a friend with poor self-control. Researchers found
the same results when people observed someone who was successfully exercising self-control (in this case, eating carrots while staring
at a plate of warm and aromatic chocolate chip cookies).[5] So the next
time you need a little extra strength, you can try thinking about someone you know who excels when it comes to resisting temptation. It
also doesn't hurt to befriend other high achievers, since their self-
control skills can (almost literally) rub off on you.

Be careful using this strategy, however, because in particular circumstances it can backfire. Did anyone ever watch you working hard
at something and say, "I'm getting tired just looking at you"? If so,
they probably weren't kidding. Watching other people exert a lot
of self-control can either boost *or* deplete your own self-control reserves, depending on *how* you watch them. When we simply observe
someone pursuing the goal of resisting temptation, it's contagious.
However, when we mentally simulate what they are doing, imagining

their thoughts, feelings, and actions vividly in our minds *as if it were happening to us*, it can sap our own self-control strength just as if we were actually doing the work ourselves!

In a study that illustrated these opposite effects, participants were asked to read about a waiter who had arrived at work hungry but who was unable to eat on the job without the risk of getting fired. The story described in detail all the delicious foods being served and how hard it was for the waiter to resist sneaking a bite. Half of the participants were asked to simply read the story, while the other half were asked to imagine what it was like to be the waiter and to try to experience his thoughts and feelings. Next, all participants were given a test of self-control: they were given a list of twelve mid- to high-priced products (like cars and designer watches) and were asked to list how much they would be willing to pay for each. (When self-control is low, we tend to get a bit more reckless with our dollars.) The researchers averaged the prices for the twelve items and found that the people who took the waiter's perspective paid an average of over $6,000 more for each item than the passive readers! Empathy is obviously a valuable and necessary emotion—lots of good things can come from walking a mile in another person's shoes—but it can mean a significant drain on your self-control reserves. When you are tackling a particularly difficult goal, maintaining a little psychological distance can be a very effective strategy.[6]

In addition to using contagion, you can also try to give your self-control a boost by giving yourself a pick-me-up. I don't mean a cocktail—I mean something that puts you in a good mood. (Again, *not* a cocktail—I realize they can be mood-enhancing, but alcohol is definitely not self-control enhancing.) Good moods can be created in any number of ways, but gifts definitely seem to do the trick.

In one study, people who had used up some of their self-control strength were given a thank-you gift—a bag of candy tied up with a nice ribbon. Then their self-control was tested by asking them to drink as much as they could of an unpleasant beverage (once again, vinegar Kool-Aid—experimental psychologists have an odd sense of humor). The participants who had been given the mood-enhancing gift drank *twice* as much as those who were not given a gift (5.5 ounces as compared to 2.7 ounces). They even drank as much as those participants who hadn't used up any self-control strength in the first place. In other words, the good mood created by the gift caused self-control reserves to bounce back very rapidly to their normal level. The same pattern of results emerged when a good mood was created by watching a comedy video. Thinking or writing about your most important values and why they matter to you also does the trick. Really, anything that lifts your spirits should also restore your self-control strength when you're looking for a quick fix.[7]

There is one more way to boost your reserves that I want to mention, and it will probably strike you as very odd. It has to do with the (recently discovered) way in which self-control strength manifests itself in the body, physically speaking. It turns out that self-control operates, at least in part, through blood glucose.[8] That's right—your willpower is influenced by the amount of sugar that is in your bloodstream from moment to moment. Multiple studies have now shown that a person's blood glucose is significantly lower after self-control-depleting tasks like thought suppression, controlling attention, helping others, coping with thoughts of death, or suppressing prejudicial responses toward others. More important, it's not just *any* difficult activity that uses up glucose, but specifically those activities that require significant self-control.

It gets even more strange: consuming glucose through eating or drinking actually *restores* your self-regulatory strength, at least temporarily. Glucose is absorbed into your bloodstream at an average of about thirty calories per minute, and after roughly ten minutes it can be metabolized to the brain.[9] So this method needs a little time to work, but in laboratory studies it has been shown to be as effective as contagion or pick-me-ups in boosting willpower. For example, psychologists found that drinking Kool-Aid lemonade made with sugar (but not with Splenda, a sugar substitute that doesn't contain glucose) helped people whose self-control had been depleted perform as well on tasks that required accuracy and persistence as those who hadn't been depleted at all. In another study, glucose drinkers who had taken a difficult exam subsequently gave more to charity and offered more help to a classmate than Splenda drinkers (though we may like to think it comes naturally, generosity often requires a whole lot of self-control to fight off our more selfish impulses).

So if you need a little boost of willpower, consider taking steps to raise your blood glucose. It's important to keep in mind, though, that consuming protein and complex carbohydrates is a better way to maintain blood glucose levels over a longer period. Sugary drinks and candies may give you a burst of self-control strength, but it will burn out quickly. Plus, you don't want to increase your willpower if it means risking diabetes and unhealthy weight gain. Not to mention how it will irritate your dentist.

When There's No Gas Left in the Tank

There will be times when, after a long, busy, or unusually trying day, you are pretty much completely burned out. There's just nothing left in your self-control reserves, and the fixes I've just described aren't enough to help you battle whatever temptation you may be facing. There's a reason why most people break their diets, drink too much, or give in to the urge to smoke in the evening, rather than first thing in the morning. Recovering addicts use the acronym H.A.L.T.—Hungry,

Angry, Lonely, Tired—to remind themselves of the circumstances under which they are most likely to relapse. Each of these conditions is characterized by having lowered self-control. This is when we are most vulnerable and also when it is most important to take steps to protect your goal pursuit from bad influences.

There are, fortunately, strategies you can use to limit your need for self-control when you find it is lacking. First, remember that according to the laws of physics, bodies in motion tend to stay in motion, unless something acts to stop them. Well, the same thing can be said about human behavior, too. Your actions have a kind of inertia—once you start doing something it often takes an act of self-control to stop. This gets harder to do the longer the behavior goes on. For instance, it's easier to be abstinent if you stop at the first kiss, rather than letting things get hot and heavy. It's easier to pass on the potato chips entirely, rather than eat just one or two. Stopping before you start is an excellent strategy to keep your need for self-control to a minimum.[10]

Second, remember that *why* thinking (focusing on our long-term goals, values, and ideals) and self-monitoring (comparing how you are doing with how you want to be doing) are also excellent methods for fighting temptation. I'm a lot less likely to give into the sweet siren song of the pie in my refrigerator when I focus on wanting to have a healthy weight and look good in my jeans, or when I hop on the scale before I pick up a fork.

Third, whatever you do, don't try to pursue two goals at once that both require a lot of self-control. At least, not if you can help it. This is really just asking for trouble. You need to respect that, no matter who you are, your self-control capacity has its limits. For example, studies show that people who try to quit smoking *while* dieting, in order to avoid the temporary weight gain that often accompanies smoking cessation, are more likely to fail at *both* enterprises than people who tackle them one at a time.

Finally, here's one last strategy for overcoming a total loss of will-power: pay yourself for being good. Studies show that well-chosen incentives, ones that appeal to the specific person in question, can compensate for a lack of self-control strength by increasing overall motivation to succeed. Cash is one kind of incentive, but it is by no means the only kind. When people believe that they can learn from what they are doing, or when they are told that other people will benefit from their persistence, it can be at least as effective as more material rewards.[11]

A Final Word of Caution: Don't Tempt Fate

After reading this chapter, I hope that you are confident that you can build your own self-control muscle, boost your strength when it is low, and compensate for a loss of strength using the techniques I have described. I, for one, am completely confident that you can. But there is one sense in which too much confidence can be danger-ous, and it involves a mistake that you can easily avoid so long as you are aware of it. Recent research shows that most people overestimate their ability to control their impulses—in other words, they think they have more self-control than they actually do. The more inflated our beliefs are, the more we expose ourselves to temptation, believ-ing that we will be able to handle it easily. When we are no longer tired, hungry, or in withdrawal, we tend to lose the ability to imag-ine what those states are really like and how vulnerable we are in them. So we overestimate our control and put ourselves right in harm's way.

For example, one study looked at smokers who were in the pro-cess of quitting. Those who hadn't smoked in three weeks, and were therefore well out of the physical withdrawal phase, were asked how confident they were in their ability to resist the urge to smoke in the future. They were also asked about whether or not they actively avoided temptation—shunning those situations and places (like bars or being out with friends who smoke) that might increase their urge to smoke. The more confident the former smokers were about their ability to resist temptation, the *less* likely they were to actually avoid it. Several months later, the researchers found that smokers who avoided temptation were less likely to relapse, while those who had been so confident were far more likely to have returned to their bad habits.[12]

In the end, you are much more likely to successfully reach your goals if you do what you can to develop your self-control strength, while remaining respectful of its inherently limited nature. Understanding when it might fail you, and making plans whenever possible (see the last chapter) for how you will deal with that vulnerability when it occurs, will leave you far better prepared to rise to whatever challenges daily life throws you way.

What You Can Do

- **Use it or lose it.** Your self-control muscle is just like the other muscles in your body. When it doesn't get much exercise, it becomes weaker over time. But when you give it regular workouts by putting it to good use, it will grow stronger and stronger and better able to help you successfully reach your goals.

- **Pump it up.** To build up your self-control, take on a challenge that requires you to do something you'd honestly rather not do. Give up high-fat snacks, do a hundred sit-ups a day, stand up straight, try to learn a new skill. When you find yourself wanting to give in, give up, or just not bother—don't. Start with just one activity, and make a plan for how you will deal with troubles when they occur ("If I have a craving for a snack, I will eat one piece of fresh or three pieces of dried fruit"). It will be hard in the beginning, but *it will get easier.* As your strength grows, you can take on more challenges and step up your self-control workout.

- **Give it a rest.** Muscles get tired. Remember that your self-control strength does get depleted when you're using up a lot of it. Immediately after you've put it to the test, you will be more vulnerable than you usually are to temptations, distractions, and other pitfalls that can throw you off track. If you can, don't ask too much of yourself until your strength has had a chance to bounce back.

- **Catch some control.** When you need a boost, try using *contagion.* Just observing someone exerting self-control, or thinking about a person you know who's loaded with it, will give you a surge of self-control strength. (But be careful to avoid too much empathy—imagining what it is like to be in that other person's shoes as they tax their self-control muscle can end up weakening yours even more!) Good moods also enhance self-control, so try giving yourself a (nonalcoholic) pick-me-up to replenish your reserves.

- **Try a little something sweet.** Self-control relies, at least in part, on the amount of glucose in your bloodstream. The best way to maintain a constant supply over the long haul is by eating protein and complex carbs, but when you need a quicker fix, try a snack or drink made with sugar (but *not* with artificial sweeteners like Splenda). It takes about ten minutes for the sugar to be metabolized to the brain, so give it a little time to work. And remember that sugar from simple carbs burns out quickly, so don't count on it lasting too long.

- **Stop before you start.** When self-control reserves are low, it's important to use strategies that keep your need for self-control to a minimum. Remember that it is harder (and requires more willpower) to stop any action once you've gotten started than it is to just not start in the first place. (It's easier to pass on the potato chip bag altogether than it is to stop at one or two chips.) Other strategies that can help you include *why* thinking about your goal, stronger self-monitoring to make sure you are staying on track, and using other incentives (like payments or rewards) to boost your motivation to succeed.

- **Don't tempt fate.** No matter how strong your self-control muscle becomes, it's important to always respect the fact that it is limited, and if you overtax it you will temporarily run out. Don't try to take on two challenging tasks at once, if you can help it (like quitting smoking and dieting at the same time). And don't put yourself in harm's way—many people are overly confident in their ability to resist temptation, and as a result they put themselves in situations where temptations abound. Why make it harder on yourself if you don't have to?

CHAPTER 11

Keep It Real

IF THERE'S ONE PEARL OF WISDOM YOU WILL FIND IN JUST ABOUT every self-help book, it's that it is *really, really* important to be confident and optimistic when trying to reach all your goals. You are constantly being told to "Believe in Yourself!" "Visualize Success!" and "Stay Positive!" They practically shout it at you. And I'm not saying that they're wrong, exactly.

It is true that, for some goals, believing you will succeed really gets your motivational juices flowing. But notice that I said "some" goals. You now know that there are *many* kinds of goals, and while optimism is just what the doctor ordered for some of them, it's not all that necessary or helpful for others. In this chapter, I'll tell you more about when optimism is a good strategy and when it's a very *bad* one. I'll show you when it pays to think positive, and when you should tamp down your expectations to avoid the pitfalls of too much bravado. You'll learn the difference between *realistic* optimism (often an essential ingredient for success) and *unrealistic* optimism (an illusion that feels good but can cause trouble). You'll also get some tips to help you psych yourself up to succeed when a sunny outlook is what's called for, and all you're seeing is rain.

Always Look on the Bright Side of Life . . .

For years, it seemed to social psychologists that when it came to optimism, you really couldn't get too much of a good thing. Generally speaking, optimism is the belief that things are going to work out well for you—perhaps because you have confidence in yourself and your abilities, or maybe because you believe that God or destiny is on your side. Some people call this "positive thinking," and without a doubt it has a very clear upside. Just to give you a feel for *how* good optimism seems to be, here is a sample of some of the amazing benefits research has shown it to predict: greater physical health, lower risk of mortality among cancer patients, faster recovery from bypass surgery, greater likelihood of obtaining prenatal care, less postpartum depression, less severe depression after a stressful life event, better adjustment to college among first-year students, and better coping with infertility and conception difficulty. It's hard to find a life challenge that doesn't seem to improve in the presence of a positive outlook.

As if that weren't enough, optimists even have better romantic relationships! Studies of committed couples show that optimists are much more likely to work through problems with their partner without resorting to attacking and blaming. These more effective (and less abrasive) problem-solving techniques lead them to experience far greater happiness and fulfillment in their relationships over time.[1] In every area of their lives, optimists are more likely to confront obstacles that stand in the way of achieving their goals in an active, direct manner, rather than becoming passive or avoiding the issue. Believing that they will ultimately succeed, they persist longer and can be more likely to reach their goals as a result.

Another, less well-known benefit of optimism has to do with the ways in which we prioritize our goals. Some goals are much more important to each of us than to others. These are typically the ones that have the greatest ability to impact our lives. Often, they are the goals with the biggest "payoff"—the ones offering the most valuable rewards for you personally. Other goals we may set for ourselves are of relatively minor importance in comparison. For example, the pay-off I receive from achieving my goal to be a good mother or a suc-cessful psychologist is far greater than what I get from achieving some of my lesser goals, like cleaning out my refrigerator or figuring out how to program my TiVo.

It makes sense that to maximize your happiness, you should devote more time, energy, and enthusiasm to the more important goals, sacrificing the lesser ones when necessary. This is exactly what optimists do. In essence, they are not only better at achieving many goals, but they are also better at juggling *multiple* goals. For example, a study of aerobic exercisers revealed that the more the participants valued the goal of doing aerobic exercise, the more the *optimistic* participants worked out. For those with a more pessimistic outlook, the amount of time spent exercising wasn't at all related to its per-sonal value. Other studies have produced similar results, with goals as diverse as making friends and getting good grades. Again and again, we find that optimists devote more time and energy to the goals that really matter, and less to the ones that don't.[2]

Optimists are also more sensitive to positive information in their environment.[3] They are more likely to see the silver lining, to turn even a terrible experience into a not-so-bad one. Because they are able to see the good in almost any situation, they are particularly gifted when it comes to coping with life's hiccups.

But Beware the Dark Side . . .

More recently, it's become clear that being an optimist isn't really all wine and roses. It turns out that always expecting the best leaves you vulnerable to certain types of mistakes—mistakes a pessimist would never make.

For instance, because they believe that success is inevitable, optimists are less likely to think through all the possible outcomes of their actions. They are less likely to adequately prepare and more likely to engage in risky behavior. (Insert any one of countless possible references to overly confident American government officials, and the trouble they've gotten us into, right here.) For example, when optimists gamble, they are quite likely to *increase* their wagers after a string of losses, believing that success is awaiting them on the next shuffle or roll of the dice.[4] Given that almost every game in a casino is designed so that the odds heavily favor the house, this is a strategy that delights the management while leaving the optimist with a far lighter wallet.

Pessimists, on the other hand, expect the worse, so they are far more likely to prepare for many possibilities, including the possibility that things may go badly. After a few rounds of losses, gambling pessimists begin to lose faith that they will win and therefore stop playing. In fact, it's very unusual to see a true pessimist enter a casino of their own free will in the first place.

Optimists and pessimists also differ in the kind of thinking they do *after* a poor performance. When you have failed to reach a goal in the past, did you ever wonder afterward what would have happened if you had done things differently? These "what-ifs" and "if onlys" are what psychologists call *counterfactual* thinking, and that's something both optimists and pessimists are very likely to do when things don't go their way. The "what-ifs" they consider, however, are very different. Pessimists think about how they could have succeeded if they had done things differently ("It would have worked if only I had . . ."), and this turns out to be very useful for future performance, because it allows you to be better prepared for what will happen next time. Optimists, on the other hand, tend to think about how they could have screwed things up *even more* ("It would have been even worse if I hadn't . . ."). This kind of counterfactual thinking serves only one purpose—to make you feel better about failing. While lifting your spirits is an understandable goal, particularly when there are no future performances or when circumstances are out of your control, it's definitely not going to help you to improve and to ultimately reach your goal.[5]

The most troubling form of optimism is what psychologists call *unrealistic* optimism. This is more than just psyching yourself up to believe you can succeed—it's a total unwillingness to look the objective facts of reality in the face. It is also remarkably common. A landmark study by psychologist Neil Weinstein, published thirty years ago, showed that most college-aged Americans believed themselves to be significantly more likely than their peers to one day own their own home, make a large starting salary, travel around Europe, and live past eighty. They also believed that they were less likely than their classmates to develop a drinking problem, get divorced, contract a venereal disease, get fired from their job, or have a heart attack.[6]

It's a kind of variation on the Lake Wobegon effect—not only do we all think that we are above average in our abilities, but we also think good fortune will smile on us more than it will smile on everyone else. This kind of unrealistic optimism is most likely seen in cases of controllable events (e.g., becoming seriously overweight), rare events (e.g., going bankrupt), or relatively benign occurrences (e.g., doing less well on an exam that you expected). But notice that when it comes to controlling your weight, managing your finances, or preparing for your exams, there are effective steps that can be taken to prevent failure. Of course, you aren't particularly likely to take these steps if you think you'll never have these problems in the first place.[7]

Years ago, I dated an aspiring New York actor who waited tables at a Times Square tourist trap in order to pay the rent while waiting for his "big break." I only ever saw him in one production, soon after we started dating—an off-off-off (how many times can you say "off"?) Broadway production of *Romeo & Juliet*. He was quite good, and at the time I thought he might just have a future in acting. He certainly believed his success was inevitable—he had, he told me, "star quality." The only problem was, he never auditioned for anything. (It turned out that a friend had gotten him the Romeo job.) Months went by, while his stack of glossy black-and-white headshots lay totally undisturbed, gathering dust. (*He* also spent most of that time gathering dust on my sofa.) He was "waiting for the right part to come along"—something worthy no doubt of his yet unknown awesome talent. While I realize that sometimes a young actor is "discovered" by a roving director or producer, most successful actors will tell you that it takes years of hard work and a mountain of glossy headshots to make it in that grueling business. The last I heard of him, my former boyfriend was still distributing pasta dishes and house salads, waiting for Steven Spielberg to wander in and offer him a starring role. His odds are not good.

The difference between unrealistic optimism, which is usually unproductive and sometimes dangerous, and *realistic* optimism, which is critical for achieving many of our goals, lies in *why* you are optimistic. When you are optimistic because you believe you can exert some control over whether you succeed or fail, by putting in the necessary effort, making plans, and finding the right strategies, that's realistic. It's also empowering and highly motivating. If, on the other hand, you are optimistic for reasons that are beyond your control, like relying on some fixed ability ("I'll succeed because I'm smarter than other people") or luck ("I'll succeed because things always work out for me"), it can be harmful. Odds are, you won't prepare for the task the way you should, and you will be too quick to give up when things start going badly for you.

The difference between realistic and unrealistic optimism was nicely demonstrated in a study of incoming college freshmen. The researchers measured the students' optimism when they arrived on campus, and found that many were strongly optimistic but not particularly realistic. Half of those high in optimism were given a special intervention, called *attributional retraining*. "Attributions" are the explanations we come up with for our successes and failures—what we believe to be the underlying causes. In the retraining, the students were taught that it's better to attribute your performance to how much effort you put in and which strategies you use, rather than to how smart or talented you are. The researchers also explained that even ability-related performance (like math skill) is changeable and will improve over time with learning. This intervention turned the unrealistic optimists into realistic optimists, who became confident in their ability to *make success happen*, rather than simply assuming that it would.

The results of the retraining were remarkable. Those highly optimistic students who received attributional retraining completed their first year with a GPA average equivalent to a B, compared to a C average among highly optimistic students who received no training! These results, and others like it, show that it's a very good idea to be optimistic about your future, so long as you understand that your actions are directly responsible for making success a reality.[8]

If you are concerned that the confidence you feel about reaching your goal might not be realistic, there are a few questions you can ask yourself to find out. Going through this process can help you turn that unrealistic optimism into a more realistic optimism that will actually work in your favor.

1. Ask yourself *why* you think you will do well. For example, if you are heading into a job interview and you feel you have an advantage over other candidates, think about why you have that advantage. It may help to write it down so that you can fully articulate the reasons.

2. How likely are other people to have that advantage as well? For example, if you think you are likely to land the job because you are so smart, or because you graduated from a good school with a good GPA, consider the fact that there may be other applicants who are also very smart, with good GPAs from good schools. Will you really stand out? Is that *realistic*?

3. Now, think about how you can take control over whether you succeed or fail. What actions can you take to increase your chances of landing the job? How can you prepare for the interview so that you will do your best? How can you *make success happen*? Taking steps to ensure that you will reach your goal will give you the authentic, realistic, and well-deserved optimism you need to do your best.

There are two more points that I want to make about the dangers of optimism. I have already discussed them both in previous chapters, but I think they are worth reiterating. First, remember that optimism is a bad idea when you are pursuing *prevention goals*. Anytime you see a goal in terms of safety and danger, anytime you are focused on what you have to *lose*, you are better off motivating yourself with thoughts of what could go wrong rather than with confidence that everything will go right.

Second, remember that there is a big difference between believing you will succeed and believing success will come *easily* (Chapter 1). In fact, believing success will come easily is another case of *un-*

realistic optimism—it just isn't realistic to think that you will achieve any meaningful and worthwhile goal without lifting a finger. Reaching yours goals takes careful thinking, preparation, and effort. The good news is that each one of us has what it takes to make that happen, which is cause for optimism indeed.

Increasing Optimism

Sometimes, believing that you will succeed is essential if you want to achieve your goal. This is particularly true for promotion-focused goals—those that we see in terms of what we have to *gain*. How can you increase your optimism, and grow more confident that you will reach your goal, when you are feeling a little unsure of yourself?

For one thing, you can take advantage of the strategies used by psychologists in their studies of attributional retraining. Most people feel unsure about their chances for success because they feel that they lack the *ability* to succeed. More often than not, they are dead wrong. Question your assumptions. Consider other possibilities. For example, is reaching this goal *really* about ability, or is it more about putting in the effort, persisting through the difficulty, and using good strategies like planning? If it's the latter (and it almost always is), then it is absolutely within your power to achieve that goal. It can be helpful to think about some role models—people who have succeeded in achieving the same goal. You'll find that high achievers, without exception, need to work hard and plan well to accomplish their goals, and that is something anyone can do.

For another, you can also boost your confidence by taking a page out of your own past. Reflect on some of your past successes—the challenges you faced and the strategies you used to overcome them. It can be very helpful to take about ten minutes and write about an accomplishment you are particularly proud of, and how you pulled it all off. Sometimes, when you are feeling insecure, all it takes is a little reminder of how capable you really are to change your point of view.

A third strategy I strongly recommend is using the strategy of *if-then* planning to identify and challenge any negative thoughts as they occur. As a part of your plan, decide which specific optimistic thoughts you will use to replace the pessimistic ones. For example, "If I start to doubt myself, then I will tell myself that I have what it takes to succeed!" As I mentioned in Chapter 8, this technique has been shown to be very effective in dealing with disruptive thoughts, and it will strengthen your optimistic outlook over time if you continue to use it.

As a fourth strategy, what about "visualizing success"? I won't name names, but it seems like there are an awful lot of self-help books out there telling people that if they just picture what they want in their minds, it will somehow happen. That would be great if it were true, but scientifically speaking, there really isn't much evidence for it. On the other hand, visualization can be very helpful, if you imagine the *steps you will take in order to succeed*, rather than the success itself. Mentally simulating the process of achieving the goal, rather than the hoped-for outcome, not only results in a more optimistic outlook, but in greater planning and preparation. Picture yourself doing what it takes to succeed, and you will soon find yourself believing that you can.[9] The best part is, you'll be absolutely right.

What You Can Do

- **Some optimism is good.** Optimism has loads of benefits. It increases motivation, helps you prioritize, and better equips you to handle the curveballs that get thrown your way.

- **Some optimism is dangerous.** Optimism can also lead to some costly mistakes—not thinking through all the possible consequences of your actions, failing to adequately prepare, taking unnecessary risks. After a setback, optimists are more likely to try to make themselves *feel* better, rather than figure out how they could *do* better next time around.

- **Know the difference.** The key is to understand the difference between *unrealistic* optimism and *realistic* optimism. Unrealistic optimism is a confidence in things you can't actually control—like a fixed ability, fate, or luck. If you believe you will succeed because you are naturally smart, or lucky, or that you have "star quality," you are just asking for trouble. Unrealistic optimists don't take the steps they need to succeed, and they don't have the first clue what to do when things start to go wrong.

- **Keep it real.** Realistic optimism is confidence in things you *can* actually control. It's believing that you will succeed because you will *make success happen,* by putting in effort, staying motivated, and using the right strategies. Realistic optimists are less likely to make those costly mistakes and far more likely to ultimately achieve their goals.

- **If it isn't real, then make it real.** When tackling a goal, make sure the optimism you are feeling is realistic. When in doubt, use the method I outlined in this chapter (identifying *why* you believe you will do well, challenging any unrealistic assumptions, replacing them with plans for steps you can take to bring about your own success).

- **Take the focus off ability.** To increase your optimism, the trick is often to replace any doubts about your *ability* to suc-

ceed with the realization that, much more often than not,
reaching a goal is actually about effort, persistence, and planning. It can be helpful to consider role models who achieved
the same goal—high achievers succeed because they work
hard and work smart, and that is something anyone can learn
to do.

- **Take a page from your past.** Another strategy to boost your
  optimism is to think about your own past achievements. A
  reminder of how capable you really are can do wonders for
  your confidence.

- **Don't visualize success.** Instead, visualize the steps you will
  take in order to succeed. Just picturing yourself crossing the
  finish line doesn't actually help you get there—but visualizing
  how you run the race (the strategies you will use, the choices
  you will make, the obstacles you will face) not only will give
  you greater confidence, but also leave you better prepared for
  the task ahead. And that is definitely *realistic* optimism.

CHAPTER 12

Know When to Hang On

In my career as a researcher and a teacher, I've seen very smart people give up on a new task or subject the moment it became difficult, and I've seen people of seemingly modest ability fight their way through to the end and succeed. When you study achievement, one of the first things you learn is that innate ability (to the extent that there is such a thing) has surprisingly little to do with success. Persistence, on the other hand, has *a lot* to do with it. One of the most common reasons we fail to reach our goals is that we give up on them way too soon and for all the wrong reasons.

How can you increase your persistence? In this chapter, I'll share with you several strategies you can use to better equip yourself for the long hauls. First, I'll highlight the kinds of goals (ones I mentioned in previous chapters) that create a mind-set to help you deal more effectively with a steady stream of challenges and obstacles. Start with the right goal, and you will have already increased the chances that you'll stick it out for as long as it takes.

It's also true that people explain their successes or failures in significantly different ways, and that these differences influence your persistence. For instance, do you think that getting an A on a test or getting a promotion at work is mostly about being smart, working hard, or being lucky? The answer matters because it determines what it will *mean* to you when success doesn't come quickly or easily. It won't surprise you to learn that people who cope with a challenge by thinking "I need to work harder" persist much longer than the ones who think "I'm unlucky" or "I'm stupid."

We'll take a look at how the beliefs *you* hold about what it takes to succeed, and the kinds of goals you've chosen to pursue, have impacted your persistence in the past. We'll also consider the impact of *culture* on persistence and see how these same ideas can go a long way toward explaining the much talked-about gap in achievement between Asian and Western students.

However, as important as persistence is for success in just about every aspect of life, I really don't think I could, in good conscience, write a book about how to achieve your goals without acknowledging that *sometimes* you really do need to throw in the towel. You honestly can't win them all. And just as it can be difficult to hang in there, it can also be very, very difficult to know when to quit.

As it turns out, learning when to give up on a goal is also a very necessary part of living a happy, healthy life. So in this chapter, I will also tell you how and when you should *dis*engage from goals that are too difficult or too costly to attain. You'll learn how to make good decisions about whether to pursue a goal or let it go—decisions based on evidence, not fear and faulty logic. Just as important, you'll learn how to feel good about, and benefit most from, deciding to move on with your life.

How to Keep On Keepin' On

Just as there are people who have more self-control than others, there are also people who are much better at hanging in there when the going gets very tough. Psychologist Angela Duckworth calls this quality "grit," and writes that "the gritty individual approaches achievement as a marathon: his or her advantage lies in stamina." Grit is a combination of both long-term commitment and persistence, and is measured by your agreement with statements like "I have achieved a goal that took years of work" and "I finish whatever I begin."

When hearing a word like *grit*, you probably think of some of the extraordinary individuals who have overcome nearly insurmountable obstacles against all odds—people like Lance Armstrong or Nelson Mandela (and, if you are a movie buff, John Wayne). But ordinary people can be gritty too, and studies show that grittiness is strongly associated with higher achievement. For example, differences in grit predict the level of education individuals obtain in their lifetime. Students with more grit earn higher college GPAs. Grit predicts which cadets will stick out their first grueling year at West Point. Grit even predicts which round contestants will make it to at the Scripps National Spelling Bee! (That last finding turns out to be mostly due to the fact that gritty spellers do more studying before the competition than nongritty ones.)[1]

In a nutshell, it's great to have grit. The good news is that, just as you can build up self-control strength, you can also increase your ability to persist in the face of challenge if you want to. If you aren't all that gritty now, you can learn to be.

First, you can start by choosing goals that will naturally increase your grit. *Getting-better* goals put the emphasis on progress and improvement, rather than on *be-good* perfection and validation (see Chapter 3). These goals allow you to still get a sense of accomplishment and optimism out of how far you've come, even when you still have a long way to go, and that's a terrific way to enhance grit. Similarly, goals that are *autonomously chosen*, and pursued for their own sake, also heighten your grit. When a goal authentically reflects your own preferences, values, and desires, you want it more, and you can enjoy the pursuit (no matter how long it may take) nearly as much as you enjoy finally achieving the goal.

Just think of all the academics who toil away for most of their lives in obscurity, hunched over desks piled high with books and papers. Many spend years, even decades, in search of a mathematical solution, a chemical reaction, or definitive proof that Shakespeare's plays were written by some other guy. You would think they'd be miserable, but most of the time they are far from it. Their gritty perseverance in pursuit of some particularly elusive piece of knowledge comes naturally because academics get to *choose* the problem they spend their lifetime trying to solve.

Another way to increase your grit is to make sure you are attributing your successes and failures to the right causes. Believing that your less than perfect performance is the result of low ability, particularly when you are someone who feels that ability can't be changed, makes you much more likely to think badly of yourself, feel anxious and depressed, and lose confidence that you will reach your goal.[2] Imagine you get your first performance review at your new job, and your manager tells you that your communication skills "need improvement." Now, if you believe that your shyness or awkwardness is unchangeable, that you are stuck exactly as you are, how motivated will you be to work on improving those skills and getting a better review next time? *No one* feels gritty when they have lost all hope for success.

If, however, you believe that you performed poorly because you didn't try hard enough to get your ideas across, or that you didn't approach communicating with your coworkers in the right way, then you are far less likely to feel bad and far more likely to work on the problem and keep on trying. And that's very gritty, indeed.

It turns out that this grittier way of thinking is not only better for you, but it is usually objectively more correct. Failures that are caused solely by a totally unchangeable ability are quite rare. I'm not saying they don't happen—for instance, I have to admit that because of my height (I'm five foot five), I can never dunk a basketball in a regulation hoop without the use of a ladder or special shoes with springs or tiny rockets. So if I make dunking my goal, I'm going to end up disappointed. But even if I can't dunk, I *can* learn to be a better basketball player, because playing any sport well has a lot to do with determination and proper training. Natural abilities and giftedness exist, but any coach will tell you they are not nearly as important as effort and practice. Improvement is *always* possible.

So why, then, do we blame our failures on low, unchangeable abilities if they are really not only changeable, but rarely to blame in the first place? Why are we so quick to think that we aren't smart, strong, or talented enough to reach our goals? If our lack of effort, planning, persistence, and poor choice of strategies are the real culprits, why don't we realize it? The answer seems, at least in part, to be cultural. Every culture has its own particular set of values and beliefs, and as children we absorb these values and beliefs without even realizing it. Western societies, for example, tend to place a great deal of emphasis on measuring, and celebrating, ability—and nowhere is that more true than in the United States. Americans are fascinated by stories of geniuses, prodigies, and the "naturally gifted." We celebrate people who we believe have special abilities and tend to see those who work hard to succeed as less innately capable. (This is why no one likes being called "book smart"—the implication being that students who are really diligent about their schoolwork do so because they aren't very bright. This is one of the more idiotic misconceptions I've ever come across.) It's not surprising, really, that people who grow up in a culture that sees success as a sign of ability would then proceed to blame their own failures on a lack of it. But it doesn't have to be that way—and in some parts of the world, it isn't.

What Asians Do Differently

The *Trends in International Mathematics and Science Study* (*TIMSS*) is an international survey of student achievement in forty-eight countries, conducted every four years. The U.S. Department of Education uses this information to keep track of how American students are doing relative to students around the world. In 2007, the last time that the study was conducted, U.S. eighth-graders were once again significantly outperformed by their peers in China, Korea, Singapore, and Japan (as they have been since the survey was first conducted in 1995). This leaves educators and government officials scratching their heads. Do Asian students consistently outperform American students in mathematics and science because they are born with capabilities that American students lack? It may be tempting to think so, but if you did you'd be 100 percent wrong. The differences are cultural, not genetic. And if you wanted to narrow it down to the single most influential cultural difference between East Asian and American students, it would be this: Americans believe in *ability*, and East Asians believe in *effort*.

Most East Asian educational systems are founded on a bedrock of Confucian doctrine, which heavily emphasizes the importance of effort.[3] Some well-known educational proverbs include:

> *Talent and will come first in study; will is the teacher of study and talent is the follower of study. If a person has no talent, it [achievement] is possible. But if he has no will, it is not worth talking about study.*
>
> —Xu Gan, *Zhong Lun*

> *Being diligent in study means devoting one's effort to it for a long time.*
>
> —Confucius, *Zi Zhang* chapter

One of my fellow graduate students at Columbia, who had been born and educated in Korea, once told me that Koreans have an expression, *sugo haseyo*, that is used to congratulate someone on a job well done. It literally means "work hard." The message it conveys is that no matter how well you have done, you can always try to do better. (To which a typical American response would be, "Gee, thanks a lot.")

Not surprisingly, Asian students are much more likely to blame their poor performances (as well as their successes) on the effort they put in to them. For example, Japanese college students who were led to believe that they had failed on an anagram task were most likely to choose "lack of effort" rather than "lack of ability," "task difficulty," or "luck" as the most important cause.[4] In another study, researchers found that Chinese mothers cited "lack of effort" as the predominant cause of their child's failure in mathematics, while American mothers tended to blame failure on ability, training, luck, and effort equally.[5]

Asian children are explicitly taught that hard work and persistence are the keys to success. It makes sense, therefore, that they would excel in subjects like math and science, which require determination and long hours to master. Too often, American students labor under the (mistaken) belief that doing well in math and science is a matter of possessing some innate ability—as if some people are just born capable of long division. When they first encounter a difficult concept or a problem that they don't know how to solve, they jump to the (mistaken) conclusion that they don't have what it takes to do well. Teaching our children how to hang in there, and helping them to understand what it *really* takes to succeed, would go a long way toward closing that achievement gap.

Now that I've hammered home the importance of persistence, it's time to take a look at the flip side of the coin.

Know When to Fold 'Em

There are of course times when you actually do need to seriously consider giving up on a goal. The trick, it turns out, is to make sure you are doing it for the *right* reasons. Most people give up on their goals because they don't believe they have what it takes to succeed, and I hope by now you realize that they are almost always wrong. You do have what it takes to succeed—or if you don't have it *right now*, you can get it. So why, then, is it still in your best interest sometimes to abandon a goal you are truly capable of achieving?

There are two very good reasons to disengage from a goal (and neither of them have anything to do with ability). The first is that, like it or not, there are only so many hours in a day. You can have all the ability in the world, you can be a genius in every possible sense, and you would still have limited resources to use to achieve all your goals. You only have so much energy. You only have so much time. *Everyone* needs to make choices, because doing it all is just not physically possible. Reading this book will help you make *better* use of your time, but it won't actually change the fact that you've got somewhere between sixteen to eighteen hours a day at your disposal. (I am a huge proponent of sleep, so let's make it sixteen.)

This is a dilemma that most working parents know only too well. If you have a job that requires you to work sixty hours a week, you are going to lose time with your kids. That is simply a fact. And if, as I have tried, you attempt to get away without day care or a full-time nanny, your work is absolutely going to suffer for it. Sometimes, rather than pursuing several goals at a time but not being particularly successful at any of them, it's best to give yourself a break and recognize that your time and energy are limited. When that happens, focus on what's most important to you, and let the rest of it go (at least until a more opportune time comes along).

The second good reason to abandon a goal is that you find it is just costing you too much. Circumstances change, and goals can become unexpectedly difficult or unpleasant to pursue. Many times, you find that you didn't fully understand what you were getting yourself into. When that happens, the smart *and* healthy thing to do is to reevaluate your choices.

Back in 2003, my soon-to-be husband was teaching philosophy to undergraduates at Washington University in St. Louis. It had been two years since he had graduated with his Ph.D. in philosophy from Columbia. By all accounts, he should have been very happy. He had never seriously considered pursuing any other profession since childhood. (This is a guy who read, and *liked*, Bertrand Russell when he was fourteen.) But by the second year into his career as a young academic philosopher, he had made a troubling discovery: he hated it. Not the philosophy, but the teaching of it. And while many academics "put up with" teaching as part and parcel of academia, the problem for Jonathan was that philosophy professors typically have to teach *a lot*. Science professors can get away with only one or two courses per semester, but in philosophy three or four is more the norm. All that teaching left him drained, and with too little time for actual philosophizing—not enough, Jonathan felt, to make his teaching duties more palpable.

His final decision to give up his career in philosophy came after a long, painful, and brutally honest self-evaluation of his strengths and his shortcomings. (My husband is Minnesotan, so being *dishonest* would have probably been much harder.) It meant rethinking what he would do with his life—rethinking who he *was* as a person. Painful, too, was the thought of disappointing all the people who had supported him and believed in his clear potential. It was, without question, a brave decision—and it was also the right one for him. Sometimes, the very best thing we can do for ourselves is to abandon the goal we thought we always wanted, when the costs of achieving it reveal themselves to be too great to pay.

In the presence of constant doubt and distress, it really should be pretty easy to give up on a goal that's giving you trouble. But of course, it isn't easy at all. Abandoning a goal can be *very* hard to actually do. Perhaps you have already sunk a lot of time and energy into it and don't want to feel that it was all wasted. Maybe you aren't yet convinced that the goal is truly unreachable. Or maybe you just don't want to feel like a failure. Just as we sometimes give up too soon, it's also true that we often don't know when, or how, to quit.

You may also have an even harder time giving up a goal that is related to some important aspect of your self-image. The roles that we play in our day-to-day lives make up a big part of how we see our very identity. If you are a doctor, or a mother, or a teacher, you probably often think of yourself in those terms. So when you are pursuing a goal as a doctor (e.g., healing a patient), or a mother (e.g., getting your toddler to sleep through the night), or a teacher (e.g., reaching a difficult student), and you fail, it's not only disappointing—it's also a threat to your sense of who and what you are.

The ability to disengage is really critical for your happiness and well-being, and fortunately it too is something you can learn to do. To give up a goal successfully, you need to take two steps. First, you need to decide if giving up is really what's best for you. Try asking yourself the following questions (it can be very helpful to write out the answers):

1. *Why am I having a hard time reaching this goal?* Figure out what it would take to be more successful. It is:
   a. more time
   b. more effort
   c. a new approach

    d. help from an expert

    e. greater self-control

    f. a better plan

If the answer is "I don't *have* what it takes," you are wrong. You do have what it takes. Start again.

2. *Am I able to do what it takes? Can I find the time, or the energy, or the help I need?* If the answer is "no," you should seriously consider giving up the goal.

3. *Will doing what it takes cost me too much? Will it make me unhappy? Will I need to sacrifice too many other goals that are important to me?* If the answer is "yes," you should seriously consider giving up the goal.

Once you've gone through this process and made the decision to give up the goal, try your best not to dwell on it. Ruminating about a goal that you couldn't reach keeps the goal active in your unconscious mind. Understandably, your unconscious gets very confused ("Are we done with this goal, or aren't we?") and never fully disengages from it.[6]

The second step you need to take is very important, and it's the one we most often neglect. But taking this step is the key to increasing your happiness and overcoming regret. You need to *find a goal to take its place*, assuming you don't already have one. If your career isn't working for you, what kind of job will you start looking for? If you are hating your step aerobics classes, what other options does your gym offer that you might enjoy more? Thinking of leaving your (un)romantic partner? How will you fill the hours that you used to spend together? Studies show that disengaging from our goals seems to be far more adaptive when it leads to, or is tied to, the taking up of *other* goals. Replacing a goal that doesn't work for you with one that actually *will* help you to stay engaged and to maintain your sense of purpose and identity. It will keep you moving forward, rather than looking back.[7]

What You Can Do

- **Got grit?** People who are willing to make commitments to long-term goals, and be persistent in the face of difficulty, are far more likely to be successful than those who are less gritty.

- **Get grit!** You can increase your grittiness by choosing the right goals: *get-better* goals and *autonomously self-chosen* goals create a mind-set that makes hanging in there for the long haul much easier.

- **Blame your effort, not your ability.** If you believe that you are having a hard time reaching your goal because you lack the necessary ability, and that you can't do much to change that . . . well, there's no way to put this nicely: you are wrong. Effort, planning, persistence, and good strategies are what it *really* takes to succeed. Embracing this knowledge will not only help you see yourself and your goals more accurately, but also do wonders for your grit.

- **You can't have it all.** While it's almost never a good idea to abandon a goal because you think you lack the *ability* to achieve it, that doesn't mean that it's never in your best interest to give up on a goal. It's important to recognize that you only have so much time and energy at your disposal to achieve your goals, and sometimes that means something's got to give.

Don't be afraid to abandon a goal when achieving it becomes practically impossible.

- **Sometimes the price isn't worth paying.** It's also perfectly okay to walk away from a goal, even when it's something you've really wanted and could in fact reach, when the costs of achieving it reveal themselves to be too great. Some sacrifices aren't worth making—they are too painful, or they require you to give up too much.

- **Out with the old, in with the new.** Knowing when to give up a goal that is just too difficult, or too costly, to attain is an essential part of being a healthy, satisfied person. To make the process not only easier, but even more rewarding, be sure to replace your old goal with a new one. This will enable you to maintain your sense of engagement and purpose, and to keep moving forward with your life.

CHAPTER 13

Give the Right Feedback

Feedback is very important and necessary to reach our goals—without it, we would be groping in the dark, not knowing whether we were on the right path. If you are a parent, a teacher, a coach, or a manager, then part of your job is providing that feedback for others. You need to reinforce what they're doing right, as well as point out where they are going wrong, and help them stay motivated to keep on course. Unfortunately, as you have no doubt discovered in your own experience, not *all* feedback is particularly helpful. Some of it is more or less useless. Worse yet, some feedback is actually counterproductive, and you might well have been better off saying nothing at all. Even with the best intentions, giving someone praise or criticism can really backfire, and most people have a hard time figuring out why.

There is a science to giving feedback, a reason why some things work and others don't. It is neither mysterious nor random. Knowing what to say and what *not* to say isn't a matter of possessing some innate gift or talent. If you've screwed it up in the past (and who hasn't?), then you can learn to do a better job giving feedback from now on. In this chapter, we'll focus on how you can use what you've learned about the common pitfalls of goal pursuit to give the *right* kinds of feedback to your employees, students, children (and anyone else you care about)—helping them to stay motivated and on the right track.

Ask yourself: Before reading this book, did you think that it was nicer to tell someone that he performed poorly because he didn't put in enough effort, because he approached the task the wrong way, or because the type of work really wasn't his strong suit? Is it always a good idea to offer your help, even when it isn't asked for? If you want to praise a student or an employee, should you tell her that she is smart, or that she worked hard, or that you admire her persistence? Should you dole out lots of compliments, or reserve them only for praising major accomplishments? If you ask ten experienced managers or ten seasoned teachers to answer these questions, they will probably give you ten different sets of answers.

I don't deny that giving good feedback can be a bit complicated. Praise people for having high ability, and they will feel like a superstar—only to plummet back to earth if the going gets tougher. Praise for effort can sometimes make students feel stupid, but it can also make them better able to face a challenge down the road. Praise for minor accomplishments can actually *undermine* performance. But don't worry—as I said before, feedback is a science, and there are principles at work here. In the pages that follow, I'll outline some simple rules you can use to help you decide what to say and how to say it.

When Things Go Wrong

It's never easy to tell people that they aren't doing as well as they could be. No one likes to be the bearer of bad news, and giving constructive criticism is a particularly difficult skill to master. Most people make the all-too-understandable mistake of thinking that protecting the recipient's *feelings* is paramount. We say "it's not your fault" or "you tried your best" or "you're just not well suited for this kind of thing," regardless of whether or not any of those statements are accurate, because we don't want the person to blame himself and feel terrible for it.

From a motivational standpoint, that's shortsighted. Feeling bad is not just an unfortunate consequence of hearing honest feedback, it is a *necessary* consequence. Anxiety and sadness serve a key motivational function—they make your brain want to take action to get rid of them. Negative feelings focus attention and resources on the task at hand. They are like fuel for your fire. And taking away a person's sense of responsibility for a poor performance also robs them of their sense of control—if you aren't responsible for what you've done in the past, how can you possibly improve your performance in the future? Now, I'm not saying you should go out of your way to make employees or students (or yourself) feel awful when they are struggling—far from it. The point is that motivationally effective feedback is often not all that fun to hear, and that is okay. You shouldn't shy away from saying what people need to hear, for their own sake, because you're too worried about the fallout.

The key to giving good feedback when someone is having difficulty is to keep her believing that success is still within her reach. Nothing saps motivation quite like self-doubt. (This is particularly true when you are dealing with a promotion-minded person. People who see their goals in terms of gain are very sensitive to pessimistic criticism.) So when you are giving negative feedback, there are a few important points to keep in mind, in order to make sure that the recipient will truly benefit.

First, you want to be as **specific** as possible about what went wrong, so that both you *and* the receiver avoid overgeneralizing the problem. When we attribute our poor performances to broad abilities ("I'm not good at math") rather than specific skills ("I need to brush up on statistics"), we are more likely to lose confidence and not bother even trying to improve. Don't tell others that they have lousy communication skills—tell them what, specifically, they need to work on. What exactly do they need to say (or not say)? *How* do they need to say it?

> **Instead of saying:** *Bob, you are a poor communicator.*
> **Say:** *Bob, I'd like to have a better sense of the progress you are making on your projects and how you are managing your time. Let's set up a brief weekly meeting so you can keep me informed.*

(Bob probably already knows he's a poor communicator, so just reminding him of that will do nothing but reinforce his shortcomings. Instead, pointing out exactly what he can do to improve his performance will leave him feeling empowered—this is a specific change he can make.)

It's also good to keep in the back of your mind that when it comes to negative feedback, people with low self-esteem are even more likely to overgeneralize what they hear than those with high self-esteem. We once had a guest speaker come to give a talk in my department at Lehigh, who, despite being very well known for his work, was more than a little insecure about it. At the end of the talk, one of my colleagues asked for clarification of something the speaker had said, and he responded by storming out of the room. When asked about it later, he replied in total seriousness and with *complete* certainty that my colleague had literally called him a moron. Somehow, his brain had turned "How did you measure self-esteem in that study?" into "You are an idiot." Now, this is not a problem you can avoid entirely. But you'll want to be particularly careful to be specific when giving negative feedback to someone who's already showing signs of being down on himself.[1]

When we feel out of control, it leads to pessimism and eventually to depression. Feeling in control, on the other hand, leads to self-confidence and optimism. So when you are offering criticism, make sure you take pains not to undermine the receiver's sense of control over his own performance. It's best not to try to take him off the hook for a poor performance, no matter how tempting that may be. We need to feel responsible for our failures, in order to feel that it is *also* within our power to do things differently. Don't shy away from telling someone that he didn't work hard enough, or needs to try a different approach, if you honestly feel that's the case. But keep confidence high by pointing out the changes that are within your student's or employee's power to make.

> **Instead of saying:** *Don't worry about failing your chemistry exam, Jane. You're just not a "science" person—but look at how great you are at writing!*
>
> **Say:** *Jane, I don't think you studied for your chemistry exam the way you needed to. You are not applying yourself the way you do with your writing. Let's talk about how much time you're devoting to chemistry, and the methods you're using to study, to see how you can improve your performance next time.*

Sadly, there are times when a student or employee does work hard and still fails to reach her goals. In these instances, it's particularly tempting to try to make the individual feel better by praising all the effort she put in. "Don't feel bad—you tried your best!" we say. As well-meaning as this kind of feedback is, you should go out of your way to avoid it. First, studies show that praising hard work when it doesn't pay off can easily make the recipient feel even more stupid—exactly the opposite, really, of what you are trying to do. When serious effort leads to failure, avoid praise and stick with purely informational feedback. What can be done differently? If effort isn't the problem, then ineffective strategies are most likely to blame. Would better planning help? When it is your responsibility to dole out feedback, you need to remember that helping your students or employees figure out how to do it *right* is just as important as letting them know what they are doing *wrong*.

When Things Go Right

Is there really such a thing as *bad* praise? Most people will readily admit that criticism can be constructive or harmful but tend to balk at the idea that there is a right way and a wrong way to say "good job!" In fact, praise can be motivating *or* undermining, depending on what you say and how you say it. In some studies, praise has been shown to increase confidence and determination, as you might expect it to. When praised, we often enjoy what we are doing more, and we engage in a task more willingly. On the other hand, praise also can create excessive pressure to continue performing well, discourage risk-taking, and decrease feelings of autonomy. So how do we say "good job!" in a way that fuels the fire, rather than accidentally putting it out?

In a 2002 review of the many dozens of studies on the effects of praise, psychologists Jennifer Henderlong and Mark Lepper found that in order to have a positive influence, feedback for a job well done should be guided by five rules.[2]

> **Rule #1**: Praise should be **sincere**—or, at the very least, it
> should *seem* sincere. The clearest indicator of insincerity

is an obvious ulterior motive. If people feel that you are trying to manipulate them into doing something, or protect them from feeling bad about themselves, your praise will be seen as insincere. Praise is also more likely to seem disingenuous if it is highly effusive ("This is the greatest quarterly report I've ever seen!"), so be careful not to gush too much.

Also, try to avoid being overly general ("You are *always* so generous!")—it makes it too easy for the recipient to come up with counterexamples ("What about all the times when I tipped less than 15 percent?"). Whenever possible, be *specific* about what exactly is being praised.

> **Instead of saying:** *Amazing job this year, Phil! You are an ideal employee.*
>
> **Say:** *Phil, I was really impressed by the way you handled the Stevens account. That was a difficult situation, and you rose to the challenge. I appreciate all the hard work you put in this year—you exceeded my expectations.*

Don't praise hard work when there wasn't any, and don't praise high ability when someone is just learning—you aren't fooling anyone, and it will be experienced as more embarrassing than motivating. Praise for minor achievements ("Wow, Joe—your handwriting is so easy to read!") also tends to make you look phony or, worse, make the recipient feel stupid ("Why would she compliment my handwriting? She feels sorry for me—she thinks I'm an idiot."). No one wants to be praised for something he didn't actually do, for something he did badly, or for something that doesn't even deserve praise.

Also, if you want to appear sincere, be sure that you don't contradict your praise with other, nonverbal behavior. If you avoid making eye contact, or if you pause too long before you begin to speak (as if you are searching for what you should say), the receiver will wonder why your actions don't mesh with your words. Finally, praise should be used somewhat sparingly, so that it seems genuinely contingent on good performance—though you should absolutely feel free to praise someone when it's well deserved.

> **Rule #2:** The praise that you give should emphasize, when-ever possible, behaviors that are under the recipient's con-trol. Praising a person for abilities or qualities that seem innate or unchanging can lead to problems when things get difficult. Just think about it: say to a child who does well on an exam, "Nice job, Tommy! You are so smart!" and what will Tommy think the next time he *doesn't* do so well? Praise for hard work, persistence, use of good strategies, and determination, on the other hand, reinforces the idea that these are the key ingredients for success and makes the recipient more resilient in the face of dif-ficulty.

The importance of Rule #2 was vividly shown in a series of stud-ies conducted by Carol Dweck and Claudia Mueller. Fifth-graders were given a set of relatively easy problems to work on and then praised for their good performance.[3] Half of the students were given praise that emphasized ability ("Wow, you did really well. You must be really smart at this!"), while the others were given effort-focused praise ("Wow, you did really well. You must have worked really hard!"). Next, all the students were given a very difficult set of prob-lems, and no one in the study got more than one out of ten of those correct. Finally, the researchers gave the students one last set of problems, similar in difficulty to the first set.

Dweck and Mueller found that the children who had been praised for smartness did *far worse* on the third set of problems when compared to the first. Having been told that their good performance on the first set made them "smart," they were quick to conclude that their poor performance on the second set made them *not* smart. These students lost confidence and motivation, and their final performance suffered for it.

A very different pattern emerged for the children who had been praised for effort—they performed *better* on the third set than they had on the first set. Having been told that doing well was about effort, their experience with difficulty on the second set prompted them to ramp up their efforts and work even harder. These students *gained* confidence and motivation, and they achieved even more.

I will readily admit that it *feels* a lot better to get ability praise than it does to be praised for effort. Who wouldn't rather be complimented for their brilliance than for their hard work? We all instinctively know this, which has a lot to do with why we are so quick to dole out ability praise. But you have to ask yourself, what is really more important—feeling good or being well equipped to achieve your goals? If the answer is the latter, then you need to adjust your praise accordingly.

I am not, for the record, saying that you can never compliment someone's ability—my parents told me I was smart when I did something well, and I have said the same thing to my own children. The important thing to remember is to avoid giving ability praise *in isolation*—it's okay to tell someone that they are talented, so long as you *also* praise the hard work and strategy use that is required in order to make use of that talent. You want to avoid the impression that success is all about ability, because it really never is. Success is almost always about taking the right steps, persisting, and staying motivated, and you need to be sure to give credit where credit is really due.

Instead of saying: *Nice job, Tommy! You are so smart!*

Say: *Nice job, Tommy! I'm so proud of how hard you studied for this exam. You have learned so much!*

Rule #3: When you praise, avoid comparing the recipient to others. This rule is closely related to Rule #2, because comparison almost always make people think in terms of ability, ignoring the contributions of more controllable factors like effort and strategy. Studies show that when students and employees are made explicitly aware that their performance is being compared to others', it makes them more likely to focus on *being good*—on validating their skills and abilities, rather than on developing them. When praise emphasizes comparisons, we become self-conscious and worried about continuing to prove ourselves, and that can actually interfere with our future achievement.

Instead, when you praise someone, try emphasizing personal mastery over competition. Rather than comparing your students or employees to others, try comparing their current performance to *their own past performance*. Praise for improvement reinforces the idea that the focus should always be on *getting better*.

Instead of saying: *Dan, you are the best graduate student in this department!*

Say: *Dan, you have come a long way since you began this program. You have really developed into a first-rate scholar!*

Rule #4: Praise should be given in a way that doesn't undermine the recipient's sense of autonomy. Remember that rewards and pressures are often experienced as controlling—they take the focus off of doing something for its own sake. Telling someone "If you keep this up, you will get this prize" or "Continue to do well, and I will think you are great" puts the emphasis on external validation, like getting money or earning love. The last thing you want is for an intrinsically motivated student or employee, someone who actually enjoys and is interested in what she is doing, to start working just to get the praise (and the other good things that may go with it). Keep your praise focused on the task itself, and try to be "autonomy-supportive" by acknowledging the recipient's feelings and choices.

Instead of saying: *Annie, if you continue to get grades like this in math, I will be so proud.*

Say: *Annie, I am so proud of you. And I'm glad to see how much you are enjoying math!*

Rule #5: Praise should always convey attainable standards and expectations. Recognizing people's accomplishments is a great way to motivate them to keep up the good work—but sometimes, in our enthusiasm, we get a bit carried away. We want our students, our employees, and our loved ones to know that we think they can do *anything* if they put their minds to it. We are trying to build up their confidence with our praise, but instead we may be inadvertently signaling that we expect more from them than they can actually achieve.

Referring to a promising student as "bound to go to Harvard" or to a talented young athlete as "a future Olympian" might sound like harmless compliments, but if you hear them too often, it's easy to start feeling that people expect nothing less of you. I'm not saying you shouldn't set the bar high, but you want to make sure your praise is realistic. Thousands of brilliant and accomplished high school seniors are rejected from Harvard every year, and only the tiniest fraction of extraordinary athletes can earn the privilege of representing their country at the Olympics (just imagine—if you are the fourth-fastest guy *in America* that year, you are probably too slow).

Remember that it's far better to encourage your students and employees to set difficult but *possible* goals. Instead of Harvard or the Olympics, a promising student can be told that he is "bound to go to a good college or university," and a talented athlete may be told that she might be "able to play at the college level." Assuming that they continue to work hard, of course . . . which is also something you might want to mention.

> **Instead of saying:** *If you can continue playing this well, then I expect to see you in the Major League!*
> **Say:** *Great job—you have so much potential! Now, let's talk about how you can really challenge yourself and improve your game.*

When it comes to giving good feedback, you owe it to your students, employees, and all the other people you care about to think very carefully about what you want to say. Our words have a far greater motivational impact than most of us realize, and that's a responsibility that should be taken seriously. If there are people who look to you for answers, be sure you are sending them the right message—one that empowers and inspires, while offering them the practical guidance they need to keep moving forward.

What You Can Do

- **Speak the truth.** Be careful not to let concerns about bruised feelings keep you from telling people what they need to hear. Telling individuals that "it's not their fault" or that "they did their best" may spare their feelings, but it will also leave them feeling powerless and unmotivated. Taking responsibility for failure, when your effort or strategies are to blame, also leaves you empowered to do things differently in the future.

- **Stay positive and practical.** When giving criticism, it's important to convey that you believe the recipient can succeed if he takes necessary action. Be as specific as possible about the nature of the problem and what steps the person can take to solve it.

- **Praise should seem sincere.** In order for praise to enhance, rather than undermine, motivation, it has to be seen as sincere. Praise that is too effusive, too general, or too frequently given is likely to seem disingenuous. Reserve your compliments for achievements that are authentic, well executed, and deserving of your admiration.

- **Praise what they do, not what they are.** Praise should emphasize behaviors that are under the recipient's control. Highlight hard work, good strategy use, determination, and persistence rather than praising abilities that are seen as fixed or innate.

- **Avoid comparing to others.** Avoid praise that explicitly compares your students or employees to their peers. Instead, compare their current performance to their own past performance, in order to emphasize the value of improvement and keep the focus on *getting better.*

- **They shouldn't be doing it for the praise.** Don't allow praise and rewards to undermine autonomy—acknowledging the recipients' own choices and feelings will keep them focused on the task for its own sake, protecting their powerful intrinsic motivation to succeed.

- **Once again, keep it real.** Praise (and criticism, for that matter) should always convey realistic, attainable standards and expectations. Be careful not to let exuberant language ("You can be the best ever!") create an atmosphere where your student, child, or employee feels too much pressure to be perfect.

Epilogue

I HAVE A STRONG AVERSION TO MAKING PREDICTIONS ABOUT PRETTY much anything with absolute certainty. Perhaps this is due to years of scientific training, when it was imprinted on my brain to make no statements that the data didn't actually support. Or maybe I just don't like going out on a limb. It has frequently been pointed out to me how much I hate being wrong. (To which I respond, "Who doesn't?")

That being said, I feel perfectly comfortable with the following prediction about you, even though I don't know you personally, and I make it with 100 percent certainty: you can be more successful in reaching your goals than you have been in the past.

Every principle of motivation I described in this book, every piece of advice I have offered, is entirely within your power to use to your advantage. It is my hope that, after reading these chapters, you have gained some insight into all the things you have been doing right all along. Even more important, I hope you have been able to identify the mistakes you have made that have derailed you as well as what you can do differently from now on.

There is no pitfall in goal pursuit that doesn't have a solution: you can increase your self-control and compensate for it when it is low, you can make more effective plans, you can learn how to be realistically optimistic, you can increase your grit. You can rethink the goals themselves—reframing them in ways that will make them easier and more enjoyable to pursue. You can embrace the strategies that work for you, and abandon the ones that don't. If you have to, you can walk away from a goal for the *right* reasons, and do it in a way that will make you a happier and healthier person.

I know that you can do these things, because *anyone* can. It doesn't take any special qualities or gifts. And you don't need to become a *different* person to become a more successful one. What it does take is knowledge of what really works, the willingness to do what it takes, and a little practice. If you read this book, you have the knowledge. Just picking up this book in the first place shows that you have the willingness. Now it's time to put it all into action.

You are ready. You are set. Now go.

Acknowledgments

THIS BOOK WOULD NEVER HAVE BEEN WRITTEN, AND CERTAINLY NEVER published, without the unwavering support and excellent guidance I received from my good friend and agent (in that order) Giles Anderson. Giles, you are the second-greatest guy I ever met in a bar.

Academic writers are, by and large, awful. We make up words for things when there are perfectly good English words already available. We make ideas sound complicated when they are in fact simple and straightforward. We are trained for years in the art of making interesting ideas sound really, really boring. So, for saving me every time I succumbed to old habits, I must thank my amazing and patient editor, Caroline Sutton.

I am enormously grateful to the many friends and fellow psychologists who have helped me to explore and understand the principles of motivation found throughout this book. I need to particularly thank my colleagues at Columbia, NYU, and Lehigh—especially Shawn Guffey, Gordon Moskowitz, Peter Gollwitzer, Gabriele Oettingen, Jason Plaks, Dan Molden, and Joe Cesario.

As a graduate student, I had the rare privilege of training under two extraordinary and generous mentors. I thank Tory Higgins for taking my lame half-baked ideas and molding them into something that might actually work (while convincing me that the credit was somehow mine.) Kurt Lewin may have said that there is nothing so practical as a good theory, but Tory made me believe it.

From Carol Dweck I learned so many things, but most relevant to this book, she taught me the importance of two skills overlooked by most academics—how to tell a good story, and how to tell it in plain language, using actual English words. That turned out to be really useful.

I am grateful to my husband, Jonathan Halvorson, who overcame his natural propensity for being, at best, *cautiously* optimistic, as well as his aversion to effusive praise, in order to become the most ardent and vocal supporter of this book and my decision to write it. It also turns out to be handy to have married a philosopher when you're trying to figure out if what you've written actually makes sense. The man can spot a hole in an argument a mile away.

My father, George Grant, taught me to read when I was five by sitting me down next to him on the couch and reading me *The Little Engine That Could* approximately seven thousand times. I don't think it's a coincidence that I ended up writing a book about motivation and persistence thirty years later. So thank you, Pop, for the inspiration (and also for the whole learning-to-read thing, which I don't think I appreciated at the time.)

If you enjoyed *Succeed*, then you really should probably be thanking my mother, Sigrid Grant. She has been my sounding board, cheerleader, and toughest critic for thirty-six years, and she played each one of those roles with some frequency while I was writing this book. She went over every word, changing many of them for the better. So thank you, Mom, for your enthusiasm, your patience, and your willingness to tell me that earlier drafts of some chapters "sounded like a high school book report." I don't know what I would do without you.

Notes

Introduction

1. R. F. Baumeister, E. Bratslavsky, M. Muraven, and D. M. Tice, "Ego-Depletion: Is the Active Self a Limited Resource?" *Journal of Personality and Social Psychology* 74 (1998): 1252–65.
2. From the January 2009 issue of *O, The Oprah Magazine.*
3. M. Muraven and E. Slessareva, "Mechanisms of Self-Control Failure: Motivation and Limited Resources," *Personality and Social Psychology Bulletin* 29 (2003): 894–906.
4. M. T. Gailliot, E. A. Plant, D. A. Butz, and R. F. Baumeister, "Increasing Self-Regulatory Strength Can Reduce the Depleting Effect of Suppressing Stereotypes," *Personality and Social Psychology Bulletin* 33 (2007): 281–94.

Chapter 1

1. E. Locke and G. Latham, "Building a Practically Useful Theory of Goal Setting and Task Motivation," *American Psychologist* 57 (2002): 705–17.
2. G. Latham and E. Locke, "New Developments in and Directions for Goal-Setting Research," *European Psychologist* 12 (2007): 290–300.
3. Items adapted from R. Vallacher and D. Wegner, "Levels of Personal Agency: Individual Variation in Action Identification," *Journal of Personality and Social Psychology* 57 (1989): 660–71.
4. R. Vallacher and D. Wegner, "What Do People Think They're Doing? Action Identification and Human Behavior," *Psychological Review* 94 (1987): 3–15.
5. Y. Trope and N. Liberman, "Temporal Construal," *Psychological Review* 110 (2003): 403–21.

6. S. McCrea, N. Liberman, Y. Trope, and S. Sherman, "Construal Level and Procrastination," *Psychological Science* 19 (2008): 1308–14.

7. T. Parker-Pope, "With the Right Motivation, That Home Gym Makes Sense," *New York Times*, January 6, 2009.

8. G. Oettingen, "Expectancy Effects on Behavior Depend on Self-Regulatory Thought," *Social Cognition* 18 (2000): 101–29.

9. D. Gilbert, *Stumbling on Happiness* (New York: Knopf, 2006), p. 27.

10. G. Oettingen and E. Stephens, "Mental Contrasting Future and Reality: A Motivationally Intelligent Self-Regulatory Strategy," in *The Psychology of Goals*, G. Moskowitz and H. Grant, eds. (New York: Guilford, 2009).

Chapter 2

1. Items adapted from C. S. Dweck, C. Chiu, and Y. Hong, "Implicit Theories: Elaboration and Extension of the Model," *Psychological Inquiry* 6 (1995): 322–33.

2. C. S. Dweck, *Mindset* (New York: Random House, 2006).

3. Y. Hong, C. Chiu, C. Dweck, D. Lin, and W. Wan, "Implicit Theories, Attributions, and Coping: A Meaning Systems Approach," *Journal of Personality and Social Psychology* 77 (1999): 588–99.

4. C. Erdley, K. Cain, C. Loomis, F. Dumas-Hines, and C. Dweck, "Relations among Children's Social Goals, Implicit Personality Theories, and Responses to Social Failure," *Developmental Psychology* 33 (1997): 263–72.

5. J. Beer, "Implicit Self-Theories of Shyness," *Journal of Personality and Social Psychology* 83 (2002): 1009–24.

6. R. Nisbett, *Intelligence and How to Get It* (New York: W. W. Norton, 2009).

7. L. Blackwell, K. Trzesniewski, and C. Dweck, "Implicit Theories of Intelligence Predict Achievement across an Adolescent Transition: A Longitudinal Study and an Intervention," *Child Development* 78, no. 1 (2007): 246–63.

8. R. Nisbett, *Intelligence and How to Get It* (New York: W. W. Norton, 2009).

9. J. Bargh, P. Gollwitzer, A. Lee-Chai, K. Barndollar, and R. Troetschel, "The Automated Will: Nonconscious Activation and Pursuit of Behavioral Goals," *Journal of Personality and Social Psychology* 81 (2001): 1014–27.

10. J. Shah, "Automatic for the People: How Representations of Significant Others Implicitly Affect Goal Pursuit," *Journal of Personality and Social Psychology* 84 (2003): 661–81.

11. H. Aarts, P. M. Gollwitzer, and R. R. Hassin, "Goal Contagion: Perceiving Is for Pursuing," *Journal of Personality and Social Psychology* 87 (2004): 23–37.

Chapter 3

1. Items adapted from H. Grant and C. Dweck, "Clarifying Achievement Goals and Their Impact," *Journal of Personality and Social Psychology* 85 (2003): 541–53.

2. A. J. Elliot, M. M. Shell, K. Henry, and M. Maier, "Achievement Goals, Performance Contingencies, and Performance Attainment: An Experimental Test," *Journal of Educational Psychology* 97 (2005): 630–40.

3. L. S. Gelety and H. Grant, "The Impact of Achievement Goals and Difficulty on Mood, Motivation, and Performance," unpublished manuscript, 2009.

4. H. Grant and C. S. Dweck, "Clarifying Achievement Goals and Their Impact," *Journal of Personality and Social Psychology* 85, no. 3 (2003): 541–53.

5. D. VandeWalle, S. Brown, W. Cron, and J. Slocum, "The Influence of Goal Orientation and Self-Regulation Tactics on Sales Performance: A Longitudinal Field Test," *Journal of Applied Psychology* 84 (1999): 249–59.

6. K. A. Renninger, "How Might the Development of Individual Interest Contribute to the Conceptualization of Intrinsic Motivation?" in *Intrinsic and Extrinsic Motivation: The Search for Optimal Motivation and Performance*, C. Sansone and J. M. Harackiewicz, eds. (New York: Academic Press, 2000), pp. 375–407.

7. A. Howell and D. Watson, "Procrastination: Associations with Achievement Goal Orientation and Learning Strategies," *Personality and Individual Differences* 43 (2007): 167–78.

8. R. Butler and O. Neuman, "Effects of Task and Ego Achievement Goals on Help-Seeking Behaviors and Attitudes," *Journal of Educational Psychology* 87 (1995): 261–71.

9. H. Grant, A. Baer, and C. Dweck, "Personal Goals Predict the Level and Impact of Dysphoria," unpublished manuscript, 2009.

Chapter 4

1. E. T. Higgins, "Beyond Pleasure and Pain," *American Psychologist* 52 (1997): 1280–1300.
2. J. Keller, "On the Development of Regulatory Focus: The Role of Parenting Styles," *European Journal of Social Psychology* 28 (2008): 354–64.
3. A. Y. Lee, J. L. Aaker, and W. L. Gardner, "The Pleasures and Pains of Distinct Self Construals: The Role of Interdependence in Regulatory Focus," *Journal of Personality and Social Psychology* 78 (2000): 1122–34.
4. J. Shah and E. T. Higgins, "Expectancy X Value Effects: Regulatory Focus as Determinant of Magnitude and Direction," *Journal of Personality and Social Psychology* 73 (1997): 447–58.
5. J. Förster, H. Grant, L. C. Idson, and E. T. Higgins, "Success/Failure Feedback, Expectancies, and Approach/Avoidance Motivation: How Regulatory Focus Moderates Classic Relations," *Journal of Experimental Social Psychology* 37 (2001): 253–60.
6. E. T. Higgins, R. S. Friedman, R. E. Harlow, L. C. Idson, O. N. Ayduk, and A. Taylor, "Achievement Orientations from Subjective Histories of Success: Promotion Pride versus Prevention Pride," *European Journal of Social Psychology* 31 (2001): 3–23.
7. J. Norem, *The Positive Power of Negative Thinking* (New York: Basic Books, 2001).
8. P. Lockwood, C. H. Jordan, and Z. Kunda, "Motivation by Positive or Negative Role Models: Regulatory Focus Determines Who Will Best Inspire Us," *Journal of Personality and Social Psychology* 83 (2002): 854–64.
9. L. Werth and J. Förster, "How Regulatory Focus Influences Consumer Behavior," *European Journal of Social Psychology* 36 (2006): 1–19.
10. E. T. Higgins, H. Grant, and J. Shah, "Self-Regulation and Quality of Life: Emotional and Non-emotional Life Experiences," in *Well-being: The Foundations of Hedonic Psychology*, D. Kahnemann, E. Diener, and N. Schwarz, eds. (New York: Russell Sage Foundation, 1999), pp. 244–66.
11. E. Crowe and E. T. Higgins, "Regulatory Focus and Strategic Inclina-

tions: Promotion and Prevention in Decision Making," *Organizational Behavior and Human Decision Processes* 69 (1997): 117–32.

12. N. Liberman, L. C. Idson, C. J. Camacho, and E. T. Higgins, "Promotion and Prevention Choices between Stability and Change," *Journal of Personality and Social Psychology* 77 (1999): 1135–45.

13. A. L. Freitas, N. Liberman, P. Salovey, and E. T. Higgins, "When to Begin? Regulatory Focus and Initiating Goal Pursuit," *Personality and Social Psychology Bulletin* 28 (2002): 121–30.

14. R. Zhu and J. Meyers-Levy, "Exploring the Cognitive Mechanism That Underlies Regulatory Focus Effects," *Journal of Consumer Research* 34 (2007).

15. D. Molden, G. Lucas, W. Gardner, K. Dean, and M. Knowles, "Motivations for Prevention or Promotion following Social Exclusion: Being Rejected versus Being Ignored," *Journal of Personality and Social Psychology* 96 (2009): 415–31.

16. E. T. Higgins, "Regulatory Fit in the Goal-Pursuit Process," in *The Psychology of Goals*, G. Moskowitz and H. Grant, eds. (New York: Guilford, 2009).

17. H. Grant, A. Baer, E. T. Higgins, and N. Bolger, "Coping Style and Regulatory Fit: Emotional Ups and Downs in Daily Life," unpublished manuscript, 2010.

18. J. Förster, E. T. Higgins, and A. Taylor Bianco, "Speed/Accuracy in Performance: Tradeoff in Decision Making or Separate Strategic Concerns?" *Organizational Behavior and Human Decision Processes* 90 (2003): 148–64.

19. D. Miele, D. Molden, and W. Gardner, "Motivated Comprehension Regulation: Vigilant versus Eager Metacognitive Control," *Memory & Cognition* 37 (2009): 779–95.

20. L. Werth and J. Förster, "The Effects of Regulatory Focus on Braking Speed," *Journal of Applied Social Psychology* (2007).

21. P. Fuglestad, A. Rothman, and R. Jeffery, "Getting There and Hanging On: The Effect of Regulatory Focus on Performance in Smoking and Weight Loss Interventions," *Health Psychology* 27 (2008): S260–70.

22. A. L. Freitas, N. Liberman, and E. T. Higgins, "Regulatory Fit and Resisting Temptation during Goal Pursuit," *Journal of Experimental Social Psychology* 38 (2002): 291–98.

23. A. D. Galinsky and T. Mussweiler, "First Offers As Anchors: The Role of Perspective-Taking and Negotiator Focus," *Journal of Personality and Social Psychology* 81(2001): 657–69.

Chapter 5

1. R. Ryan and E. Deci, "Self-Determination Theory and the Facilitation of Intrinsic Motivation, Social Development, and Well-being," *American Psychologist* 55 (2000): 68–78.
2. M. E. P. Seligman, *Authentic Happiness* (New York: Free Press, 2004).
3. M. Hagger, N. Chatzisarantis, T. Culverhouse, and S. Biddle, "The Processes by Which Perceived Autonomy Support in Physical Education Promotes Leisure-Time Physical Activity Intentions and Behavior: A Trans-Contextual Model," *Journal of Educational Psychology* 95 (2003): 784–95.
4. G. C. Williams, V. M. Grow, Z. R. Freedman, R. M. Ryan, and E. L. Deci, "Motivational Predictors of Weight Loss and Weight-Loss Maintenance," *Journal of Personality and Social Psychology* 70 (1996): 115–26.
5. G. C. Williams, Z. R. Freedman, and E. L. Deci, "Supporting Autonomy to Motivate Patients with Diabetes for Glucose Control," *Diabetes Care* 21 (1998): 1644–51.
6. R. M. Ryan, R. W. Plant, and S. O'Malley, "Initial Motivations for Alcohol Treatment: Relations with Patient Characteristics, Treatment Involvement and Dropout," *Addictive Behaviors* 20 (1995): 279–97.
7. A. Greenstein and R. Koestner, "Autonomy, Self-Efficacy, Readiness and Success at New Year's Resolutions," paper presented at the meeting of the Canadian Psychology Association, Ottawa, Ontario, Canada, 1994.
8. E. L. Deci, J. Nezlek, and L. Sheinman, "Characteristics of the Rewarder and Intrinsic Motivation of the Rewardee," *Journal of Personality and Social Psychology* 40 (1981): 1–10.
9. D. I. Cordova and M. R. Lepper, "Intrinsic Motivation and the Process of Learning: Beneficial Effects of Contextualization, Personalization, and Choice," *Journal of Educational Psychology* 88 (1996): 715–30.
10. E. J. Langer and J. Rodin, "The Effects of Choice and Enhanced Personal Responsibility for the Aged: A Field Experiment in an Institutional Setting," *Journal of Personality and Social Psychology* 34 (1976): 191–98.

11. R. M. Ryan, S. Rigby, and K. King, "Two Types of Religious Internalization and Their Relations to Religious Orientations and Mental Health," *Journal of Personality and Social Psychology* 65 (1993): 586–96.

Chapter 7

1. T. Chartrand, J. Huber, B. Shiv, and R. Tanner, "Nonconscious Goals and Consumer Choice," *Journal of Consumer Research* 35 (2008): 189–201.

Chapter 8

1. Charles S. Carver and Michael F. Scheier, *Attention and Self-Regulation: A Control-Theory Approach to Human Behavior* (New York: Springer, 1981).

Chapter 9

1. C. J. Armitage, "Implementation Intentions and Eating a Low-Fat Diet: A Randomized Controlled Trial," *Health Psychology* 23 (2004): 319–23.
2. C. Armitage, "Efficacy of a Brief Worksite Intervention to Reduce Smoking: The Roles of Behavioral and Implementation Intentions," *Journal of Occupational Health Psychology* 12 (2007): 376–90.
3. P. M. Gollwitzer and P. Sheeran, "Implementation Intentions and Goal Achievement: A Meta-analysis of Effects and Processes," *Advances in Experimental Social Psychology* 38 (2006): 69–119.
4. C. Martijn, H. Alberts, P. Sheeran, G. Peters, J. Mikolajczak, and N. de Vries, "Blocked Goals, Persistent Action: Implementation Intentions Engender Tenacious Goal Striving," *Journal of Experimental Social Psychology* 44 (2008): 1137–43.
5. A. Achtziger, P. Gollwitzer, and P. Sheeran, "Implementation Intentions and Shielding Goal Striving from Unwanted Thoughts and Feelings," *Personality and Social Psychology Bulletin* 34 (2008): 381–93.

Chapter 10

1. A. L. Duckworth and M. E. P. Seligman, "Self-Discipline Outdoes IQ Predicting Academic Performance in Adolescents," *Psychological Science* 16 (2005): 939–44.
2. K. Vohs, R. Baumeister, B. Schmeichel, J. Twenge, N. Nelson, and D.

Tice, "Making Choices Impairs Subsequent Self-Control: A Limited-Resource Account of Decision Making, Self-Regulation, and Active Initiative," *Journal of Personality and Social Psychology* 94 (2008): 883–98.

3. M. Muraven, "Building Self-Control Strength: Practicing Self-Control Leads to Improved Self-Control Performance," *Journal of Experimental Social Psychology* 46 (2010): 465–68.

4. M. Oaten and K. Cheng, "Longitudinal Gains in Self-Regulation from Regular Physical Exercise," *British Journal of Health Psychology* 11 (2006): 717–33.

5. M. van Dellen and R. Hoyle, "Regulatory Accessibility and Social Influences on State Self-Control," *Personality and Social Psychology Bulletin* 36 (2010): 251–63.

6. J. M. Ackerman, N. J. Goldstein, J. R. Shapiro, and J. A. Bargh, "You Wear Me Out: The Vicarious Depletion of Self-Control," *Psychological Science* 20 (2009): 326–32.

7. D. M. Tice, R. F. Baumeister, D. Shmueli, and M. Muraven, "Restoring the Self: Positive Affect Helps Improve Self-Regulation following Ego Depletion," *Journal of Experimental Social Psychology* 43 (2007): 379–84.

8. M. T. Gailliot, R. F. Baumeister, C. N. DeWall, et al., "Self-Control Relies on Glucose As a Limited Energy Source: Willpower Is More Than a Metaphor," *Journal of Personality and Social Psychology* 92 (2007): 325–36.

9. R. T. Donohoe and D. Benton, "Blood Glucose Control and Aggressiveness in Females," *Personality and Individual Differences* 26 (1999): 905–11.

10. R. F. Baumeister, T. F. Heatherton, and D. M. Tice, *Losing Control: How and Why People Fail at Self-Regulation* (San Diego, Calif.: Academic Press, 1994).

11. M. Muraven and E. Slessareva, "Mechanisms of Self-Control Failure: Motivation and Limited Resources," *Personality and Social Psychology Bulletin* 29 (2003): 894–906.

12. L. Nordgren, F. van Harreveld, and J. van der Pligt, "The Restraint Bias: How the Illusion of Self-Restraint Promotes Impulsive Behavior," *Psychological Science* 20, no. 12 (2009): 1523–28.

Chapter 11

1. K. Assad, M. Donnellan, and R. Conger, "Optimism: An Enduring Resource for Romantic Relationships," *Journal of Personality and Social Psychology* 93 (2007): 285–97.

2. A. Geers, J. Wellman, and G. Lassiter, "Dispositional Optimism and Engagement: The Moderating Influence of Goal Prioritization," *Journal of Personality and Social Psychology* 96 (2009): 913–32.

3. S. C. Segerstrom, "Optimism and Attentional Bias for Negative and Positive Stimuli," *Personality and Social Psychology Bulletin* 27 (2001): 1334–43.

4. B. Gibson and D. Sanbonmatsu, "Optimism, Pessimism, and Gambling: The Downside of Optimism," *Personality and Social Psychology Bulletin* 30 (2004): 149–59.

5. L. Sanna, "Defensive Pessimism, Optimism, and Simulating Alternatives: Some Ups and Downs of Prefactual and Counterfactual Thinking," *Journal of Personality and Social Psychology* 71 (1996): 1020–36.

6. N. D. Weinstein, "Unrealistic Optimism about Future Life Events," *Journal of Personality and Social Psychology* 39 (1980): 806–20.

7. P. Harris, D. Griffin, and S. Murray, "Testing the Limits of Optimistic Bias: Event and Person Moderators in a Multilevel Framework," *Journal of Personality and Social Psychology* 95 (2008): 1225–37.

8. J. Ruthig, R. Perry, N. Hall, and S. Hladkyj, "Optimism and Attributional Retraining: Longitudinal Effects on Academic Achievement, Test Anxiety, and Voluntary Course Withdrawal in College Students," *Journal of Applied Social Psychology* 34 (2004): 709–30.

9. I. D. Rivkin and S. E. Taylor, "The Effects of Mental Simulation on Coping with Controllable Stressful Events," *Personality and Social Psychology Bulletin* 25, no. 12 (1999): 1451–62.

Chapter 12

1. A. L. Duckworth, C. Peterson, M. D. Matthews, and D. R. Kelly, "Grit: Perseverance and Passion for Long-Term Goals," *Journal of Personality and Social Psychology* 92, no. 6 (2007): 1087–1101.

2. B. Weiner, *An Attributional Theory of Motivation and Emotion* (New York: Springer-Verlag, 1986).

3. R. D. Hess, C. Chih-Mei, and T. M. McDevitt, "Cultural Variations in Family Beliefs about Children's Performance in Mathematics: Comparisons among People's Republic of China, Chinese-American, and Caucasian-American Families," *Journal of Educational Psychology* 79, no. 2 (1982): 179–88.

4. K. Shikanai, "Effects of Self-Esteem on Attribution of Success-Failure," *Japanese Journal of Experimental Social Psychology* 18 (1978): 47–55.

5. R. D. Hess, C. Chih-Mei, and T. M. McDevitt, "Cultural Variations in Family Beliefs about Children's Performance in Mathematics: Comparisons among People's Republic of China, Chinese-American, and Caucasian-American Families," *Journal of Educational Psychology* 79, no. 2 (1982): 179–88.

6. N. Jostmann and S. Koole, "When Persistence Is Futile: A Functional Analysis of Action Orientation and Goal Disengagement," in *The Psychology of Goals*, G. Moskowitz and H. Grant, eds. (New York: Guilford, 2009).

7. C. Wrosch, M. F. Scheier, G. E. Miller, R. Schulz, and C. S. Carver, "Adaptive Self-Regulation of Unattainable Goals: Goal Disengagement, Goal Re-engagement, and Subjective Well-being," *Personality and Social Psychology Bulletin* 29 (2003): 1494–1508.

Chapter 13

1. M. H. Kemis, J. Brockner, and B. S. Frankel, "Self-Esteem and Reactions to Failure: The Mediating Role of Overgeneralization," *Journal of Personality* 57 (1989): 707–14.

2. J. Henderlong and M. R. Lepper, "The Effects of Praise on Children's Intrinsic Motivation: A Review and Synthesis," *Psychological Bulletin* 128 (2002): 774–95.

3. C. M. Mueller and C. S. Dweck, "Praise for Intelligence Can Undermine Children's Motivation and Performance," *Journal of Personality and Social Psychology* 75 (1998): 33–52.

Index

abandoning goals, 216–21
abilities
    effort vs. ability, 205, 207–8, 209,
        212–13, 214–15, 220, 230–31
    and entity beliefs, 34–38, 40, 42,
        50, 56
    and feedback, 226
    and grittiness, 212–13
    and incremental beliefs, 34–38,
        41–42, 50
    malleable nature of, 40–42
abstract thinking, 7–9, 134, 135
accuracy, 99–100, 103, 133–34, 139
achievement
    and difficult goals, 6–7
    emotional responses to, 93–94
    and feedback, 233–34, 235
    and grittiness, 211
    and optimism, 91
    and promotion-focused goals,
        85, 86
    triggers for, 147

active learning, 69–70
aggression, 145–46
Allen, David, 171
American Dream, 83
anger, 192
anxiety
    and if-then planning, 180, 181
    and mastery vs. performance
        mind-sets, 75
    and motivation, 24
    and promotion vs. prevention
        mind-sets, 93, 94, 103
    and relationships, 97
apathy, 126
approval, 79
Asians, 214–15
assistance, 70–71, 75
athletes, 180
attention, 190
attributional retraining, 203, 205
autonomy
    autonomous help, 70–71

autonomy (*cont.*)
autonomy-supportive, 112,
113–14, 123, 233
creating the feeling of choice,
116–19
and creative tasks, 134–35, 139
defined, 121
and enjoyment, 136, 139
and feedback, 232–33, 236
and goal acceptance, 143
and grittiness, 211–12, 220
and happiness, 139
human need for, 108, 109, 121, 137
and internalization, 119–21
and motivation, 109, 112–15,
122–23, 134–35
and rewards, 236
satisfying the need for, 122
of students, 112–14
and superficial goals, 110
and why vs. what mind-sets, 12

Baer, Allison, 72, 98
Bargh, John, 44–45
Baumeister, Roy, xviii
Beer, Jennifer, 39
being good. *See* performance goals
and mind-set (*being good*)
beliefs, 32, 50
The Biggest Loser, 144–45
blood glucose, 190–91, 195–96
Bolger, Niles, 98
brand names, 146
breast self-examination, 176
*Bright-Sided: How the Relentless
Promotion of Positive Thinking
Has Undermined America*
(Ehrenreich), 91
Butler, Ruth, 70, 148

caution, 95, 103
Centers for Disease Control and
Prevention (CDC), xii
cervical cancer screenings, 176
Chartrand, Tanya, 146
children
and beliefs about personality, 38
and creating the feeling of choice,
115–19
and effort vs. ability, 215
and feedback, 231
and goal contagion, 154
and happiness, 137–38
implicit theories of, 38
and intelligence, 40–41
and internalization, 119
and motivation, 111–12, 114, 116,
137–38
and promotion vs. prevention
parenting, 82–83
and rewards, 114–15
and role models, 154
See also students
choice
creating the feeling of choice,
115–19
and goal acceptance, 143, 155
See also autonomy
choosing goals. *See* goal assignment
Clinton, Bill, 132–33
commitment to goals, 25, 160
competence
and happiness, 139
human need for, 108–9, 121, 137
and internalization, 119–20
and promotion vs. prevention
mind-sets, 89
satisfying the need for, 122
and superficial goals, 110

competing goals, 163–65, 169

competition, 136

concrete thinkers, 7–9

confidence

and creating the feeling of choice, 117

and expectations of difficulties, 20–24

and feedback, 231

and mental contrasting, 24–27

and personal control, 227

and promotion vs. prevention mind-sets, 102, 126

and self-control, 193–94, 196

and vigilance, 89, 103

See also optimism

Confucianism, 214

conservative bias, 95, 103

consumerism, 146, 189

contracts, 143–45, 155

control

and feedback, 225, 227

and incentives, 113, 114

and internalization, 120

and motivation, 113, 114, 115, 122

and optimism vs. pessimism, 227

and personal choices, 113

and superficial goals, 110

Cordova, Diana, 116–17

counterfactual thinking, 200–201

creativity, 95, 134–35, 139

criticism, 79. *See also* feedback

cues. *See* triggers

culture, 213, 214

deadlines, 115, 122

death, thoughts of, 190

Deci, Edward, 108, 110, 112

decision making, 15, 143, 185

defensive pessimism, 90

depression

among college students, 149–50

and mastery vs. performance mind-sets, 71–74, 75

and personal control, 227

and promotion vs. prevention mind-sets, 93

desirability information, 15, 17–18, 29

detail orientation, 103

difficult tasks and goals

and choosing goals, 128–31, 138

and depression, 74

and mastery vs. performance mind-sets, 64–66, 75, 129–31, 138

and positive thinking, 20–24, 29–30

and promotion vs. prevention mind-sets, 99, 100, 129, 138

and specific goals, 129

and speed-accuracy trade-offs, 99

and the value of challenging goals, 4–7, 28–29, 129

and why vs. what modes of thinking, 9–10, 12, 13–14, 129

discrepancy reduction, 165–66

disruptive thoughts, 206

distractions, 100, 103, 163, 169

"do-your-best" goals, 4, 28

Duckworth, Angela, 174, 211

Dweck, Carol

on beliefs about ability, 35, 37

on beliefs about personality, 38

on feedback, 230–31

on intelligence, 41

Dweck, Carol (*cont.*)
  on mastery vs. performance goals,
    67–68, 72

eagerness, 86, 96
Eastern cultures, 83
easy goals, 126, 138
Edison, Thomas, 61
education, 112–14, 116–17, 149–50.
    See also students
effort vs. ability
  challenging assumptions about,
    205, 220
  and feedback, 230–31
  and grittiness, 212–13
  and optimism, 205, 207–8
  and persistence, 209, 213,
    214–15, 220
Ehrenreich, Barbara, 91
Elliot, Andrew, 63
emotional responses to success and
    failure, 93–94, 103
empathy, 189–90, 195
encouragement, 86–88
enjoyment
  and autonomy, 136, 139
  choosing a goal for, 139
  and mastery vs. performance
    mind-sets, 68–70, 75, 135–36,
    139
  and rewards, 136
entity beliefs, 34–38, 40, 42, 50, 56
environment
  importance of, 50–51
  and intelligence, 40–42
  limits of, 48
  triggers in, 32, 43, 44–48, 51,
    145
evaluation, 148–49, 155, 232

exercise
  and if-then planning, 176
  and intrinsic motivation, 112–13
  and missed opportunities, 162
  and self-control, 186–87
  triggers for, 147
Expectancy Value Theory, 22, 84–85
expectations for success
  and defensive pessimism, 90
  and expectations of difficulty,
    20–24
  and feedback, 87–88
  and mastery vs. performance
    mind-sets, 65–66
  and promotion vs. prevention
    mind-sets, 84–86
expedient help, 70–71

failure
  emotional responses to, 93–94,
    103
  expectations of, 23
  explanations for, 212–13
  and feedback, 74, 227–28, 235
  and grittiness, 212–13
  and intentions, 160
  and performance mind-sets (*being
    good*), 61, 70
  and persistence, 209–10
  and positive thinking, 21
  and resilience, 128–29
  and self-control, xiii–xiv
  and willpower, xiii–xiv
false alarms, 94, 95, 97
fame, 110, 111, 122, 137, 139
feasibility information, 18, 29
feedback, 223–36
  and discrepancy reduction,
    165–66

negative feedback, 86, 224–28, 235

positive feedback, 86, 228–34, 235

and promotion vs. prevention mind-sets, 86–88

and self-esteem, 226–27

self-monitoring, 166–67, 169

specificity in, 225–26, 235

financial gain, 106, 110, 111, 122, 137, 139

food and self-control, 186. *See also* weight loss

Förster, Jens, 86–87, 92

framing, 147–49, 155

future, influence on decision making of, 14–20, 29

Gailliot, Matthew, xxi

gains

and creative tasks, 134

emotional responses to, 93–94

and framing, 155

and parenting styles, 82–83

and promotion-focused goals, 78, 102

and relationships, 96, 97

and speed-accuracy trade-offs, 133, 139

Galinsky, Adam, 100–101

gambling, 200

Gelety, Laura, 64

generosity, 191

getting better. *See* mastery goals and mind-set (*getting better*)

Getting Things Done (Allen), 171

gifts, 189–90

Gilbert, Dan, 24

glucose, 190–91, 195–96

goal assignment, 125–39

for accuracy, 134, 139

for creativity, 134–35, 139

for difficult tasks, 128–31, 138

for easy tasks, 126, 138

for enjoyment, 135–36, 139

for happiness, 136–38, 139

for procrastination, 127–28, 138

for speed, 133, 139

for temptation, 131–33, 138

goal contagion, 149–54

described, 46–48

effectiveness of, 150–54

and mastery (*getting better*) interventions, 149–54

and role models, 51, 150–54, 156

and self-control, 195

goals, prioritization of, 198–99

goals for others, 141–56

and the direct approach, 142–45

and framing, 147–49, 155

and goal contagion, 149–54, 156

and triggers, 145–47, 155

goal shielding, 163–65, 169, 180

Gollwitzer, Peter, 44–45, 173, 174, 176, 179

good performance. *See* performance goals and mind-set (*being good*)

Green, David, 114

grittiness, 211, 212–13, 220

habits, 179

H.A.L.T.—Hungry, Angry, Lonely, Tired, 191–92

happiness, 105–23

and abandoning goals, 216–20

choosing a goal for, 139

and creating the feeling of choice, 115–19

happiness (*cont.*)
  and difficult goals, 6–7
  and human needs, 107–9, 121,
    137–38, 139
  and internalization, 119–21, 123
  and intrinsic motivation, 109,
    111–15, 122
  and matching strategies to goals,
    98
  and promotion vs. prevention
    mind-sets, 93–94
  and superficial goals, 109–11,
    122, 137, 139
health, 109
Hearts of Gold, 105–6
helping others, 190
Henderlong, Jennifer, 228
Higgins, Tory
  and matching strategies to goals,
    97–98
  and promotion vs. prevention
    mind-sets, 78, 81, 87, 89,
    147–48
  and reactions to failure, 93–94
high-performance cycle, 7
home-gym equipment, 22
human needs
  described, 107–9
  and happiness, 107–9, 121,
    137–38, 139
  and internalization, 119–20
  and superficial goals, 109–11, 137
  See also autonomy; competence;
    relatedness
hunger, 191–92

Idson, Lorraine Chen, 87
if-then planning, 174–75, 176–80,
  181, 206

implementation intentions, 174
implicit theories, 33, 34–35, 38
importance of goal setting,
  3–30
  and distant- vs. near-future plans,
    14–20, 29
  and positive thinking, 20–28,
    29–30
  and specific and difficult goals,
    4–7, 28–29
  and why vs. what mind-sets, 7–14,
    29
impulsivity, 11–12
incentives. *See* rewards and
  incentives
incremental beliefs, 34–38, 41–42,
  50
independence, 83. *See also*
  autonomy
inhibition, 164–65
intelligence
  and competence, 108
  entity theory of, 34–38, 40, 42,
    50, 56
  incremental theory of, 34–38,
    41–42, 50
  malleable nature of, 40–42
  and performance mind-sets
    (*being good*), 59–61
  and rate of success, 58–59
Intelligence and How to Get It
  (Nisbett), 40
intentions, 160
interdependence, 83, 121
internalization, 119–21, 123, 145
intrinsic motivation, 111–15
  and autonomy, 109, 112–15,
    134–35
  and creative tasks, 134–35

defined, 109
effectiveness of, 109, 112, 122
and enjoyment, 139
and feedback, 233
inhibition of, 114, 115, 122
and rewards, 114–15, 122, 233
inverse-effort rule, 36

judgment, 148, 155

KIPP (Knowledge Is Power Program)
    charter schools, 40–41
Koenigsberger, Deborah, 105

Lake Wobegon effect, 201
Langer, Ellen, 117
Latham, Gary, 4–7
Lepper, Mark, 114, 116–17, 228
Liberman, Nira, 15, 17, 18, 19
Locke, Edwin, 4–7
loneliness, 110, 192
long-term goals, 11
losses
    and framing, 155
    and parenting styles, 82–83
    and prevention-focused goals, 79,
        102
    and relationships, 96, 97
    and speed-accuracy trade-offs,
        133, 139
    and value of the goal, 85
love, pursuit of, 81–84

mastery goals and mind-set (*getting
    better*)
    about, 61–62
    advantages of, 63–64, 76
    and assistance, 70–71
    and depression, 71–74, 75

and difficult tasks and goals, 62,
    64–66, 75, 129–31, 138
and enjoyment, 68–70, 75,
    135–36, 139
and evaluation, 148–49
and feedback, 232, 235
and framing, 148, 155
and goal contagion, 149–54
and grittiness, 211
and happiness, 137
and persistence, 66–68
and students, 66–68, 148–54
McCrea, Sean, 19
mental contrasting, 24–27, 30
Mindset (Dweck), 35
misregulation, 168
missed opportunities, 160–63, 169,
    177, 180
Molden, Dan, 96–97
monitoring, 115, 122
mood boosters, 189–90, 195
motivation
    and autonomy, 109, 112–15,
        122–23, 134–35
    and children, 111–12, 114, 116,
        137–38
    and creating the feeling of choice,
        115–19
    and defensive pessimism, 90
    and feedback, 165, 231
    and internalization, 119–21, 123
    and mental contrasting, 30
    and performance vs. mastery
        mind-sets, 63–64
    and planning, 171, 179
    and promotion vs. prevention
        mind-sets, 86–88, 102–3
    and rewards, xx–xxi
    student motivation, 112–14

motivation (*cont.*)
  undermining, 111–15
  and why vs. what mind-sets, 9–14,
    20, 29
  See also intrinsic motivation
Mueller, Claudia, 230–31
multiple goals, 192, 196, 199
Muraven, Mark, xx, 186

necessity to act (state), 25
negotiation, 100–101, 103
New Year's resolutions, xii
Nisbett, Richard, 40, 42, 114
Norem, Julie, 90
nursing home residents, 117–19

Obama, Barack, xvi, xvii
obstacles to goals
  and defensive pessimism, 90
  and if-then planning, 181
  and mastery vs. performance
    mind-sets, 74
  and mental contrasting, 24, 27, 30
  and optimism, 102
  and positive thinking, 21, 23
  and promotion vs. prevention
    mind-sets, 100, 102
  and why vs. what modes of
    thinking, 15–16
Oettingen, Gabriele, 23, 24, 26, 174
opportunities to act on goals, 160–63
optimism, 197–208
  and attributional retraining, 203,
    205
  benefits of, 198–99, 206
  and counterfactual thinking,
    200–201
  dangers of, 199–205, 207
  and gains-oriented thinking, 134

  increasing optimism, 205–6
  and personal control, 227
  and promotion vs. prevention
    mind-sets, 89–92, 101, 102,
    103, 204, 205
  realistic optimism, 202–3, 204,
    207
  unrealistic optimism, 201–5, 207
  and value of the goal, 199
  See also confidence
others, choosing goals for. *See* goals
  for others

parenting, 82–83, 116, 130–31
Parker-Pope, Tara, 22
passivity, 69
performance goals and mind-set
  (*being good*)
  about, 59–61
  advantages of, 63–64
  and assistance, 70–71
  and depression, 71–74, 75
  and difficult tasks and goals,
    64–66, 75, 129–31, 138
  and easy tasks, 126, 138
  and enjoyment, 68–70, 75,
    135–36, 139
  and evaluation, 148–49, 155
  and feedback, 232
  and framing, 148, 155
  and persistence, 66–68
  and students, 66–68, 148–54
persistence, 209–21
  and abandoning a goal, 216–21
  and difficult goals, 5
  and effort vs. ability, 209, 213,
    214–15, 220
  and explanations for successes/
    failures, 209–10

and grittiness, 210–12, 220
importance of, 30
and mastery vs. performance
    mind-sets, 56, 66–68
and pre-med students, 66–68
and why vs. what mind-sets, 20
personality, beliefs about, 38–39,
    50
pessimism
    and counterfactual thinking,
        200–201
    defensive pessimism, 90
    and gambling, 200
    and personal control, 227
    and promotion vs. prevention
        mind-sets, 89–92, 103
    and value of the goal, 199
    See also prevention-focused goals
        and mind-set
physical aptitudes, 50
planning, 171–81
    effectiveness of, 173–75
    if-then planning, 174–75, 176–80,
        181, 206
    and missed opportunities, 177
popularity, 110–11, 122, 137
The Positive Power of Negative
    Thinking (Norem), 90
positive thinking, 20–28, 29–30, 91,
    198. See also optimism
power, 110
praise. See feedback
prejudice, 190
pre-med studies, 66–68
pressure, 107, 115, 120, 135
prestige, 137, 139
prevention-focused goals and mind-
    set, 77–104
    about, 78–79

and being loved/staying safe,
    81–84
and conservative bias, 95–96
and cultural context, 83
and difficult goals, 99, 100, 129,
    138
and easy tasks, 126
and emotional responses, 93–94,
    103
and feedback, 86–88
and framing, 148
loss-orientation of, 79, 82–83, 85,
    96, 97, 102, 155
and motivation, 86–88
and optimism vs. pessimism,
    89–92, 101, 103, 204
and parenting styles, 82–83
and procrastination, 91, 95, 103,
    127, 138
and relationships, 96–97
and risk taking, 94–95, 97, 101,
    103, 134
and role models, 90–91
and shopping, 92–93
and speed-accuracy trade-offs, 99,
    103, 134, 139
strategies that match, 97–98, 104
strengths/weaknesses of, 98–102
and temptation, 103, 132–33, 138
and value of the goal, 85, 86
prioritization of goals, 198–99
procrastination
    choosing a goal for, 127–28
    and performance vs. mastery
        mind-sets, 69
    and prevention-focused goals, 91,
        95, 103, 127, 138
    and why vs. what mind-sets, 19,
        127, 138

promotion-focused goals and
    mind-set, 77–104
  about, 78
  and the American Dream, 83
  and being loved/staying safe,
    81–84
  and creative tasks, 134–35, 139
  and cultural context, 83
  and difficult goals, 99, 100
  and easy tasks, 126, 138
  and emotional responses, 93–94,
    103
  and feedback, 86–88
  and framing, 148
  gains-orientation of, 78, 82–83,
    93–94, 96, 97, 102, 155
  and likelihood of success, 85
  and motivation, 86–88
  and negotiation, 100–101, 103
  and optimism vs. pessimism,
    89–92, 102, 103, 205
  and parenting styles, 82–83
  and relationships, 96–97
  and risk taking, 94–95, 97, 101,
    103, 134
  and role models, 90–91
  and self-doubt, 225
  and shopping, 92–93
  and speed-accuracy trade-offs, 99,
    103, 133, 139
  strategies that match, 97–98, 104
  strengths/weaknesses of, 98–102
  and value of the goal, 85
public commitment, 144–45, 155
public image, 110
punishments, 82–83, 122, 135, 136

realistic thinking and goals, 5,
    24–27, 28–30, 91–92

rebelliousness, 46
rejection, 96–97
relatedness
  and autonomy, 121
  and happiness, 139
  human need for, 108, 137
  and internalization, 119–20
  satisfying the need for, 121–22
relationships
  and beliefs about personality,
    38–39
  goals related to, 109
  and happiness, 137
  human need for, 108, 109, 119,
    121–22, 137
  and interdependence, 83, 121
  and loneliness, 110, 192
  and mastery vs. performance
    mind-sets, 76
  and optimism, 198
  and promotion vs. prevention
    mind-sets, 81–84, 96–97
  and superficial goals, 110–11
relaxation, 93–94, 103
religious behaviors, 120–21
resilience, 128
rewards and incentives
  and autonomy, 236
  and creative tasks, 135
  and enjoyment of tasks, 136
  and feedback, 236
  and happiness, 107
  and intrinsic motivation, 114–15,
    122, 233
  and performance mind-sets (being
    good), 126
  and promotion vs. prevention
    mind-sets, 82–83
  and self-control, xx–xxi, 193, 196

risk taking, 94–95, 97, 101, 103, 134
Rodin, Judy, 117
role models
    and goal contagion, 51, 150–54,
        156
    positive and negative role models,
        90–91
    and promotion vs. prevention
        mind-sets, 90–91
    and self-control, 188–89
Ryan, Richard, 108, 110, 112, 120

saboteurs of goals, 159–69
    and feedback, 165–67, 169
    and goal shielding, 163–65, 169,
        180
    and misregulation, 168
    and missed opportunities, 160–63,
        169, 180
    and underregulation, 167–68
sadness, 93–94
safety, pursuit of, 81–84
self-control, 183–96
    and blood glucose, 190–91,
        195–96
    capacity limits of, 192
    contagiousness of, 188–89
    depletion of, 191–93, 196
    and empathy, 189–90, 195
    fatigue of, xvii–xix, 185, 192
    and goal contagion, 195
    and if-then planning, 179–80
    and multiple goals, 192
    nature of, xvii–xix
    overestimation of, 193–94, 196
    and recovery, 187–88, 189–90,
        195
    and rewards or incentives, xx–xxi,
        193, 196

and role models, 188–89
strengthening, xxi, 163–65,
    184–86, 194–95
struggles with, xiv–xvii
and temptation, 132, 193–94,
    196
and underregulation, 167
self-determination, 108, 116
self-fulfilling prophecies, 60–61
self-monitoring, 166–67, 168, 192,
    196
self-worth
    external evidence of, 110
    and happiness, 137
    and mastery mind-sets (getting
        better), 62
    and performance mind-sets (being
        good), 59, 60–61
Seligman, Martin, 112
Shah, James, 45–46
Sheeran, Paschal, 176
Sherman, Steven, 19
shopping, 92, 146
signal detection, 94–95
Slessareva, Elisaveta, xx
smoking and smoking cessation
    and failure rates, xii–xiii
    and intrinsic motivation, 113
    and planning, 176
    and promotion vs. prevention
        mind-sets, 100
    and self-control, 193–94
    and triggers, 48–49
specificity in goals, 4–7, 28, 129
speed-accuracy trade-offs, 99, 103,
    133–34, 139
sports, 83, 180
stress, xviii–xix
Stroebe, Wolfgang, 164–65

students
   and attributional retraining, 203
   and creating the feeling of choice,
      116–17
   effort vs. ability in, 214–15
   and evaluation, 148–49, 232
   and feedback, 230–31
   and goal contagion, 149–50
   and intrinsic motivation, 112–14
   and mastery vs. performance
      mind-sets, 66–68, 148–54
   and persistence, 66–68
   See also children
Stumbling on Happiness (Gilbert), 24
sugar, 190–91, 195–96
superficial goals, 109–11, 122, 137,
   139
surveillance, 115, 122, 135

talent. *See* abilities
team sports, 83
temptation
   choosing a goal for, 131–33, 138
   and competing goals, 164–65
   and goal inhibition, 164–65
   and goal shielding, 169
   and if-then planning, 179–81
   and prevention-focused goals,
      103, 132–33, 138
   and self-control, 132, 193–94, 196
   and why vs. what mind-sets,
      11–12, 138
threats, 115
time, influence on decision making
   of, 14–20
triggers, 44–48
   effectiveness of, 44–48, 145–46
   and encouraging goals in others,
      155

   incorporation of, 48–49, 51,
      146–47
   and weight management, 164–65
Trope, Yaacov, 15, 17, 18, 19

unconscious goal pursuit
   advantages of, 42–43
   and environmental cues, 32, 43,
      44–48, 51, 145 (*see also*
      triggers)
   and if-then planning, 178–79
   incorporation of, 48–49
   and motivating others, 145–47
underregulation, 167–68
unrealistic goals, 25–26

vague goals, 4, 28, 129
validation
   and depression, 74
   and entity beliefs, 35–36, 50
   and happiness, 110, 122, 137
   and mastery vs. performance
      mind-sets, 59–61, 75
   and types of goals, 107
Vallacher, Robin, 10–11
VandeWalle, Don, 68
vigilance
   and confidence, 89, 103
   and defensive pessimism, 90
   and motivation, 86, 90
   and relationships, 96
   and temptation, 132
visualization, 206, 208

wealth, 106, 110, 111, 122, 137, 139
Wegner, Dan, 10–11
weight loss
   and competing goals, 164–65
   and failure rates, xii–xiii

and feedback, 166–67
and intrinsic motivation, 113
and planning, 172, 174, 175–76, 179–80
and promotion vs. prevention mind-sets, 100
and self-control, xiv, xv
and specificity in goals, 128
and triggers, 48
Weight Watchers, 167
Weinstein, Neil, 201
well-being, 89
Werth, Lioba, 92
Western cultures, 83
why vs. what mind-sets, 9–14

and autonomy, 12
and difficult goals, 9–11, 12, 20, 29, 129
and distant- vs. near-future plans, 14–19
and motivation, 9–14, 20, 29
and procrastination, 19, 127, 138
and self-control, 192, 196
and temptation, 11–12, 29, 132, 138
willpower, xiii–xiv, 179. *See also* self-control
Winfrey, Oprah, xix
worry, 24